Introducing Emotional Freedom Techniques

Christine Moran

Speechmark

First published in 2012 by

Speechmark Publishing Ltd, Sunningdale House, 43 Caldecotte Lake Drive, Milton Keynes, MK7 8LF, United Kingdom

Tel: +44(0)1908 277 177 Fax: +44(0)1908 278 297

www.speechmark.net

Copyright © Christine Moran, 2012

002-5663/Printed in the United Kingdom by CMP (uk) Limited

British Library Cataloguing in Publication Data
A catalogue record for this book is available from the British Library

ISBN 978 0 86388 779 6

FSC
www.fsc.org
MIX
Paper from
responsible sources
FSC® C004309

EFT on a page

TH – top of head

EB – beginning of eyebrow

SE – side of eyebrow

UE – under eye

UN – under nose

Ch – middle of chin

CB – beginning of the collarbone

UA – under arm
(10cm under the armpit)

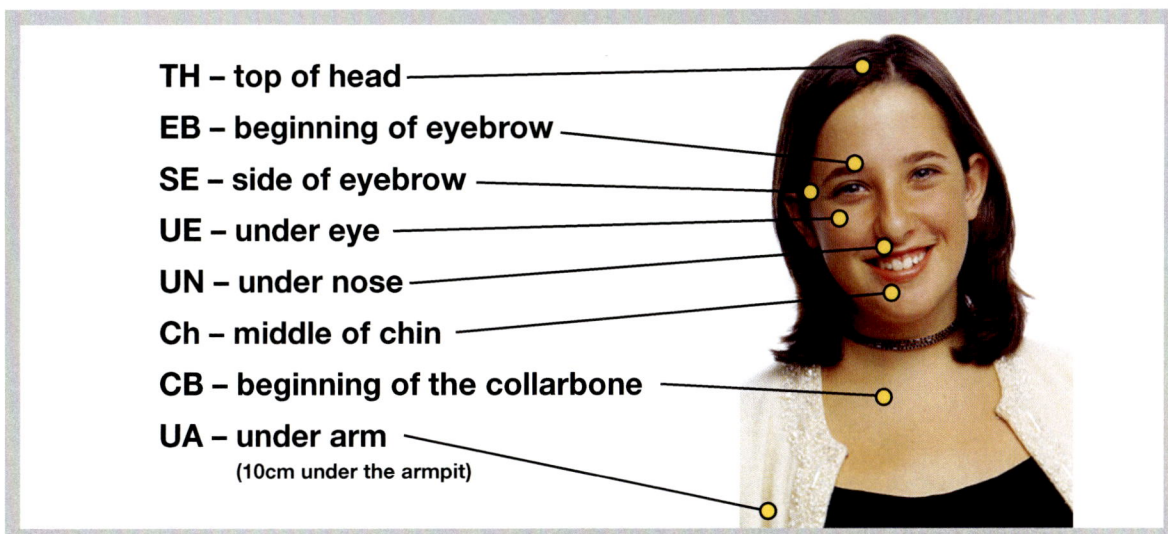

1. Think about an issue that bothers you. On a scale of 1-10 assess how much the issue bothers you now as you start to think about it? (0 means I am not bothered at all and 10 means a huge amount).

2. To create a set-up statement describe how you feel out loud and finish the sentence with something accepting about yourself. For example, *'Even though, I am really scared about the test, I love and accept myself'* Repeat this statement three times while you tap firmly with three fingers on your friendly point of your other hand.

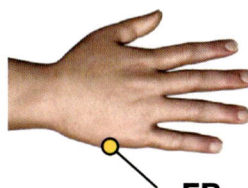

FP – friendly point

3. Now shorten this statement to a reminder phrase. This helps your mind and your body to keep 'tuned in' will you continue with a tapping round. To start a round of tapping, say the phrase over, eg. *'really scared about the test'* while you tap about seven times on top of the head. Repeat tapping and saying the words on each point, EB, SE, UE, UN,CH, CB and UA. This completes one round of tapping. Follow with another tapping round.

4. When you have finished the second round of tapping, relax your body and mind. Breathe in slowly and deeply. Let out the breath slowly and deeply as you relax.

5. Now check how you feel on the aspect you have just been focusing on. Select a number on the 0–10 scale that shows much the feeling is now. If the feeling has gone down but not gone away completely yet, there is more you can do.

6. Ask yourself 'How do I feel about it now about this aspect of the issue. Is it the same feeling? Would I describe it differently now? Focus on the exact words to create a new statement to reflect the remainder left. Follow again from step 2. Your new statement may say something like, *'Even though I still have some of this scared feeling in me, I accept myself'.*

7. After completing a couple more rounds of tapping check your 0-10 level again. Keep repeating from step 2-6 until you are down to zero on this aspect of the issue.

8. Continue to use EFT on another aspect of the issue, for example, *'Even though I feel under pressure to do well, I love and accept myself'*, and carry on from step 2 for as long as you wish.

Contents

Chapter 5 Easing the journey **79**

Chapter 6 Road blocks and alternative routes **92**

Chapter 9 Taking charge of anger **147**

Chapter 10 Easing fears, phobias and anxieties **161**

Introduction

Over the last 20 years as a self development coach for adults and children I have taken pleasure in assisting people to discover their own powerful skills and resources – to be at their best whatever that has meant for each individual. Yet while sharing my time with clients who became happier and more fulfilled, somehow I felt that there must be simpler ways to help people unlock their potential, to heal or to develop.

In 2005 I stumbled across what I now regard as that missing link in the form of a set of techniques called Emotional Freedom Techniques (EFT), developed by Gary Craig. These appeared to provide clever and effective ways for people truly to acknowledge and address their personal blocks. Using the techniques they become naturally guided to be present in the most happy, healthy and abundant existence possible.

Initially the techniques did seem too good to be true, however my scepticism was replaced by fascination as I observed regular dramatic results. Thankfully in this book I am thrilled to share with you my experiences along with the discoveries and rapid progress made by my clients in the last six years. Hopefully you are enticed to explore and enjoy what EFT has to offer for you. All the names of the clients in the case studies have been changed to protect anonymity.

The term EFT describes a set of deceptively simple strategies that are used by people to free themselves of reactions they would rather not have, allowing them to be at their best in any situation. EFT is not a healing power but an approach that facilitates change. The techniques are safe, quick and non-invasive, and can be used as self-help or with a practitioner. EFT is gaining significant recognition as the most effective and the fastest emotional healing and personal growth technique to have been developed in recent decades.

In this book you will read about the evolution of EFT and explore the basis of all negative emotion. You may be surprised at the vast range of uses to which EFT can be put and the benefits it can bring.

Emotional Freedom Techniques

EFT has been coined 'psychological acupressure', in which specific acupuncture or acupressure points are stimulated through a gentle fingertip tapping method. While tapping, you verbally explore, express and release 'emotional issues' and naturally reach awareness of alternative ways of feeling and thinking. EFT addresses the mind and the body at the same time.

As you will read in this book EFT, or 'tapping' as it is more commonly referred to, is a meridian-tapping technique, one branch of energy psychology. It is used by individuals for self-help to address problems or issues and as an everyday energy-clearing technique as part of a healthy lifestyle choice. In addition, it is used in session with qualified practitioners to treat more complex or confusing issues. It can be combined effectively with other therapeutic approaches or used as a stand-alone approach.

Tapping is practised by a wide variety of therapists and health practitioners in many parts of the world, and by individuals in all walks of life, to reduce stress rapidly. The applications are extensive. Just as EFT is applicable to helping a small child with temper to calm themselves, it is equally suited to the elimination of severe lifelong trauma in an adult.

As a society – practitioners and self-helping individuals alike – we are just waking up to what EFT has to offer in providing rapid resolution of psychological ailments and disease symptoms, improvement in performance and permanent positive change, for example in relation to fears, phobias and stress-related issues. EFT has the potential to alleviate chronic diseases and to ease illnesses and psychological conditions with an efficiency and speed that conventional treatments can scarcely touch.

The opportunities offered by EFT in terms of emotional health and healing have made the best therapeutic alternatives seem quite inadequate. With EFT it is possible to deliver radical reduction in stress in minutes, with the very favourable side-effects of vibrant health, increased productivity and optimum wellbeing. Companies, hospitals, schools, support agencies, charities, clinics, humanitarian organisations and sport teams across the world are investing in cost-effective, safe and valuable EFT programmes.

The benefits to be gained from the energy meridian-based EFT are undeniable and the weight of evidence supporting EFT is rapidly changing perceptions. There were many years of research before acupuncture was approved by the British Medical Association (BMA) and offered on the National Health Service (NHS) in the UK (Silvert, 2000). To date, little funding for evidence-based EFT research has been available, but the outstanding results reported worldwide have accelerated demand for investigation. In the UK the National EFT Research Programme is collaborating on a variety of EFT projects within several sectors to gather evidence on the efficacy of the approach. Evidence-based research and the reputation of EFT is expanding rapidly in the UK within the NHS, education and social care. In the US, the Soul Medicine Institute,[1] a non-profit-making organisation, is also undertaking comprehensive and rigorous scientific studies of EFT.

Some NHS trusts are using EFT and acceptance is growing. The potential for integrating EFT with other modalities is considerable, particularly CBT and EMDR which have some similar elements. Tapping derivatives have been used for several years by highly respected clinicians such as Dr Phil Mollon, a clinical psychologist and an advanced practitioner of meridian energy therapies at the mental health unit of the Lister Hospital, Stevenage, England, who trained at the Tavistock Clinic and the Institute of Psychoanalysis. Mollon (2007, p127) suggests that combining acupoint tapping with talk therapy 'vastly enhances the effectiveness of psychotherapy'.

Therese McGoldrick, head of a behavioural psychotherapy unit within NHS Forth Valley, Scotland, has used EFT with trauma patients for several years. In this region EFT is accepted among general practitioners (GPs) and psychiatrists and is widely used by staff members of the community psychiatric team, the suicide intervention team, crisis line workers, psychologists and ward staff. Theresa McGoldrick is a member of the research team that carried out the first British comparative controlled trial of a form of psychotherapy used widely in the treatment of trauma known as eye movement desensitisation and reprocessing, or EMDR,[2] and cognitive behaviour therapy (CBT) in post-traumatic stress disorder (PTSD). Her team has been carrying out a similar pilot trial comparing EFT and EMDR in PTSD. The Scottish Government Health Department has expressed a keen interest in the peer reviewed publication which is in preparation at time of print.

---

1 The Soul Medicine Institute was set up by Dawson Church PhD, in California, USA.

2 EMDR stands for eye movement desensitisation and reprocessing. It is a form of psychotherapy used widely in the treatment of trauma.

I dedicate this book to all my family. I thank especially my two wonderful daughters Kayti and Rachel who both grasp each new day like a precious gift, my husband Frank who reminds me daily of what is important in life and my mum – my first and finest inspiration.

Part 1

Getting into gear with emotional freedom techniques

Chapter 1
The Energy Universe

Chapter 1 The Energy Universe

Energy is never created, never destroyed, but only transformed, changed to another state.

'Everything in the universe is energy and radiates energy'

Albert Einstein expressed the science that sages have understood for thousands of years: that everything in our material world – animate and inanimate – is made of energy. The earth is one enormous arena of energy fields. Modern devices, including the electocardiogram, electocepalogram, electromyogram and magnetic resonance imaging all rely on the strength and distribution of tiny electromagnetic charges in the body in order to function.

Where is the source to this energy? Many describe it or point to it as a universal life force, or source energy. The concept of a universal energy flow is not a new one. The ancient Chinese called this flow qi (pronounced 'chi'); the ancient Hindus called it *prana*. Eastern medicine has worked with an energetic model for thousands of years. The disciplines that developed in those two cultures – t'ai chi and yoga, respectively – are based on the art of tuning into the flow of energy and using it to centre the self. When we are centred we feel and experience harmony not only with ourselves but also with others, and with our entire environment. When we are at our best we are balanced with the universal flow of energy. The effect of our body's subtle energy system on our health and wellbeing will be explored in later chapters.

Universal life energy permeates every living thing, including the air, our planet, the atmosphere and all of nature. The flow of this energy connects everything that exists, and is being constantly absorbed by humans at every moment. It is naturally flowing through us and we are this energy.

We are energy

The human body is a microcosm of universal life energy, a unified field of energy interacting with other surrounding energy fields. We are connected to the universe atomically: humans are made up of the same atomic materials as the universe. When we understand this we can begin to realise that we are energy and energy is flowing through us all the time with all of its inherent possibilities.

We can increase the inward natural flow of this energy if we are feeling drained, if we want to heal ourselves or others, or if we are doing specific energy work. Because this vital energy is what keeps us alive and healthy, the ability to increase it at will is a good thing to know.

Perhaps our physical realm – our physical system, our physical body – is an extension of our spiritual realm. Emerging research and changing perspectives have brought science and spirituality closer together in a theoretical sense. Quantum physicists, for example, are now validating ancient ideas of energy, which necessitates new thinking about health and illness.

Energy vibrates at different rates of speed and because of this it takes on different consistencies. Everything that appears solid is actually made up of swirling molecules which are vibrating at different frequencies into their current forms – solid, liquid or gas. The condition of your energy self, that is, the vibrations it radiates, shapes both your present moment and your future. Like energy attracts, and you are a living, breathing magnet attracting exactly what your energy self is radiating. Whatever you are feeling, you are vibrating, and therefore attracting. The electrons and atoms in your body make waves of living energy which ripple and spread themselves into patterns. Your body's vibrational frequency changes at various physical and emotional states – becoming stronger or weaker depending on your mental state.

Emotions have unique vibrations just as physical objects do. When you are laughing and having fun, your body's vibrations are lighter (higher and faster). When you are tired and sick your vibrations are heavier (slower and lower). You know how when you are in love you feel 'energised', 'high', as though you are 'walking on a cloud'? When you are negative and depressed, you feel sluggish: you are 'feeling low', 'heavy', you 'feel down'. Your emotional vibrations are giving your body a slower, lower vibration. Measures can be expressed scientifically, as described for example in the book *Molecules of Emotion* by Dr Candace Pert (1997) and studies ran at Heart Math Institute in California.

Measurements of our body's frequencies record our electromagnetic energy in vibrations or pulses. With every pulse your electromagnetic energy both broadcasts and attracts. Your energy field transmits your vibrations and draws other similar vibrations magnetically into your energy field. You are constantly broadcasting your own energy and attracting other energy – this is Newtonian physics.

Each single thought is energy, and grouped together our thoughts create unique neural networks in the brain. To some readers the concept that 'our thoughts create our world' will be new. Much of this book explores how our minds are susceptible to constant physical reconstruction through our patterns of thought. Quite simply, we create our reality with thinking.

Energy psychology: your body's energy system

Energy psychology applies principles and techniques for working with the body's physical energies to facilitate desired changes in emotions, thoughts and behaviours.

Energy psychology has its earliest roots in Eastern cultures where pathways of energy running through the body were used as the source of diagnosis and the focus for relief of physical pain and disease. These pathways, although invisible to the naked eye, may be accessed to relieve emotional pain and subconscious blocks to health, happiness and success.

Not only are our bodies composed of energy, but energy fields surround and move through our bodies. Energetic pathways and centres regulate and interact with cells, organs, thoughts and emotions to comprise our entire physical and emotional being. Energy psychology works with these pathways and centres and with the surrounding energy fields to improve both physical and emotional wellbeing.

All energy techniques – whether physiological (for example acupuncture or acupressure) or psychological – are based on the understanding that the most fundamental cause of physical or emotional disease is located within the body's energy system. This book explores this concept in detail, focusing on one branch of energy psychology, the most widespread meridian-tapping technique, EFT. We will investigate why feeling overwhelmed by circumstances or becoming enraged by the way we are being treated result in specific reactions in our body's energy system, and why these reactions translate into negative emotions – fear, anger, anxiety – and into long-term health issues. We will dig deep to understand why the feelings and reactions that are triggered by circumstances such as these are almost always linked to old, outdated energy patterns or limiting beliefs about our world. You will discover why the concept of being affected by past negative programming warrants more than a passing acknowledgment. You will also discover a pain-free, non-invasive approach that has already helped millions of people to be permanently free from the issues that were making them stuck.

Energy meridians

Fundamental to EFT is the existence of our energy system in the body, a matrix within the physical body functions which acts as a network between the physical and the more subtle energy body. The system consists of 14 main meridians, six pairs of meridians are located bi-laterally, which means one on each side of the body. The remaining two meridians are: the governor vessel, which runs up the spine and over the head; and the conception vessel, which runs up the centre of the front of the body. Appendix 1 summarises the path and main functions of each energy meridian. Collectively, energy meridians form a network called the energy meridian system which passes through the organs and connective tissues of the body (see Figure 1). The system forms a matrix within the physical body functions and acts as a network between the physical and the more subtle energy body.

Bioelectric energy, which is essential to nourish and energise the body, flows through each meridian, connecting organs and surrounding tissues. As mentioned above, in Chinese medicine this energy is called *qi*, pronounced 'chi'. Along the pathway of each meridian there are specific locations where the meridian intersects with the surface of the skin. These points are known as acupoints. At these points, compared with other places along the meridian, a lower electrical resistance (or higher conductivity) can be recorded on the skin. The flow of the qi or bioelectric energy can be accessed and altered with relative ease at acupoints. When we are 'in balance' the qi easily follows the specific directional pathways through the meridians, accessing all our connective tissue and organs throughout our body. If we are not in balance, the energy flow becomes sluggish or 'stuck', resulting in lower readings at the acupoints.

Acupoints also have specific energetic functions that affect individual organs and systems. In Chinese medicine they can be used to access data about the meridian and the functional status of its associated organs or tissues. All the meridians are accessed and stimulated via a small number of easy-to-access acupoints during an EFT routine. You will read more about these 'tapping points' later in the chapter.

In traditional Chinese medicine, energy meridians and specific points along each meridian are associated with emotions representing that we are 'in-balance' or 'out-of-balance'. A summary of emotions associated with the energy meridians is available in Appendix 2. When energy flows easily through each meridian, positive health and wellbeing follows. When a meridian is 'blocked' and energy is sluggish, this gives rise to negative emotions and physical symptoms. The effect is cumulative and damaging. You will learn how to ease away negative emotions and physical symptoms by addressing these blockages using EFT. You do not need information given in Appendix 2 to use EFT effectively, but you may find it interesting to read; it is referred to again in case studies in later chapters.

Figure 1 **The main meridian pathways**

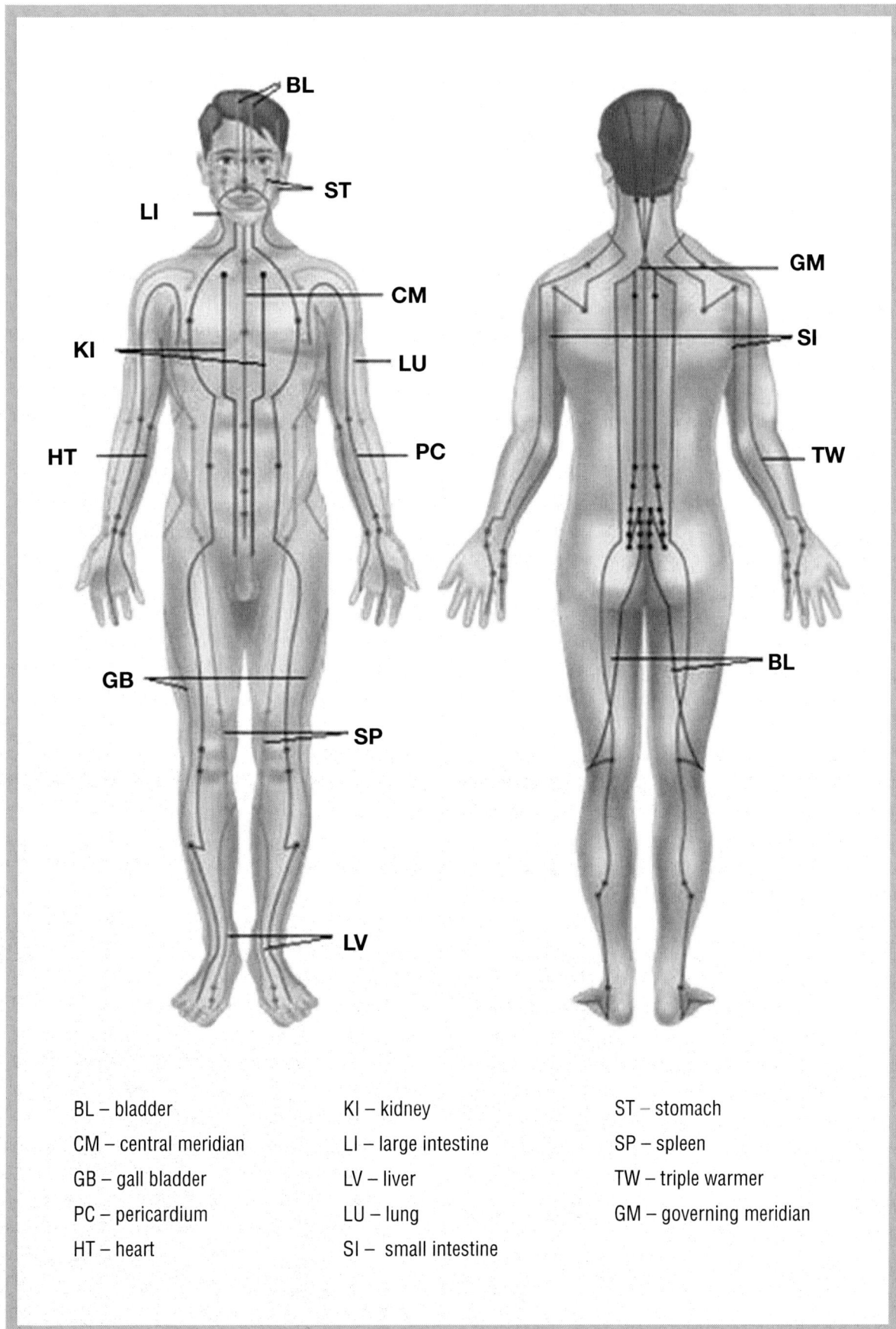

BL – bladder
CM – central meridian
GB – gall bladder
PC – pericardium
HT – heart

KI – kidney
LI – large intestine
LV – liver
LU – lung
SI – small intestine

ST – stomach
SP – spleen
TW – triple warmer
GM – governing meridian

How EFT developed

EFT was introduced in 1995 by Gary Craig, who had skilfully combined elements of a number of efficient techniques from across the globe ranging in time from ancient practices to the modern day. As a modern meridian therapy, the history of EFT goes back no more than a few decades. However, in order to have a true perspective of the development of EFT it is important to consider the historical roots of energy therapies.

Early energy therapies

The earliest origins of energy therapies developed independently but alongside each other in China and Japan respectively. However, similar therapeutic concepts that are equally as old or even older than the Chinese and Japanese therapies can be traced to many parts of the world.

> *Energy psychology is a contemporary application of methods that are at least 4500 years old.*
> *(Feinstein et al, 2006)*

There is evidence that acupuncture-like treatment was carried out by groups as far apart as the Bantu in Africa and the Inuit in the Arctic, but these are difficult to date. The earliest well-dated instance seems to be a mummified body of a man found in the Alps (Dorfer et al., 1999). Discovered in 1991, the body was preserved in a glacier in the Alpine Oetz valley between Austria and Italy. The corpse has been reliably dated to c.3200 BC, and it carries 15 groups of tattoos that correspond to the meridian lines used in acupuncture to treat stomach complaints and arthritis. Computer tomography (a non-destructive x-ray inspection technique enabling detailed analysis of the internal structure) has revealed that the iceman suffered from arthritis of the lumbar spine, and extensive research on his corpse has shown that he also suffered from worms and diarrhoea.

These findings raise interesting questions about the possibility that the very early practice of therapeutically intended acupuncture originated long before the medical tradition of ancient China (c.1000 BC) and that its geographical origins were Eurasian rather than East Asian, consistent with far-reaching intercultural contacts of prehistoric humankind. Acupuncture is usually considered to be Chinese therapy. There is a history of continuous practice there from at least 1000 BC to the present day, and in its pure form it has been incorporated into Western medicine. It is from the fruitful fusion of Eastern and Western ideas that 'modern' energy therapies, including meridian therapies, have sprung.

Modern energy therapies

The modern history of meridian tapping began in the 1960s with Dr Richard Goodheart, founder of applied kinesiology and a leading chiropractor. By testing the strength or weakness of certain muscles, kinesiologists can determine which meridians, organs or bodily systems need to be rebalanced. Goodheart discovered that he could use acupuncture points beneficially for physical conditions by light finger 'tapping' on them instead of using acupuncture needles.

The Australian psychiatrist Dr John Diamond, building on the pioneering work of his close friend and colleague Goodheart, took this discovery a step further and coined the term acupuncture emotional system (AES) to name the system delineating the relationship between emotions and acupuncture meridians. He introduced the use of verbal affirmations while the patient stimulated the acupuncture points. This was a major advance because it introduced into the process a psychological tool; however the treatment method lacked a cohesive 'engine' to drive it forward with real effectiveness. That engine was supplied in the 1980s by Dr Roger Callahan, a cognitive psychologist specialising in anxiety disorders.

Callahan started to apply his knowledge of kinesiology and acupuncture to psychological issues. His breakthrough was with a phobia client when he discovered that by tapping certain acupuncture points while encouraging the patient to focus on the negative feelings it was possible not only to relieve emotional distress but also to cure the psychological problems.

Knowing that he had hit on something quite extraordinary, Callahan started to carry out research with all kinds of phobia and later into many other emotional problems. With his background knowledge of the links between specific emotions and meridians, he developed a complete system and concluded that there was a correct tapping sequence for every negative emotion and emotional-based physical issue. He used extensive muscle testing to determine the protocol for each individual. In time, Callahan named his documented, tried-and-tested tapping sequences 'algorithms', and his treatment later became known as thought field therapy, or TFT. This was the first energy therapy technique based on using the energy system of the body to relieve emotional stresses and negative thoughts and feelings. Callahan's work was brilliant and groundbreaking, but was also complex and difficult to master because different algorithms were required for each of the numerous disorders studied.

In the early 1990s Gary Craig, who originally trained in TFT with Callahan, unveiled a major development in meridian-tapping techniques which he called emotional freedom techniques, or EFT. Craig simplified the numerous complex algorithm combinations for different types of emotion to form a single algorithm method. He combined this with other key techniques, mainly from neurolinguistic programming (NLP) methodology, which added significantly to its efficacy, and the first EFT manual was made available.

EFT in action

EFT is effective with issues that arise from any part of life. It does not matter how intense or how long ago the issue began. Applications can address present or past concerns and adapted to clear negative disruption around the thought of future anxiety. The practice of future-proof tapping means that you are able to make permanent shifts in thoughts and behaviours without being in a real panic situation. It acts deeply to help release emotional blocks, foster healing and change energy patterns.

During EFT you tap on various meridian points around your body while focusing or concentrating initially on the negative aspects of an issue. To focus on the negative while trying to rid yourself of negative feelings may seem rather counterintuitive, but this is central to the healing process. By gently recreating negative energy disruption in the body's subtle energy system, accepting the issue concerned, and then rebalancing the disruption, healing begins (see Figure 2). This central premise of EFT is summarised in Craig's 'EFT discovery statement':

The basis of all negative emotion is a disruption in the body's energy system.

Figure 2 **Removing disruption in the body's energy system**

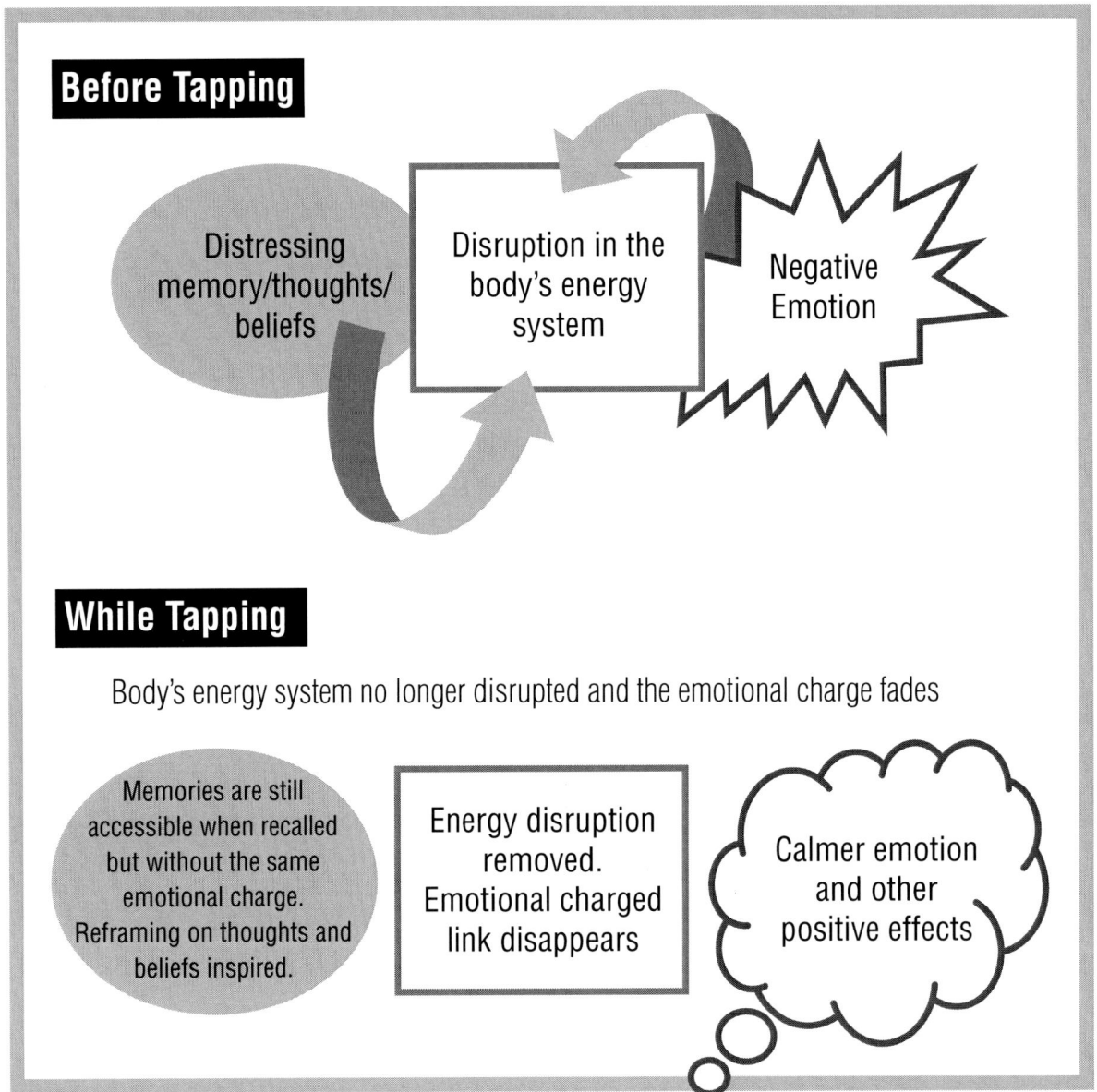

The processes that occur while EFT is being used are multilayered and are not yet fully understood.

Different perspectives are explored in Chapter 7 in more detail, while a generally accepted summary is outlined here.

Tapping specific acupoints while focusing on an issue or problem accesses bioelectric energy in the meridians, which transmits through the body/mind system and initiates many connected processes. Rebalancing any disruption in the flow of the energy system can be likened to removing a log jam in a dam. Once the disruption is removed the energy can flow more easily again around the meridian network. At the same time cognitive changes in thinking occur. Changes in a person's language are one observable indication of these cognitive changes.

An example is the use of EFT to address a phobia: following treatment it is not untypical for a person to be fairly accepting or even, in some cases, welcoming of original phobia triggers. However, while the excessive or irrational reaction is removed, the rational or commonsense reaction remains intact. This means, for example, that even though a client may have calmed a phobia of heights they still have a healthy and sensible attitude towards safety.

EFT goes far beyond just talking about feelings, experiences, struggles and rationalising an issue. Discussion alone does not have the power significantly or permanently to change a person's innermost world. The effects of distraction or a bit of attention are not sufficiently powerful to effect such lasting results. Concurrent tapping during talking and targeted questioning, however, has effects that include changes in emotions, brainwave patterns and internal physiology. Revisiting the original negative thoughts that have been transformed using EFT, no longer creates distress; instead the individual experiences a new clarity and understanding that was not accessible when they were in their earlier emotional state. As your energy disruptions are corrected, cognitive shifts occur, you are freed from the past and new energies begin to flow. In this way layer upon layer of unproductive feelings can be addressed successively, as far as you choose. From this perspective, we can consider that emotions are effective feedback devices or symptoms of blockages and disturbances in the body's subtle energy system. The combination of techniques in EFT can bring about change and balance, which in turn allows us to reprocess our inner world and operate to our best potential.

Table 1 **Typical energy system imbalances that can be corrected using EFT**

Anxiety	Anger	Fears	Cravings	Stress	Poor work performance
Phobias	Health treatment issues	Physical pain	Chronic symptoms	Lack of self-acceptance	Performance anxiety
Trauma	Inner conflict	Grief	Lack of motivation	Lack of self-worth	Poor exam performance
Post-traumatic stress disorder (PTSD)	Abuse	Insomnia	Panic attacks	Addictions	Poor sport performance
Relationships	Attachment issues	Shyness	Abandonment	Ailments	Depression
Feeling different	Limiting beliefs	Difficulties in learning	Attention issues	Lack of confidence	Unhelpful habits

People using EFT report a variety of different perspectives after an issue is resolved. Comments are extremely positive and listed here are some typical statements recorded from sessions:

'I feel … clearer'

'… more focused'

'… that I can't find the problem anymore'

'… like I can make the decisions easier now'

'… lighter'

'… more present'

'… that I am not bothered about the event/situation any longer'

'… the pain has gone!'

'… great relief'

'… calm'

'… the blocks have been lifted'

'… open to trying now'

Routes and paths with EFT

With its wide therapeutic scope, a great number of people benefit from EFT for a multitude of issues. EFT is suitable for any problem that has emotional content.

Whether or not we consciously realise it, many problems – emotional and physical – are caused by negative emotions. Problems are often supported by negative beliefs that have been formed much earlier in life. Now, any negative feeling that can be identified while using EFT can be resolved with a high degree of success. The diversity of problems and issues that can be treated with EFT means that new and effective applications for EFT are constantly being discovered.

EFT enhances any other healing or self-help tool. It can be added to the toolbox of the practitioner, whether counsellor, therapist, coach, health practitioner or an individual working with the emotional, social and behavioural health of young people. One of the many attractive qualities of EFT is that it is portable; it can be used in sessions that take place in, for example, a health practice, classroom, playground, at home or at work, on the telephone and in an emergency. Compared with other therapies, EFT sessions and programmes are relatively inexpensive, especially because relief can occur remarkably quickly. At the time of writing, as the demand is increasing worldwide, there is no doubt that this is an excellent time to train as an EFT practitioner. No medication is involved, and there is no need for surgery or needles. EFT is safe, gentle, non-invasive and suitable for all ages.

Combining current medical practices with ancient approaches provides us with a means to enhance our lives in profound and seemingly incredible ways and do it with amazing speed. The world's population is becoming more open to energy work. In a world where terror and rage are endemic, energy healing gives us access to our subtle energies, providing us with hope for health, happiness, peace and prosperity. Our physical and emotional lives can be dramatically enhanced by shifting the energies that control them. This does not mean that energy is in everything; it means that energy is everything.

The future for EFT and associated energy therapies is potentially very great. In the forthcoming chapters you will read many accounts of EFT being used to treat both emotional and physical issues. EFT programmes are also being used to reach out to help underserved populations such as vulnerable children, sufferers of PTSD and military-related stress where other help is not readily available.

Energy techniques have been used to help survivors of disasters, for example in Kosova, Rwanda, after Hurricane Katrina and following 9/11 (see Appendix 3).

While meridian-tapping techniques are now moving beyond the principles of Gary Craig's original EFT and highly skilled experts are creating tapping approaches that differ slightly, the fundamental principles nevertheless remain unchanged, and these are covered in the following chapters.

Working alone or with a practitioner

Many people use EFT very effectively by themselves for their own needs whereas others choose to seek professional help or advice. People benefit from and enjoy sessions with practitioners for a variety of reasons. People seek the help or guidance of a practitioner if they are experiencing 'blocks' arising from a range of problems: overwhelming emotions, lack of progress, getting 'stuck', trauma, abuse or mental health issues. Every day I am humbled by the changes that I facilitate in people who have tried other therapies but still feel the same way.

Advice about choosing a practitioner is offered in Chapter 5.

Compared with other techniques EFT is usually quite gentle and yet it can often achieve substantial relief. Some of the issues people bring to EFT, however, are intense and these can produce emotional or physical pain. In EFT severe reactions to memory occur only in people who are seriously emotionally damaged, and then only very occasionally, but those new to EFT should employ commonsense precautions in this regard and should not use a technique for which they are not qualified. Although EFT produces remarkable clinical results, practitioners and the public must take complete responsibility for their use of it. All commonsense approaches necessary to consulting an appropriate health professional should be taken in relation to use of EFT.

Caution and responsibility are both discussed further in Chapter 3.

If you are using EFT yourself, do inform other health care practitioners when you experience an improvement in your symptoms as a consequence of EFT. Positive reports to the medical profession about the effectiveness of EFT will help others. **Please note, however, that no matter how well EFT works for you, never use it to replace prescribed medication without proper consultation.** EFT practitioners follow regulations and ethical guidelines from their training bodies. The association AAMET[1] is the largest in the UK.

---

1 The Association for the Advancement of Meridian Energy Therapies (AAMET) is UK-based.

Chapter 2
Emotional health and wellbeing

Chapter 2 Emotional health and wellbeing

It is natural for us to strive to be emotionally healthy in our personal lives. Measures of emotional, psychological and mental wellbeing range from degrees of happiness and confidence to problem-solving ability and resilience. If you are employed in education, health or social care you probably have in place a whole range of wellbeing policies and targets for the people in your care. Achieving these goals on a practical and cost-effective basis, however, can be a tough challenge.

The key message in this chapter is that your consistent thoughts become your reality. We will explore how EFT provides a natural way to cultivate positive emotional health. We begin looking more closely at thoughts, emotions and beliefs. In later chapters we will consider the astounding effects of daily thoughts on the body, mind and even our genes, whatever our age or role in life. We will explore how EFT provides a natural way to cultivate positive emotional health. We begin by looking more closely at thoughts, emotions and beliefs.

Emotions

Emotions can be categorised in many ways, but for now consider the two principal emotions: love and fear, with all other emotions as variations of these. Our thoughts and behaviour come from either a place of love or a place of fear. Anxiety, control, inadequacy and confusion are all fear-based emotions whereas joy, caring, trust, compassion, truth, contentment and satisfaction are love-based emotions. The emotion that always underpins anger is fear – a threat exists. Fear and love, and all their variations, exist in different levels of intensity, and all varieties and intensities have a direct physical effect on our bodies as a result of chemicals released by the brain. If fear-based emotions are experienced over a long time the probability of damage to the body through illness and disease is significantly increased. But where does it all start?

It starts with a thought

We think between 40,000 and 60,000 thoughts a day. A thought is an individual electrochemical impulse that is initiated in the brain before travelling through neural networks. The associated brain chemicals that are released transmit around the body and act as messengers of the thought, instructing the body to match the thought. Thinking happy or positive thoughts produces chemicals that make us feel happy; thinking negative thoughts produces chemicals that make us feel negative. The body creates a feedback loop in which matching physiological messages return to the brain, which in turn is triggered to think similar thoughts, positive or negative. We now begin to think the way we are feeling.

It is estimated that we have negative thoughts a shocking 70 per cent of our day. We can perhaps begin to appreciate therefore the impact of niggles, irritations and stress and the overall negative effect they have on our bodies and wellbeing. Thoughts create feelings and feelings create thoughts. The cycle of thought and feeling determines how we generally feel and behave (or what we say and do); in other words, it determines our state of being. Our thoughts control our lives by determining our state of being and by controlling our actions and behaviour. This has profound implications for our health, wellness, performance and levels of achievement.

In addition, the more often a message (an electrochemical impulse) is carried in a neural network, for example in the form of a thought or an action, the easier it is for that message or impulse to be carried down the neural network. The signal and the neural connection are strengthened each time.

Chapter 7 explores further the importance of the quality of our regular thoughts as we consider how they are driven into our subconscious, becoming 'hardwired' and automatic.

Good vibrations?

As we saw in Chapter 1 our thought vibrations have a moment-by-moment and cumulative effect on health and wellbeing. Your choice counts – always. Simple choices produce profound results. So where do you focus – on the dirt in the alley or the blossoms on the trees, on the criticism of others or on their cooperation and support, on pain and suffering or on health and happiness?

Criticism and an experience of failure are not visible but they are non-physical vibrational realities that are absorbed by the body. When you absorb a frequency into your energy body over along period of time it permanently contributes its resonance to you. A constant intake of a certain frequency literally magnetises your body to that frequency.

We can, however, control the frequency at which our bodies vibrate, and if people can control their thoughts they can also control the feelings behind those thoughts. Using EFT it becomes easier to change. We have the ability and power within us to increase our vibrational rate at whatever moment we choose. We are also capable of monitoring the energy body to locate and change imbalances before illness and disease set in.

You know when you feel energy deficit emotionally and physically by the end of the day. It is important to nourish your energy body on a regular basis as many things during the day deplete energy. When you infuse your energy body the ageing process of cell tissues slows down, you are more creative and spontaneous, and you are healthier because you are raising the vibration of every one of your other selves: the physical, the mental, the emotional and the spiritual. We will explore in detail what depletes your energy and how to enhance it using EFT in later chapters.

Your thoughts are accelerated forms of energy which directly influence not only your energy body, but the energy bodies of others. Negative thoughts vibrate at a slower rate than positive thoughts. Negative thoughts are heavier than positive thoughts. People often say *'Lighten up'* when they see you are depressed or feeling badly. After you have resolved a major negative situation you feel as though a heavy load has been lifted off you. Positive thoughts are lighter and vibrate at a much faster speed than negative ones. The way you feel when you think of negative situations is different from when you think of happy ones.

Worry, resentment, power struggles and envy all cause energy drain. Likewise, judging a person, lying, criticism, being fearful and having troublesome thoughts drains your energy body. Take a check on where you allow your energy to drain.

To be stressed about things in the past or future and not able to get your thoughts or acts together in the present means that energy is literally scattered. It means not having enough energy left to be present in current, daily life. Choosing to hold on to negative past or worrying about the future results in energy depletion – physically, mentally, emotionally and spiritually. Vibrations are low and health suffers. To operate well we need to operate in the present and with quality energy. Negative energy investments put you in debt and the price is paid by your cells, your health, your relationships, your prosperity, your present and your future.

Words are powerful accelerated forms of energy and they create vibrations. Depending on your thoughts and your words, you either give or receive positive energy, creating a healing, energising effect with circuitry that benefits both participants, or you connect your circuits to places that drain you and them of energy.

Throughout the remainder of this book we will be operating from two perspectives. First, we will adopt the habit of thinking as energy being! From this point forward, think about everything energetically. Ask yourself if what you are thinking about and the way you feel about it, mentally and emotionally, make you stronger energetically or if they deplete you and cause you to radiate and attract low vibrations? You live life better when you are conscious of your energy body. Your entire life will work better when you come from this new point of view. Where you send your mind and emotions is where you send a piece of yourself, and determines what you receive in return. Evaluate your energy self and what you are currently connecting with. If something disempowers you, disconnect. Get out or it will cost you! Literally visualise yourself disconnecting, change your thoughts and feelings to positive, and reclaim your energy for more positive use. You can make positive improvements.

Second, and equally important, appreciate that life does not deal you a hand. You are creating you, yourself, moment by moment, by what you choose to think about, speak about, and by how you feel and vibrate about these things. Choose to remove yourself from energy-draining people and situations. They get their energy by taking it away from other people. They do not have enough because they are 'victims' or have spent their energy unwisely. Choose the people and situations that lift you up and increase your energy. Practising EFT will make your journey of discovery – the transitions of your choice – easier. You are creating yourself and your future.

Your mind follows your thoughts and your behaviour follows emotions. The techniques of EFT will enable you to align all these vibrations. Fine-tuning this practice means that you will no longer be giving the universe mixed messages and you will be setting yourself on the best path forward.

Connecting with feelings

We have seen that emotions control our thinking, behaviour and actions, and that they therefore have a direct effect on our physical health. To be consciously connected with your emotions allows for a life of higher energy and is crucial for optimum, healthy wellbeing. To achieve this in reality when we are going about our daily business, however, can seem an impractical proposal.

Connecting with our feelings can seem like a complex activity. To spend time talking about how you feel does not necessarily mean that you are truly connected with or 'feeling' those feelings either. People who do not connect with their feelings are avoiding the fear of losing control or the fear of the pain involved in experiencing their emotions. Many of us dismiss difficult, painful and fear-based emotions without realising that we are doing so. We get busy, exercise more, drink or eat a little more, or just pretend that whatever has triggered a difficult emotion has not happened. All of these are examples of suppressing emotions. To disconnect from your feelings is often not a conscious decision, but ignoring, dismissing, repressing emotions are damaging to the body. Additional energy is required to keep emotions buried, which depletes the body's energy system and leaves little for other activities. When energy is being used to keep emotions stuffed down, the result is that we vibrate at a lower energy level. In addition, emotions that are not felt and released but buried within the body can lead to ailments, and may eventually cause serious and chronic illness. They can also cause major difficulties in relationships and they significantly affect our ability to grow spiritually.

Signs of avoiding feelings include:

- ignoring feelings generally
- overeating or using excessive amounts of alcohol
- using recreational or prescription drugs
- any compulsive behaviour
- always keeping busy to avoid feeling
- constant intellectualising and analysing
- keeping conversations superficial.

Similarly, ventilating emotions inappropriately, such as displaying excessive anger at something that seems relatively trivial and harmless, can be a sign of trying to control or repress emotions.

In a quest to discover why we act the way we do, we also need to take into account that our present behaviour is an accumulation of responses to events in the past. We all have experienced highly emotional negative events and we would like to think that we have dealt with them and moved on, but this may not be the full story. Emotions can remain 'locked in' even if we are not consciously aware of them. When someone says *'That doesn't bother me any more'* they are often surprised when they truly focus their mind on the issue that they feel quite so emotional. The issue may not be uppermost in their mind but this does not mean that it is not affecting them regularly. In other words, we may have dealt with a negative experience logically, but it can still be stored in our body's energy system and replayed for many years. EFT provides a safe way to focus and calm negative energy disruptions.

The acceptability of expressing emotion varies between cultures, families and gender. Sometimes we are encouraged to hide our emotions, to be ashamed of them or afraid of them, but we are born with them and must live with them. We are unable to move to higher levels of consciousness when we have repressed negative emotions.

Using EFT enables us to be true to our feelings, releasing the energy disruption around any negative feelings, rather than needing to analyse them. The natural EFT process addresses unresolved negative and buried emotion, which increases our level of consciousness and thus our awareness of who we are meant to be.

Developing values and beliefs

Our lives are shaped predominantly by our values. In simple terms our values can be described as what is important to us. They are the foundation of our character. Values are not developed overnight but formed over time, as part of the developmental process. Research by sociologist Morris Massey (1979) identifies major developmental periods that an individual will go through in the creation of values: basic programming and imprinting, modelling and socialisation. Deep-seated values are 'programmed' in at an early age and remain with us at a subconscious level, guiding our adult behaviour and determining our world view. Massey's research leads him to suggest that our major values about life are picked up during this period, and many are formed by the time we reach age 10.

In the earliest period (0–7 years) major *programming* and *imprinting* occur. During our basic programming stage (0–4 years) we soak up everything, largely without filters: at this age we may not have the ability to differentiate between information that is useful and information that is not useful – it is just information that goes straight in. By age 4 most of our major programming and personality has been formed. During the imprinting stage, around 3–4 years and up, we absorb most information by observation or by patterning unquestioningly, especially when information comes from parents. Children see, so children do. The things young children experience affect their values for life. What they see in the world around them may not be logical but it is generally accepted, internalised, and considered to be right and normal. The importance of influences on young people at this stage cannot be understated.

The next period of development (approximately 8–13 years) is when *modelling* occurs. The most powerful influences include the behaviour of friends, family, heroes and other significant people. During this period we are trying on experiences like a suit of clothes, to see how they feel. We begin consciously and unconsciously to model basic behaviours of other people. We may also begin to mimic the values of those people. The influence of our teachers may be greater than that of our parents.

One way in which a young person can form a belief is through what they hear and through what they are told. Being told frequently *'You are annoying'* may be taken literally by a young child who is unable to interpret contexts. Children easily internalise the ideas and beliefs of those around them as if they reflect reality. Being told *'You are annoying'* often enough could initiate a 'real' belief for a young person. Some of our beliefs work for us positively and are life-giving, whereas some work against us. Confusion and blind belief during this period can lead to the early formation of trauma and other problems. Massey's research leads him to suggest that our major values about life are picked up during this period, at about age 10. He suggests that our values are based on where we were and what was happening in the world at that time.

Finally during the *socialisation* period (approximately 14–21 years) relationships and social values are developed. Moving towards young adulthood and developing as individuals, young people look for alternatives to earlier programming and they naturally turn to people who seem more like them. The influence of peers is most significant, and other influences include the media, especially those parts of the media that resonate with the values of the peer group. By age 21 the formation of core values is just about complete and will not change unless a significant emotional event occurs.

Personal beliefs and belief systems

'What we are today comes from our thoughts of yesterday, and our present thoughts build our life of tomorrow: our life is the creation of our mind'
Buddhist Dhammapada

A personal belief is a thought to which we have become emotionally attached. A strong personal belief signals to the mind that we are relying on it for survival and therefore it does not change easily. A belief system is a grouping of thoughts to which we have become emotionally attached. It develops from our core values and underlies much of our behaviour.

Beliefs and core values have a very powerful effect on our lives because we use them to filter 'relevant data' from the vast volume of incoming information that is available to us via our senses. Hence our belief system influences our perceptions, or how we interpret what we see, hear and feel.

This in turn affects how we behave in our daily lives. Thus if you develop a belief such as *'I am lazy'*, your mind works to register evidence to support or confirm this belief. Even one negative belief can have a profound effect on how we operate.

Our map of the world

Our beliefs influence our behaviour without our realising it. They block out data that is contradictory. When you think about whether or not you believe something, you are referring internally to your current perspective of your world and comparing the extent to which this 'new' data fits your established understanding. You make decisions and judgements accordingly.

So we interpret information and experiences based on our expectations of them, rather than on their actual content, with the result that our interpretations may often not be as accurate as we assume. Believing is seeing: we see what we believe, which in turn makes us believe what we see. The external world that we perceive is in fact our interpretation of that world according to our beliefs. In 1933 Alfred Korzybski, published 'Science and Sanity' a thesis that discussed how we experience the world through our senses and use this external datum to build internal representations of the world within our brain. The thesis used the term 'The map is not the territory' to explain how the real world and the internalised perception are different. The phrase is very widely used in neuro linguistic programming (nlp) teaching.

A map is not the territory it represents, but if correct, it has a similar structure to the territory, which accounts for its usefulness. What this means is that our perception of reality is not reality itself but our own version of it, or our 'map'.

Our attempt to obtain peace and wellbeing can be elusive, particularly when we are using unhelpful yet familiar patterns of belief that have served us for a long time. We may not even be aware of the existence of these patterns. But beliefs are not set in stone. If we allow ourselves, we can use simple techniques to review and change our perspectives, which in turn will enable us to review and change our behaviour.

Navigating the journey with blind spots

Our beliefs are our personal reference points or rule book, and we constantly make unconscious decisions to act on the basis of these reference points or rules. Many beliefs are useful and life-affirming: *'I am generous'* might be an example. Unfortunately, we also hold beliefs that are long-standing and limiting 'blind spots', created by unhelpful perceptions about either life or ourselves. *'Never rely on anyone'*, for example, is not very life-affirming. We refer to our 'blind-spot' perceptions - our limiting beliefs - on a daily basis, which naturally can cause us to feel 'stuck in a rut'.

Case study

Jez spent much of his time helping others and taking on extra projects. Even though the choices were his, he complained that he was frustrated and unfulfilled. He was unaware why he did this to himself. Using EFT, he uncovered, much to his surprise that his belief, his internal dialogue, told him that he only had value when he was being useful. He had actually internalised this idea early in life from listening to and watching his parents. These were not Jez's personal preferences but his parents'. He discovered for himself that the underlying driver compelling him to take on these tasks was about feeling worthwhile in order to please his parents despite the passing of several decades. Jez continued using EFT to achieve a greater sense of self-worth and a modified way of helping others which more accurately reflected his 'true-self'.

As we can see from Jez's case study, our internalised beliefs do not necessarily serve us well. He was operating in conflict to his true needs. Even if the beliefs we internalise cause us to feel, for example, rejected, we often unconsciously continue to set up situations that cause us more feelings of rejection (see the section 'cleaning up graffiti', in Chapter 6). Each time this happens, we unknowingly validate these erroneous beliefs through our behaviour. Our subconscious does not differentiate between helpful and unhelpful; it simply follows the instruction it is given. Hence, we subconsciously allow ourselves to fail.

Our mind establishes beliefs over time and then draws on the world around us for evidence that they are correct. We create situations in which the mind can fulfil a belief. Consequently we are driven to prove our beliefs, most of the time without even knowing what they are. Following our rule book, we cross-match new experience with our existing beliefs. This makes us feel as though we are on the right track, even though some of those beliefs are limiting or blind. They give us a sense of the familiar comfort and control even when the resulting experience is 'hurt' or 'being stuck'.

Do you ever ask yourself why do I feel like this/act like this?

Life: a reflection of your beliefs

As we have seen, the power of personal belief can work both for us and against us, but either way, it always makes things happen. Your beliefs are creating your life each day, moment by moment. Belief will always yield a result. Whether the belief is *'I can'* or *'I cannot'*, you will always get the result that you believe you will get. You are a mind with a body.

Despite the fact that we may have limiting beliefs about ourselves or the world, we still have the power intentionally to direct our individual thoughts, to reform our thinking patterns or personal beliefs, to create the destiny we desire. Given the right environment, the subconscious mind takes fresh positive thoughts and sets about manifesting them into a new reality for us.

Become more keenly aware of the thoughts that dominate your mind at each moment, as they have a huge impact on your wellbeing. The idea of manifesting more helpful personal beliefs may sound impressive, but you may be left wondering how you can make this possible. How can you become aware? How can you elicit real change? Enter EFT.

Conceive, believe and achieve

*Your consistent thoughts become your reality. The question is,
what are you thinking about?*

What beliefs do you hold about your life? How would you like your life to be? What does this feel like? How can you influence professional and personal relationships, performance, inner happiness, health and personal wealth? Letting go of limiting beliefs vastly improves your emotional and physical wellbeing. EFT provides a natural way to become aware of our inner beliefs through sharper and expanded thinking. Using EFT, blind spots become glaringly obvious and advanced techniques can help eliminate them. EFT provides a natural and non-threatening way to identify negative beliefs that do not work in your life and to replace them with positive, constructive feelings and thoughts.

Case study

Several years ago during an exam 'stress-busting' EFT workshop for students, Claire, aged 17, who was trying to start revision, said, *'I'm no good at exams. I've got a really bad memory.'* The whole group laughed with Claire about stories of her unreliable memory. It seemed that this was or had become Claire. I was interested to find out more and invited the whole class to start tapping with Claire as we retraced her thoughts.

Claire had all the answers. *'Oh my mum, my gran, my sister and I have awful memories. My dad always says all the women in our family ...'*

She continued, *'There was this time when ...'* and as she talked in detail, we all kept tapping. In time we introduced the following set-up statements from Claire:

'Even though I never remember anything...'
'Even though my dad says that all the women in our family have awful memories...'
'Even though I have a really awful memory and I know that because of all my stories...'
'Even though I can remember in detail all the times that I have an awful memory...'

Claire said, 'Oh'. A penny had dropped and Claire's reasoning was changing simply through tapping and talking. During the natural process of EFT, she had accessed the sources of her belief, the conflicting logic and the answers within herself. We continued to tap, using more positive phrases from Claire. In the remaining chapters you will read more about the processes that occur as we tap.

>>

Case study continued

The following lesson, Claire came firing in. *'You're not going to believe it, but I have memorised all this!'* She flicked through three chapters of a challenging psychology textbook. *'Test me,'* she enthused, and I did. Her friends were genuinely impressed, to say the least. Claire had challenged her unhelpful belief using insights, and EFT had been the catalyst. This was, however, not just a one-trick event. Through her own hard work and determination Claire turned around her exam performance in all her subjects in the coming months.

Two years later I received a beautiful letter from her. She was doing well at university and was proud of the 'magic of my memory', as she put it. In this case it had taken only five minutes to change a long-term limiting belief. You will gain skills in the forthcoming chapters to use EFT to facilitate similar deep change.

I use just one of thousands of examples of EFT here to show that you can have anything you want if you give up the belief that you cannot have it. We do a bit of this in everyday life by putting on a positive front and using a little willpower, but willpower alone will not eradicate disruptions in the energy system and the effect will not last. EFT allows you to move from the negative to the positive in emotional patterns and to make natural cognitive shifts, creating peace of mind, enhanced health and greater happiness.

Emotional health and wellbeing

Positive emotional health can be described in many ways: a sense of wellbeing; engaging in life through meaningful activities and positive relationships; positive self-worth and self-esteem; the ability to be truly resilient in less than favourable circumstances; achieving balance between play and work, peace and excitement; and so on. No matter what description is used, the value of positive emotional health should never be underestimated.

Positive change is always possible but the only person who can change the way you feel is you. If you have ever found yourself thinking *'I'll be happy/peaceful/satisfied when …'* you may find that you feel dissatisfied even when you have achieved that particular goal. Changing our external world does not change how we feel; it can momentarily distract us from being dissatisfied, but no other person, no material possession, no activity can release the feelings within us. Only we ourselves can do this. If you are committed to true emotional health then EFT is an essential addition to your toolbox. If you are ready to explore more about your emotional self, then EFT can help you begin the seemingly difficult tasks of uncovering limiting beliefs and releasing buried emotions so that you can operate at your best.

Education, health and social care

Following the World Health Organization's Mental Health Declaration in 2005, there is evidence of a commitment to promoting awareness of positive emotional health in many public sectors. Substantial spending has been invested in a huge range of policies and programmes in the sectors of education, health and social care in order to provide a wide range of emotional literacy and skills training for positive emotional health. Enlightenment is one thing, but providing highly effective tools and techniques to enhance wellbeing, that are easily accessible at reasonable cost, is quite another.

Chapter 3 sets out the basic principles of EFT and then much of the rest of this book provides examples of the application of EFT to many types of issue, age group and scale of intervention.

1 Mental Health Action Plan and Declaration for Europe, signed and endorsed on behalf of ministers of health of the 52 member states in the European Region. Promoting mental wellbeing for all was the first area of action.

Chapter 3
Principles of Emotional Freedom Techniques

Chapter 3 Principles of Emotional Freedom Techniques

This chapter outlines some of the basic principles of EFT to get you tapping.

Work your way through this chapter slowly and practise to get the basics right. Advanced skills are dealt with in later sections of the book but in the meantime relax, keep an open mind and enjoy it.

Trying the routine on yourself for the first time may seem a little confusing – rather like when you first try to tap your head and rub your stomach at the same time, it feels odd. Persevere, however, and you will become accustomed to the routines so that you can perform them almost in autopilot mode.

EFT is extremely gracious. You would have to try very hard to get it so wrong that you did not see at least some results. Please remember that EFT complements qualified medical advice or treatment and is not a replacement.

Techniques and tips to get started

Techniques vary in small details between different sources of information about EFT. In time, you will select your own style. Below are a few points to bear in mind before you begin.

Take your time to practise finding the tapping points before you move on to the four steps of the EFT procedure.

The decision to use the full basic recipe or the shortcut version of EFT is a personal choice.

You can choose to tap on the points on either side of the body, left or right, or swap half-way through, because there are pairs of meridians, one on each side of the body. Most people use their dominant hand to tap on the opposite side of their body. Some people, and especially young people, choose to tap on both corresponding points at the same time, for example under both eyes at the same time instead of under just one eye.

Generally, you use the pads of a couple of fingers to tap gently but firmly on the tapping points – enough to cause a vibration in that area. Being 'spot on' is ideal, but as long as you cover the area of the point you will create a vibration to release blockages and rebalance the subtle energy in that meridian.

Beginners often ask how fast or slow, or how many times, they should tap. Ideally, you will tap in a comfortable rhythm of your choice that fits the length of time it takes to say your set-up statement or reminder phrase. A very rough estimate would be to tap about seven times, but this could increase according to the length of what you choose to say.

You will get most benefit from tapping when your body is in a relaxed state. As you tap try to relax any clenched fists, crossed legs and tense shoulders, to allow energy to flow.

To maximise electrical conduction within the energy system the body needs plenty of water. To remain hydrated drink a glass of water before you begin and have another full one by your side as you tap. After each round of tapping take a few mouthfuls and relax. Additional water is also a good idea following a session. In addition, good breathing (calm and with reasonable depth) is important. Attention to breathing, usually between tapping rounds, helps to facilitate energy shifts.

If you wear glasses you may wish to remove them – some people find that they get in the way when tapping on the points around the eye area.

The feelings caused by tapping vary from person to person and depend on the problem being treated. You will read more about this in the section 'Interpreting common reactions' later in this chapter. No reaction is harmful. Keep tapping, but do also read the section on 'Caution, responsibility and abreactions' later in the chapter.

How often you tap, and what for, is your own choice. Many people tap for a few minutes every day. More options are outlined in the section 'When to use EFT' later in this chapter. The applications and benefits are endless, and this is one of the healthiest habits you will ever practise.

Locating tapping points

Local tapping points, also known as electromagnetic points, meridian energy points or acupoints, are the places on the surface of the body that we tap during EFT. Depending on the EFT routine being used, we usually tap on 9 to 14 points. Each tapping point corresponds to an energy meridian. At certain points along each meridian the bioelectrical pathway rises to the surface. Measurement at these points shows a lower electrical resistance. Stimulation by tapping, touch or rubbing one of these electromagnetic points raises the level of energy or 'vibrational energy'. This in turn rebalances any disruption or blockage in that meridian and its associated organs. Combining the active tapping part of EFT with the communication elements, EFT becomes a powerhouse of positive change, as you will discover.

The points designated in EFT were chosen from the several hundred points that could be used because they are easy to locate and access. Before you begin the whole routine, familiarise yourself with the location of these points on your body. They are illustrated in Figure 3 and described in Table 2. Note in particular the following three points.

Sore point –SP

Used in the original EFT teaching and associated with the initial set-up procedure of EFT is the sore point (SP). The location of the sore point is vertically up from the nipple about halfway to the collarbone[1]. If you have congestion in your lymphatic system it is likely to be a little tender if you press into it. Unlike other points on your body you can gently rub this point in a circular motion with the flat pads of your fingers, instead of tapping it. It is a very effective point for the set-up phase of the tapping procedure to address psychological reversal and acceptance which is discussed in detail throughout the book. In practice the tapping point used in the set-up procedure is very often the alternative point, the friendly point (FP) as it is commonly regarded as easier to find.

Friendly point – FP

More straightforward to locate, the friendly point (FP)[2] is on the fleshy region of the side of the hand down from your little finger. You can tap with fingers of one hand on the fleshy part of the other or tap both fleshy parts together. This point is tapped during the set-up phase of the routine[3] and is also associated with the question of psychological reversals and acceptance (see Chapter 6).

Top of head point – TH

This set of points is located in a ring shape at the crown of the head. This is an important energy centre, as many meridians meet at the top of the head. Stimulating this area affects the entire energy system and in particular tunes body–mind attention to the issue being addressed using EFT. This point is highly sensitive and it is important to be gentle when tapping.

Figure 3 **Location of meridian tapping points used in EFT**

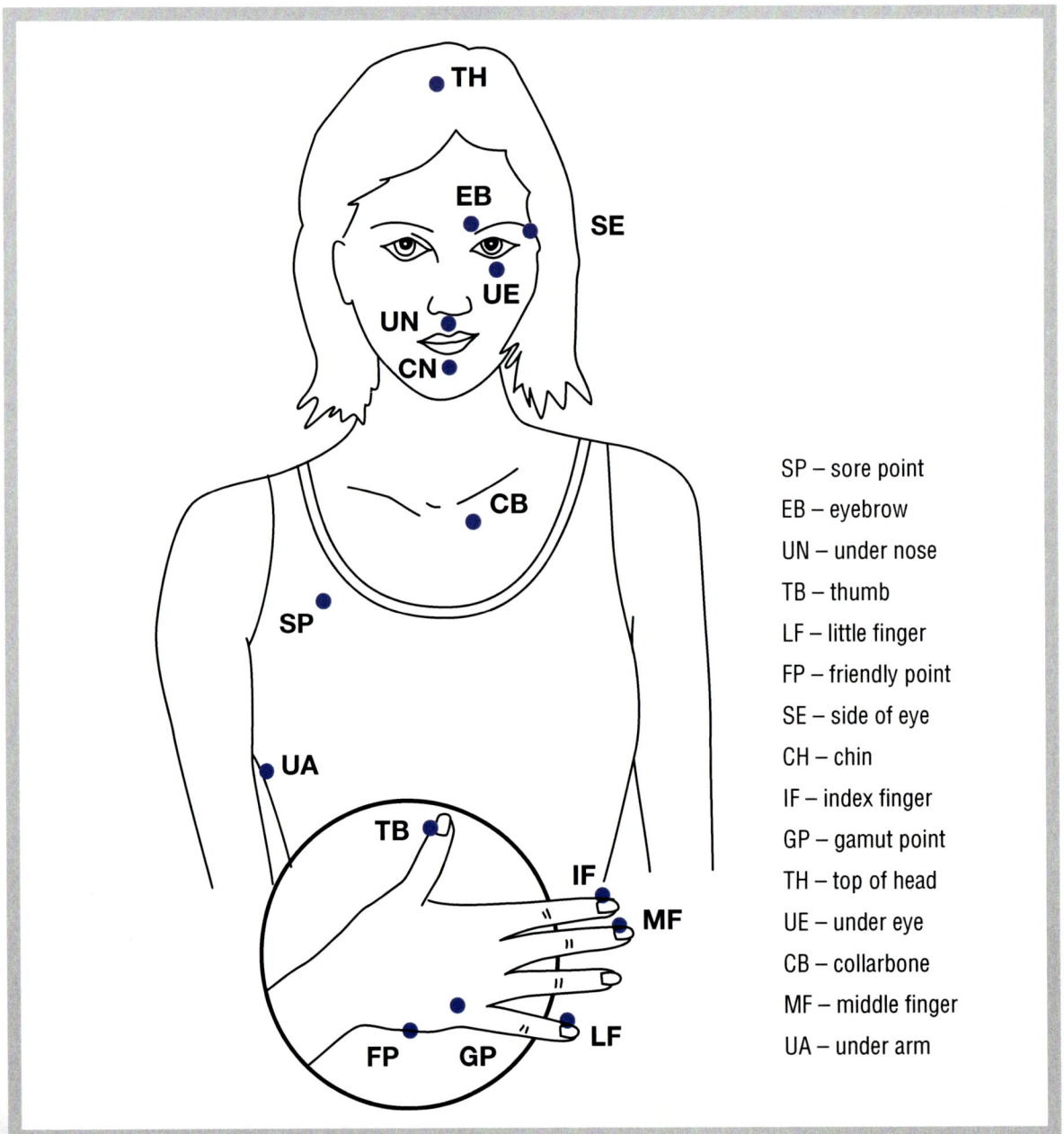

SP – sore point
EB – eyebrow
UN – under nose
TB – thumb
LF – little finger
FP – friendly point
SE – side of eye
CH – chin
IF – index finger
GP – gamut point
TH – top of head
UE – under eye
CB – collarbone
MF – middle finger
UA – under arm

Table 2 **Location of tapping points for full EFT basic recipe**

Tapping point	Location
Choose either **Sore point - SP** or	Halfway between the nipple and the collarbone
Friendly point - FP	On the soft fleshy part of the non-dominant hand, between the base of the little finger and the wrist (see note 1 below)
Top of head - TH	A set of points are located in a ring shape at the crown of the head
Eyebrow - EB	At the beginning of the eyebrow, up and over from the bridge of the nose
Side of eye - SE	At the end of the eyebrow, on the bony protrusion at the leading edge of the temple
Under eye - UE	On the bone underneath the eye, directly under the pupil
Under nose - UN	Under the nose, in the little crevice above the upper lip
Chin - CH	Just under the bottom lip, in the depression between the lip and the chin
Collarbone - CB	Just below the knob of the collarbones in the shallow depressions
Under arm - UA	About 10 cm directly below the armpit (mid bra strap location for women)
Thumb - TB	Edge of thumbnail (see note 2 below)
Index finger - IF	Edge of index fingernail
Middle finger - MF	Edge of middle fingernail
Little finger - LF	Edge of little or baby fingernail
Gamut point - GP	In the crease on the back of the hand between the little finger and the ring finger

Difficult-to-reach points

Tapping points that are difficult to reach or uncomfortable to tap need not pose a problem. If, for instance, you cannot easily reach the tapping point under your arm (UA), and so leave it out, you are not directly stimulating the spleen meridian (see Appendix 2). By tapping on the under eye (UE) point, however, you cause vibrational change not only in the stomach meridian but also in the companion organ, the spleen. This secondary stimulation to the spleen is just as effective. An EFT practitioner will be able to provide advice on alternative tapping points.

Choosing the full basic recipe or the shortcut version

The full basic recipe of EFT was first devised in the 1990s by Gary Craig and was published in the EFT manual. The recipe involves 14 elements and combines tapping, talking and some brain-balancing techniques. In time, practitioners found that they obtained the same level of success using a shortened version of EFT.

Table 3 **Example using the full basic EFT recipe**

Stage of routine	Full basic EFT recipe	Example response
1 The set-up procedure		
(a) Identify the problem	*'How does it make you feel?'*	*'Headache'*
(b) Identify aspects of the problem	List and choose one to work on	*'Thumping tightness in my left temple'* *'Slightly fuzzy'*
(c) Measure intensity using the subjective units of distress (SUD) scale	0–10 units of distress/ disturbance	*'Thumping tightness in my left temple'* SUD = 8
(d) Create an EFT set-up phrase	*'Even though I …* (problem phrase), I … (acceptance phrase)'	*'Even though I have a thumping tightness in my left temple, I love and accept myself'*
(e) Perform the set-up	(e) Perform the set-up	*'Even though I have a thumping tightness in my left temple, I love and accept myself'* x 3
2 Carry out EFT tapping routine	(i) Say reminder phrase while tapping on each tapping point TH, EB, SE, UE, UN,CH, CB, UA and continue on the finger points TB, IF, MF, LF	(i) *'Thumping tightness'* *'Thumping tightness'* *'Thumping tightness'*
	(ii) follow the nine gamut procedure – open eyes, close eyes, hard down right, hard down left, roll eyes clockwise, anticlockwise, hum, sing, hum	(ii) Concentrate on the *'thumping tightness'* as tapping
	(iii) Say reminder phrase while tapping on each tapping point TH, EB, SE, UE, UN,CH, CB, UA Take a deep breath	(iii) *'Thumping tightness'* *'Thumping tightness'* *'Thumping tightness'*

Stage of routine	Full basic EFT recipe	Example response
3 Assess the changes	Assess level of relief gained and follow suggested action on any remaining problem if necessary	*'There's no more thumping tightness in my left temple'.* SUD = 0 = complete relief on that aspect, *'but there is still a bit of a fuzzy feeling there with a* SUD = 3'
4 Address remaining aspects	Thumping tightness aspect = complete relief Fuzzy feeling aspect = 3	*'Even though I have a fuzzy feeling left in my left temple, I love and accept myself'* – perform the set-up and continue

The version you use is a matter of personal preference. Once you are confident with the basics, the beauty of EFT lies in experimenting and being creative. If you decide that tapping on all the points makes the treatment more effective, it is fine to do this and it takes only about another 30 seconds. In practice, I tend to use the shortened version most of the time. I do, however, adopt the full basic version in a certain situations, particularly when addressing traumatic memories and when working with issues that are resistant to change.

Using EFT: step-by-step procedure

Figure 4 **The EFT process**

Steps 1 and 2 form what is commonly known as a 'tapping round' or a 'round of tapping'. Steps 3 and 4 follow on, assessing and addressing the results of the tapping round. Even with basic experience it is possible to obtain good results. The four steps are:

Step 1 The set-up procedure

(a) identify the problem

(b) identify aspects of the problem

(c) measure intensity using the subjective units of distress (SUD) scale

(d) create an EFT set-up statement

(e) perform the set-up

Step 2 Carry out EFT tapping routine

Step 3 Assess the changes

Complete relief	**Partial relief**	**Intensity rises**	**Little change**
Emotional freedom from that aspect of problem. Test. If more aspects show up resume routine from Step lb	From that aspect of the problem. Create 'remaining phrase' set up and resume routine from Step lc	You are hitting a bulls eye on something. Possibly jumping aspects or accessing a deeper issue. Keep tapping on the current feeling. Read section 'Improving success rate of EFT' in Chapter 4	Many possibilities, including jumping aspect, or not being specific. Keep tapping. Skills can be fine-tuning. Read section 'Improving success rate of EFT' in Chapter 4

Step 4 Address the remaining aspects

Begin with the full basic recipe to get an idea of how the routine works. When you are able to use this full tapping routine successfully, you can move to the shortcut version.

Step 1: the set-up procedure

(a) Identify the problem

What is it that is bothering you? As you think of your problem, how does it make you feel and where do you feel it in your body? In EFT we identify the problem and focus on it to recreate the energy disruption, which is then addressed directly.

If you are new to EFT I strongly suggest that you start to practise by choosing to focus on a small problem, such as a minor irritation, a pain or a fear.

You may like to refer to the section 'An illustration of the four-step procedure in use' later in this chapter.

(b) Identify aspects of the problem

You now ponder on the problem in greater detail and identify different aspects of it. For instance, the problem may involve having to make a decision that will be unpopular. You may ask:

- What is it about the decision that bothers you?
- How do you feel about that?
- Where in your body do you get that feeling?
- Who does it involve?

Start to list the various aspects and how they affect you emotionally and physically.

Aspects of the problem to be treated are extremely important and will be explored in greater detail in Chapter 4.

(c) Measure intensity using the subjective units of distress scale

In EFT the subjective units of distress (SUD) scale, is the most common method of ranking the level of distress or disruption caused when aspects of an issue are brought to mind. The SUD scale is a simple 0–10 scale to measure the intensity of distress in response to a particular stimulus such as a memory. Distress is not always easy to quantify and is personal to each individual, which is why the technique is described as 'subjective'.

Occasionally a client may dislike or have difficulty thinking about the SUD measure. An alternative is to use the distance between your hands to indicate the size of the problem. Young people in particular create inventive ways to indicate subjectively the 'size' of how they are feeling.

Once you have focused on the problem you want to work on, you measure the level of distress or intensity that you feel in regard to each aspect. You do this both before and after a tapping round in order to obtain an accurate reflection of change. To measure the level of intensity accurately you need to 'feel in the present' rather than imagining what the measure might be. To recreate the emotion try to remember what caused you to be anxious; for example, recall the upsetting scene or imagine being in the situation again or hearing the voice of the person who caused you distress. Recreating some of the emotion recreates the associated energy disruption, which is then tapped on directly. Choose one aspect of the problem to start working on.

An alternative to the SUD rating is the validity of cognition (VOC) rating. This measure is used to address core intangible issues such as beliefs.

Chapter 6 describes the use of EFT for beliefs in more detail.

(d) Create an EFT set-up statement

In EFT we create accurate set-up statements that verbally reflect an aspect of the issue in focus. Newcomers to tapping may doubt their ability to formulate accurate set-up statements, but the guidelines are simple.

A set up statement consists of two parts:

- the first is where you acknowledge the problem

- the second is where you state your acceptance of yourself.

The set-up always[4] begins with *'Even though ...'* and continues with the issue or aspect of the issue in focus.

Be specific in describing the problem. Use the name of a person or place, or describe the location in your body where you have the experience. Saying *'Even though I felt miserable when Claire didn't want to see me ...'*, for instance, may get better results than saying *'Even though I felt miserable ...'*. Likewise, saying *'Even though I have a thumping tightness in my left temple ...'* is possibly better than *'Even though I have a headache ...'*.

Chapter 4 discusses ways of being specific in more detail.

So the first part of the set-up statement acknowledges the problem and how you feel about it now.

The second part consists of your acceptance of yourself and begins to address your willingness to let go of the problem or feeling. The traditional acceptance phrase is *'I deeply and completely love and accept myself'* or *'I accept myself'*. In effect, the acceptance phrase is saying *'Despite having this problem, I accept myself anyway'*.

To use an example, the set-up statement could be:

'Even though I have a thumping tightness in my left temple, I deeply and completely love and accept myself.'

We also need to create a reminder phrase (a short version of the aspect in focus) that will be used within the tapping round. In this example it could be: *'thumping tightness in my left temple'*.

The wording of any set-up statement needs to reflect feelings accurately. Nowhere is this more important than in the acceptance phrase of the statement. The standard acceptance phrase can be a struggle for some people who do not love, accept or even like themselves. It is essential that the whole set-up is 'true for you' or the effect of energy shifts will be minimal – all that will happen is that an inner voice will be whispering something like, *'love myself, you must be joking'*. Your energy and attention will go there instead of towards any opportunity to heal. More examples of acceptance phrases are:

'I'm a good dad' or *'I was doing the best I can'*, which may lead to *'I can learn to love and accept myself'* or *'I'm open to the possibility that I can love and accept myself'*, or *'I choose to accept myself.'*

Further assistance on self-acceptance is covered in Chapter 8.

In order for the acceptance phrase of the set-up to be effective your subconscious needs to understand what is intended. Other examples might be:

'Even though I have this burning pain in my right wrist, I deeply and completely accept myself.'

'Even though I still feel sad that I let Tom down, I accept myself, I am a fair person.'

'Although I still feel guilty because I wasn't very kind, I accept that I'm doing the best I can.'

Other styles of set-up statement include:

- The younger generations. The set-up statement is personal and specific to the individual, issue and age group. It would be unhelpful for a young child who has dyslexia, for example, to say *'Even though I have difficulty with sequences, I deeply and completely accept myself.'* Instead, the statement must make personal sense. In this case, a far more effective statement would be *'Even though I get jumbled with my days of the week, I am a good boy'*, because the child would understand and agree with what he was saying.

- Letting go and moving on. These statements indicate our intent and willingness to let go of a problem and move on to alternative ways of perceiving, feeling and reacting. They are best introduced when the negative aspects of an issue have begun to clear. Examples can be found throughout later chapters.

- Dr Carrington EFT Master introduced the Choices Method which powerfully extends the scope and power of the EFT tapping routine. The method is a way of turning around negative thoughts and has the advantage that it helps the set-up statements be believable. Choices tapping is usually introduced to the process after tapping on the initial negative feelings of an issue. So, for example, following tapping on a regular set up statement such as *'Even though I get really nervous when I have to talk to new people, I love and accept myself'*, an alternative Choice statement can be introduced such as; *'Even though I get really nervous when I have to talk to new people, I now choose to feel happy and confident when I speak to new people'*.

> Further examples of Choice tapping are outlined in Chapter 6.

> **Important note:** In the remainder of the book, whenever the set-up statement ends with '...', this indicates that it is completed with an acceptance phrase that suits a particular individual.
>
> So for instance a set-up statement that says, *'Even though I have tightness over my right eye...'*, the statement in full may be something like, *'Even though I have tightness over my right eye, I deeply and completely love and accept myself.'*
>
> Various options of suitable acceptance phrases are offered throughout the book.

(e) Perform the set-up

Repeat your set-up statement out loud three times while you either rub your sore spot or tap your friendly point (see Figure 3). This helps to remove blockages. Say the statement with emphasis.

Within the EFT routine you always start by focusing on the negative in order gently to recreate the feeling that you want to treat. For EFT to be able to target the disruption it is essential to maintain the focus.

Step 2: carry out EFT tapping routine

During Step 2 you make a decision to use either the full basic version or the shortcut version of EFT. Before this stage both versions are identical. Both options are described in greater detail below.

Option A: the full basic recipe

Tapping round

Once you have completed the set-up procedure you begin to tap using the pads of your fingers on each of the points listed below (see Table 2). While you do this you repeat your reminder phrase, for example *'Thumping tightness in my left temple'*.

- Top of the head (TH)
- Eyebrow (EB)
- Side of eye (SE)
- Under eye (UE)
- Under nose (UN)
- Chin (CH)
- Collarbone (CB)
- Under arm (UA)
- Thumb (TB)
- Index finger (IF)
- Middle finger (MF)
- Little finger (LF)

Nine gamut procedure

The nine gamut procedure is a sequence of brain-balancing exercises that help to reprocess memories. Located on the triple warmer meridian, the gamut point accesses a gateway to balance stress in many different parts of the body, notably the brain. The procedure is introduced at this stage while you continuously tap on the gamut point located between the ring finger and little finger on the back of your hand, just slightly below the knuckles (see Figure 3). The brain-balancing exercises involves humming, counting and rotating eyes, which stimulates brain functions. When eye exercises such as closing, opening and rotating are performed, the brain is directly stimulated via the connecting optic nerves. The eye movements also help to relocate trauma, thereby reducing the intensity of its effect. The nine gamut procedure helps the reprocessing of visual memories and internal dialogue. Humming engages right brain activity and counting stimulates the left brain. Full brain stimulation opens up the opportunity for new processing to be laid in multiple areas of the brain.

It is important during the other stages of the full basic version to keep repeating your reminder phrase, but you do not need to do this during the nine gamut procedure. You can just think of the phrase in your head throughout, and perhaps repeat it a couple of times. Keep your head up and face forward for the whole of the procedure. When the procedure requires you to look down or roll your eyes, move only your eyes, not your head.

The nine steps are:

- open eyes
- close eyes
- eyes hard down right (direct eyes to the 5 o'clock position on a clock face)

- eyes hard down left (direct eyes to the 7 o'clock position on a clock face)
- roll eyes clockwise (in a large circle)
- roll eyes anti-clockwise
- hum out loud (a few bars of a familiar tune, such as 'happy birthday')
- count out loud '1, 2, 3, 4, 5'
- hum again.

Tapping round

You finish with another tapping round on each of the points listed above, while again saying the reminder phrase at each point.

The full basic recipe option is sometimes referred to as a 'tapping sandwich', because two rounds of tapping surround the 'nine gamut' procedure. The recipe consists of:

full tapping round, nine gamut, full tapping round (see Table 3).

Option B: the shortcut version

If you choose the shortcut version you begin to tap using the pads of your fingers on each of the following points (refer to Table 4) while repeating your reminder phrase, for example (see Table 5); *'Thumping tightness in my left temple'*.

Table 4 **Location of tapping points for shortcut version of EFT**

Tapping point	Location
Choose either **Sore point - SP** or **Friendly point - FP**	Halfway between the nipple and the collarbone On the soft fleshy part of the non-dominant hand, between the base of the little finger and the wrist (see note 1 below)
Top of head - TH	A set of points are located in a ring shape at the crown of the head
Eyebrow - EB	At the beginning of the eyebrow, up and over from the bridge of the nose
Side of eye - SE	At the end of the eyebrow, on the bony protrusion at the leading edge of the temple
Under eye - UE	On the bone underneath the eye, directly under the pupil
Under nose - UN	Under the nose, in the little crevice above the upper lip
Chin - CH	Just under the bottom lip, in the depression between the lip and the chin
Collarbone - CB	Just below the knob of the collarbones in the shallow depressions
Under arm - UA	About 10 cm directly below the armpit (mid bra strap location for women)

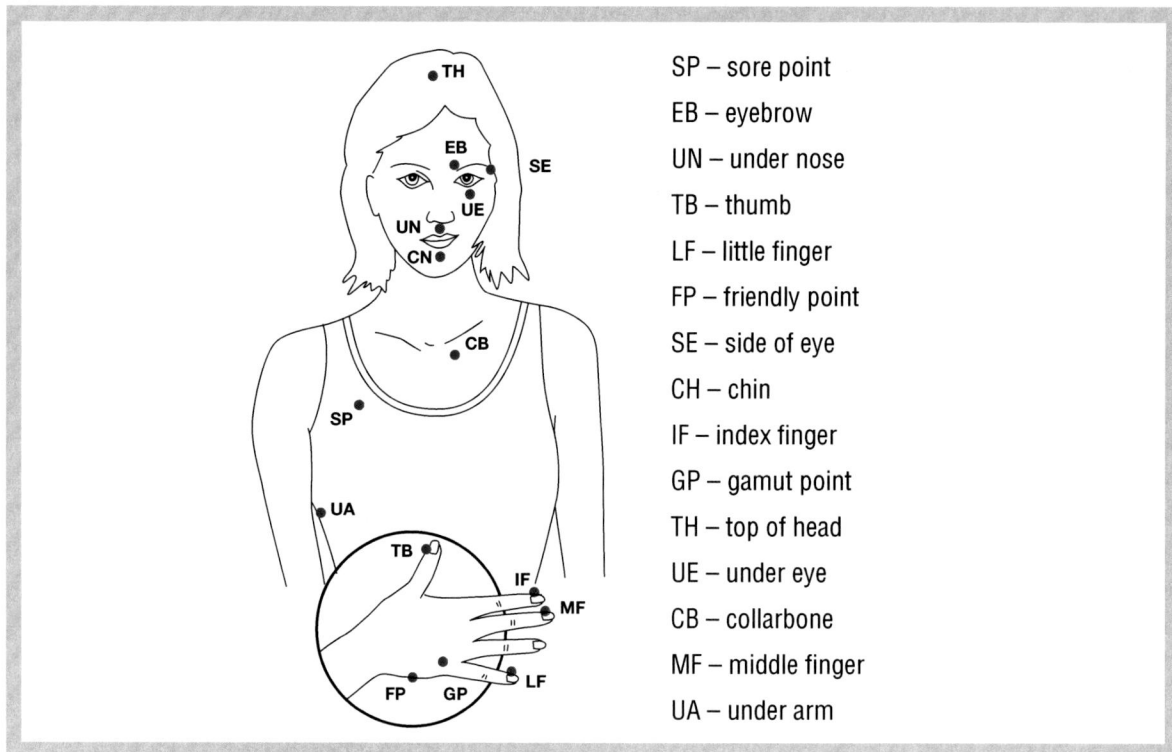

SP – sore point
EB – eyebrow
UN – under nose
TB – thumb
LF – little finger
FP – friendly point
SE – side of eye
CH – chin
IF – index finger
GP – gamut point
TH – top of head
UE – under eye
CB – collarbone
MF – middle finger
UA – under arm

Table 5 **Example using the shortcut version of EFT**

Stage of routine	Full basic EFT recipe	Example response
1 The set-up procedure		
(a) Identify the problem	*'How does it make you feel?'*	*'Headache'*
(b) Identify aspects of the problem	List and choose one to work on	*'Thumping tightness in my left temple'* *'Slightly fuzzy'*
(c) Measure intensity using the subjective units of distress (SUD) scale	0–10 units of distress/ disturbance	*'Thumping tightness in my left temple'* SUD = 8
(d) Create an EFT set-up phrase	*'Even though I …* (problem phrase), I … (acceptance phrase)'	*'Even though I have a thumping tightness in my left temple, I love and accept myself'*
(e) Perform the set-up	Rub sore point while saying set-up phrase three times	*'Even though I have a thumping tightness in my left temple, I love and accept myself'* x 3

Stage of routine	Full basic EFT recipe	Example response
2 Carry out EFT tapping routine	Say reminder phrase while tapping on each tapping point TH, EB, SE, UE, UN,CH, CB, UA Take a deep breath and relax	*'Thumping tightness'* *'Thumping tightness'* *'Thumping tightness'*
3 Assess the changes	Assess level of relief gained and follow suggested action on any remaining problem if necessary	*'There's no more thumping tightness in my left temple'.* SUD = 0 = complete relief on that aspect, *'but there is still a bit of a fuzzy feeling there with a SUD = 3'*
4 Address remaining aspects	Thumping tightness aspect = complete relief Fuzzy feeling aspect = 3	*'Even though I have a fuzzy feeling left in my left temple, I love and accept myself'* – perform the set-up and continue

- Top of head (TH)
- Eyebrow (EB)
- Side of eye (SE)
- Under eye (UE)
- Under nose (UN)
- Chin (CH)
- Collarbone (CB)
- Under arm (UA)

Inhale and then gently breathe out and relax. This completes a tapping round. Subsequent rounds of tapping may be needed depending on the outcome of Steps 3 and 4.

Step 3: assess the changes

It is essential to review the outcome of each round of tapping in order to interpret changes that have occurred and to decide what direction to take next (see Figure 4). Take a moment to check on the specific aspect of the problem for which you have been tapping. Use the SUD scale to check your level. If it is zero and you have complete relief on that aspect, you can tap for any remaining aspects by resuming the routine at Step 2. If you still have a SUD level of 1 or more, further tapping using a remaining phrase will help (refer to Step 4).

Table 6 **Example of results after tapping on one aspect – assessing change and addressing remaining aspects**

Result after tapping	SUD reading and example response	Further action suggested and example set-ups
Complete relief	SUD reading = 0 *'I have no thumping tightness in my left temple'*	Complete relief from the thumping tightness aspect of the problem Test for more aspects If more aspects of this issue show up then resume routine from Step 1b – fuzzy feeling SUD = 3 *'Even though I have a fuzzy feeling in my left temple I love and accept myself ...'* and continue until no more aspects exist
Partial relief	SUD reading = 4 *'I still have some thumping tightness in my left temple'*	Partial relief from the thumping tightness aspect of the problem Create remaining phrase set-up and resume routine from Step 1c *'Even though I still have some remaining thumping tightness in my left temple I love and accept myself'*
Virtually no change Many reasons are possible, including: jumping aspects, limiting beliefs, inexperience, reversal. See Chapter 4	SUD reading = 7 *'The thumping reduced a bit'*	If the SUD's of a specific aspect does not drop after several rounds, then explore possible reasons listed opposite and other tips in Chapter 4
Feeling worse Not common, but if it occurs can be because of: shifting aspects, inexperience or insights gained while tapping. See Chapter 4	SUD reading = 8 *'I still have thumping tightness and it has spread a bit. I think I know why the headache came on'*	Feeling worse You have hit a bulls-eye of some sort. See Chapter 4 *'Even though, I still have thumping tightness, I have an idea now why I have a headache, I love and accept myself'*

> **Notes:**
>
> Possible results gained after tapping for an aspect of a headache. Set-up statement used *'Even though I have this thumping tightness in my left temple, I love and accept myself'* SUD reading on this aspect of headache prior to tapping was 8.
>
> The 'reminder phase' and the 'remaining phrase' have different functions. The reminder phrase is a shortened version of the set-up phrase that helps you stay focused on the problem. The remaining phrase is so called as it is used in rounds following the first round of tapping when there is still remaining disruption around an aspect of the problem.

A summary of the results and further action following tapping on one aspect can be found in Table 6.

As already mentioned, the results with EFT can be rapid. It is vital to test your results before and after every couple of rounds of tapping at least. By attending closely to each aspect in turn, using suitable set-up statements and performing as many rounds as appropriate, the energy disruption reduces to zero so that when you choose to recall an aspect in order to test the results you can do so easily without experiencing emotional intensity. If any residual emotion, anxiety or discomfort still exists, measure carefully again the nature and size of the feeling and its location to create a new set-up phrase accordingly. When the SUD level is zero you want to be sure that the problem is no longer bothering you by vividly imagining or actually confronting it. If you can do this without recreating any negative feelings or anxiety, you have been successful.

It is worth pointing out at this stage that EFT never removes a memory; it simply unhooks the negative emotional charge associated with it. Like other aspects, a memory can still be recalled, but without the earlier impact.

Interpreting common reactions

As with most other therapies, recalling an emotional memory is likely to be followed by an emotional reaction – tearful, fearful, elated, according to the memory, which is a perfectly normal response. Negative reactions, such as anger, anxiety, uneasiness and sadness, or even temporary worsening of an issue, may emerge during or after an EFT session. These reactions are not side-effects of EFT, nor are they an indication that something is wrong. They can result from holding on to emotions that EFT is working to release. In fact, the emergence of these feelings indicates that EFT is having an effect.

Other noticeable changes occur when a positive reaction takes place. Example responses to a memory may include: *'It just seems a bit more fuzzy now and I'm not bothered about it'; 'I can't focus on the problem any more'; 'It seems in the distance now' or 'I have no feeling about it now, how weird!'*

Depending on the way an aspect of the problem was described originally, there may be changes to other dimensions of the memory such as colour, shape, distance, volume or size.

Step 4: address the remaining aspects

Sometimes one round of EFT is all you need to obtain complete relief, and this is not uncommon. If you get only partial relief you need to do more rounds to reduce the emotional intensity measured in SUD or VOC, and here persistence is the key. You need to alter the set-up statement slightly. Alterations will acknowledge that you still have something left to work on. A 'remaining phrase' is now introduced, and the wording will include terms such as *'remaining'* and *'still'*.

While tapping on the friendly point, or rubbing the sore spot, the 'remaining statement' could be something like *'Even though I still have some of this tightness over my right eye, I deeply and completely accept myself'* or *'Even though I have some remaining tightness over my right eye, I deeply and completely accept myself.'*

In this example the reminder phrase would be or *'still have a tightness over right eye'* or *'remaining tightness'*.

Tapping on the remaining meridian points, you might say, *'remaining tightness'*, at each of the other points:

- **TH, EB, SE, UE, UN, CH, CB, UA, TB, IF, MF, LF,** if you are using the full basic version; you do not need to include the nine gamut procedure here as it is usually used only in the initial set-up of an issue

or

- **TH, EB, SE, UE, UN, CH, CB, UA,** for the shortcut version.

(See again Figure 3, and Tables 3 and 5.)

Check the SUD scale again to see whether the intensity has diminished. If the problem is still present, repeat Steps 1 and 2.

Common questions and observations at Step 4

Take note of how you are feeling now, both physically and emotionally, and pay particular attention to any thoughts or memories that are coming to the surface. You may discover some emotional feelings, a new understanding or a logical explanation of the problem.

Even if the intensity level on this issue is lower, an associated issue, emotion or memory may be triggered. These are new aspects of the problem (see Chapter 4) and you need to address them with separate rounds of EFT.

If you are not experiencing complete relief after numerous rounds of EFT, there may be underlying problems or interferences. Again, Chapter 4 looks at this further.

How do you know that EFT is working for you? The major sign that EFT has worked is when you can think of the issue without the negative emotion being attached, or when your pain has reduced or gone. More complex testing tips are offered in the following chapters.

During EFT you may notice physical signs, more or less energy. Or you may experience sensations, such as a sigh. Muscle tension and tightness often ease because EFT helps relax your energy system. Energy moving in your physical body may give warmth or tingling in certain areas or throughout your body. Chapter 4 provides more information on calibrating vital signs when EFT starts to work. People experience different signs and sensations when using EFT. Notice what your signs are. These signs are normal and not harmful; they demonstrate that a shift is taking place, which is very good news indeed.

People often ask about the long-term effects of EFT. Aspects and issues will clear for permanent effect if EFT is done properly. EFT does not remove common sense or logic, or change your personality; it simply and beautifully rebalances the disrupted energy of negative emotions that we have chosen to focus on.

An Illustration of the four-step procedure

When you start to use EFT, keep it simple. Do not begin with a major problem. Practise, for example, on:

- a physical symptom
- an embarrassing memory
- constricted breathing
- a decision.

In this section constricted breathing provides an illustration of the four-step procedure.

EFT for constricted breathing

This exercise is often used in sessions and tasters to demonstrate gently the ease and the effect of tapping without having to approach deep or upsetting issues. In addition, it is ideal to use at times when emotional feelings become a little overwhelming. A bonus of the exercise is its benefit to the lungs and most people are genuinely surprised by the improvement in their quality of breathing.

1 Take two or three really deep breaths, breathing in through the nose and out through the mouth, taking your time and taking care not to hyperventilate. This step stretches your lungs to the extent that any further improvement in your breathing cannot be attributed to a normal 'stretching effect' of your lungs. Rather, further changes will be a result of the EFT exercise.

2 After you have stretched your lungs, take another deep breath and assess the quality of this breath on a scale of 0–10 where 10 is your estimate of your maximum capacity (depth and quality of breath). Numbers typically vary from 3 to 9 for this. The occasional person who rates their breath at 10 may find that, after EFT, they go to 12 or 15.

3 Follow either the **full version** or the **shortcut version** of tapping and perform one round of EFT, starting with a set-up statement such as: *'Even though I have constricted breathing...'* or *'Even though I can only fill my lungs to an 8 ...'* You can create your own set-up statement based on any observations you made when you tested you breath, such as soreness, tightness, sense of breath being stuck. When you have completed one round of tapping, relax.

4 Take another deep breath and assess the 0–10 quality of breath measure. In the vast majority of cases the quality of breathing (as measured by the SUD scale) has improved. Repeat Steps 3 and 4 to improve breathing quality further. Asking probing questions of yourself during the tapping may provide insights and further material to work on using EFT; examples include *'What does this ... feeling remind you of?', 'Who or what is this sensation?', 'When in your past did you feel this?'* and *'If there's an emotional reason for your constricted breathing, what might it be?'*

Caution, responsibility and abreactions

EFT compares favourably with other therapeutic procedures because of its gentle nature. Even when dealing with severe phobias or trauma, there are gentle ways to proceed. But anyone using EFT needs to be concerned to exercise caution and responsibility.

When considering working with someone else, some of the gentler techniques can be helpful. Whatever technique you use, however, the assumption is that you take full responsibility for your own use of EFT as you would naturally. Whether you are newcomer to EFT or fully trained, common sense and good judgement must prevail. Do not use EFT with people with serious issues such as severe trauma, abuse or psychiatric problems unless you have the appropriate experience. The simple rule of thumb from Gary Craig is, *'Don't go where you don't belong.'* Another of Gary Craig's is *'Try it on everything!'*, which is designed to encourage us to open up our minds to the possibilities of EFT rather than to encourage irresponsible actions.

Although potential dangers are minimal and the incidence of negative side-effects is extremely low, anyone who chooses to practise EFT on someone else should be aware of them. In a survey carried out by Gary Craig in 1997 the incidence of serious abreactions was negligible[5]; such abreaction does not happen under normal circumstances. A study published in 2009 showed that therapists prefer EFT or TFT for traumatized clients because of the noted lack of abreactions.

Reactions to EFT can include crying, upset and anger. On *very rare* occasions abreaction may result in palpitations, sweating, shaking, extreme distress or upset. An experienced professional will be skilled in addressing such responses and will apply EFT appropriately for their resolution. Again, should such responses occur, common sense must prevail:

- keep calm and explain that you will help
- ask to take over tapping on the person on all accessible points
- tap for feelings of what is happening in the body – with or without words
- instruct the person to breathe slowly and deeply
- be sure to know that these reactions are safe and harmless.

As mentioned earlier, while the results with EFT are often outstanding, never assume that EFT is taking place of prescribed medicine or any other form of healing procedure. Any client should still seek approval and advice from their GP or specialist regarding appropriate treatment and medication. EFT practitioners follow regulations and ethical guidelines from their training bodies. The association AAMET[6] is the largest in the UK.

When to use EFT

People frequently ask 'How often do I need to tap?' As mentioned earlier, this is your personal choice. I recommend tapping every day and there is no limit to what you will be able to achieve.

Table 7 **Good opportunities for tapping**

When you are 'in the moment'	If you are feeling anger, pain or anxiety, start tapping straight away and you will feel the effects immediately. Words are often not necessary as you are fully engaged 'in the moment'.
Every day	Set aside a little time every day depending on what works for you, for example: Morning boost In the shower, for an energetic boost During a walk, when you are clearing the air after a disagreement In the bathroom or anywhere you can be peaceful In the office Settling into bed (or for young people, the night-time tuck, see Chapter 14) And whenever else you need or choose to
To address an issue	Systematically to ease aspects and beliefs around an emotional or physical issue. Issues are regularly addressed and cleared by self-help. Alternatives are working with an EFT partner or in-session with an EFT practitioner
When persistence is needed	Some issues require persistence, especially chronic symptoms, addictions and cravings, and problems with many aspects
As part of the personal peace procedure	A long-term wellbeing programme (see Chapter 5)

I tap in public, not every day or every week, but when I need to. Catching your foot in a door, worrying on the way to a meeting, starting to get agitated about a decision at the doctor's, craving a cigarette are all perfect opportunities to tap 'in the moment'. Whenever possible tap during or immediately after an emotional upset or an anxious time, or when you are in pain. It is at such times that your body's energy system is disrupted, stress hormones rise and other negative effects are in action. Tapping 'in the moment' helps immediately to reverse the effects of the stress response and starts the process of letting your mind and body re-enter a safer, non-threatening mode.

Try any EFT shortcuts or release points (see next section) that work for you to help soothe and calm yourself. Many people, find tapping on the collarbone, for example, is good for anxious feelings. If you are unwilling to tap (even furtively) in front of others then perhaps you can pop to a bathroom for a few moments. Many school children with whom I have worked tap under the desk in class, just on their friendly point. Tapping silently and breathing gently is very often enough for them to regain calm or to focus concentration.

The powerful 'feel good' factor of getting back in control, calming yourself and taking the edge off anxious moments is empowering and rewarding. Take note of what caused the negative feelings: where you were, who you were with and what was said. Collecting data like this will be very useful if you choose to continue tapping at home for a particular issue, memory or feeling that runs a bit deeper.

Finding a release point

Case study

Aidan had begun to use EFT to work through some deep resentment and rage issues connected to his work performance. Recently he felt that he had been hugely let down by a long-term work partner. Aidan found the one-to-one EFT session beneficial in working through the layers and the core of an issue that had been bothering him for many years.

About a month later, he visited one of my workshops to learn some more from other keen tappers. During the workshop, I had intended to explore emotions associated with meridians. First, I asked if any of them had identified their 'release point'.

Many clients have found their 'release point' through using EFT on a regular basis. Typically, they may find the point that allows them that sigh of relief or perhaps the release of fear. This may be your experience too, although it need not be. Remember that it takes only a couple of minutes to tap a round, so it is hardly an ordeal. In addition, by doing a round of tapping you are giving all your meridians, organs and functions a quick 'energy circuit workout'.

Aidan was the first to share, *'I've no idea whether it's relevant or not,'* he said, *'but ever since I started using EFT for anger, I have been feeling much less bothered about the whole thing and I can see things more clearly from my partner's perspective. But what I have found is that I have kept finding myself tapping on the side of my eye and getting relief, without really thinking about it. I thought it was a bit weird and kind of ignored it. Could this be my "release point"?'*

Check out the emotions associated with the side of the eye point (SE) on the gall bladder meridian (see Appendix 2).

Once you identify your release point, or a few points that especially help you, then you can employ these to your advantage more often. You can also use them on their own as a cut-down of a full tapping routine. This is of particular advantage in more public places. You might tap surreptitiously on the friendly point (FP) while you are in a queue to calm yourself down, or tap quietly on the collarbone point (CP) before going into a nerve-racking interview.

If you find you are too busy to use EFT on a regular basis, check to see whether you could be using avoidance tactics. Busy people do not necessarily have the chance to look at their underlying problems and may indeed use their busy-ness to avoid doing so.

> Try using EFT to give yourself permission (see Chapter 6), to stop or slow down. Your body will thank you for it in both the short and the long term.

Information signposts

The following is a summary of some of the common questions raised by people who are new to tapping. Follow the signposts to access more detailed explanations. I recommend that you revisit this section often as you learn more about EFT and its surprises.

Q **'What will EFT work for and will it work for me?'**

A Emotional EFT addresses any negative emotion by rebalancing disruption in the body's energy system. Applied correctly, EFT works for anyone who is interested in change even if they are unsure of the source of their issues or unwilling to disclose a lot of detail. EFT works and this is no less the case for sceptics as long as there is a positive intent.

Q **'How can one technique be effective on such a wide range of problems?'**

A Remember the discovery statement behind EFT: the basis of all negative emotion is a disruption in the body's energy system. Any condition, issue or behaviour that has an emotional component will benefit from removing the disruption caused by negative emotions. Since EFT removes the disruption, you can apply the same technique to a huge range of issues.

Q **'How lasting are the results? Perhaps EFT is just distraction. Won't my problem just return later?'**

A When EFT is used skilfully a problem will be removed permanently. If this is not the case it is usually because there are hidden aspects of the problem that require specific treatment. In these instances there is always the option of engaging a qualified and experienced practitioner.

Many people – in fact, most newcomers – have difficulty believing that EFT will work. You do not have to believe in it for it to work. Just try it! This is what makes the results all the more impressive and the possibility that the placebo effect is at work is weakened. As for results being due to distraction, the very opposite is the case. In order for EFT to work you are required to be sensitive to the problem and not to think of something else. The effects of distraction wear off rather quickly. Try telling an EFT client who has permanently shaken off panic attacks and depression, after 35 years and endless other therapies and medication, that the effect is due to distraction.

Q **'I'm not sure if it fits with my beliefs and perspective on life.'**

A You may wonder how EFT fits with cultural and religious beliefs and with your individual perspective on life. As stated earlier, EFT is not a healing power, but a set of techniques that neatly facilitates a change, a shift in our energy and consciousness. These techniques become embedded in the foundations of our personal beliefs or spiritual path. Whether or not you are religious, connect with whatever you believe is the true source of healing. As you align the use of EFT with your own beliefs and perspectives or with the power greater than yourself, interesting things happen.

'It is a rare find to have such a powerful, yet easy to use set of techniques that is inclusive of all perspectives and beliefs',

Jo Powell, inclusion leader

Within the acceptance phrase of the set-up statement many people add their gratitude to their beliefs. So, for example, they might say, *'Thank you ... [*God, Spirit, Universe, Higher Power, Source, Divine Power ...] *for the many gifts in my life.'* The section on the law of attraction in Chapter 8 discusses gratitude.

'Thank you ... for resolving that disagreement so quickly'; 'I appreciate ... for my vibrant health and energy'; 'Thank you ... for all the blessings I have in my life today'; 'Thank you ... for bringing me such peace in my life' or 'Thank you ... for sending me this learning.'

EFT can be adapted in a wide variety of ways to suit your perspective and beliefs:

- appreciating yourself
- tapping in gratitude for positive intentions
- handling your mistakes with compassion
- using future thanks, for instance, *'I look forward to being surprised about the possibility of ...'*
- accessing your goals.

Q **'It seems a bit weird: can it do any harm?'**

A At first, it can seem weird. Initially, unless you are already familiar with meridians or energy psychology, the changes brought about by EFT might seem to be outside your comfort zone and belief system. Be open-minded and give yourself a chance to discover more. EFT is perfectly safe, as has already been stressed, although basic common sense needs to be used when addressing certain types of issue.

Q **'It seems too simple for it to be effective.'**

A The basics of tapping take only a few minutes. Do not be misled by the simplicity of these techniques. Chapter 7 outlines our rapidly advancing understanding of what can be observed when we tap.

Q **'The tapping is bogus, it's the talking that's makes the difference.'**

A If talking were the active component, the success rate of EFT would be in line with standard talk therapies, but in skilled hands it is much higher. I have worked with hundreds of clients who have had plenty of talk therapy but have failed to get permanent relief despite having all possible learning and insights required to let their issue go. The combination of techniques in EFT provides a powerhouse of effect.

Q **'I am sceptical, but I do want to deal with my issues and live my life differently. Will EFT work even though I have this lack of belief?'**

A As long as there is the desire to have a different outcome, EFT will work when it is applied skilfully. Our mind and body have a natural desire to move towards the positive. In addition, EFT is still effective with people who are unable to express their feelings accurately, because it addresses the underlying energetic disruption. The positive outcome of using EFT with clients who have difficulties in learning, or who are vulnerable or are unable to express emotions is very encouraging. The presence of a state called psychological reversal will, however, hinder progress if not addressed. Chapter 6 explores the way in which EFT addresses psychological reversal.

Q **'What if I don't do it right, will it still work?'**

A Any form of tapping will have a beneficial effect on your energy system as an energy workout. The more that focused EFT skills and techniques are implemented correctly, the more effective EFT will be. At worst, there will be only partial improvement on an issue rather than significant shifts. Although the EFT routine is very simple in its basic form, until you get used to it you may, for instance, tap the points in a different order or miss a point. You will be relieved to know that you can switch from left to right, or move from the top of your head to your collarbone to under your eye, and still find that EFT works. Many people also worry or get confused about the set-up phrases used in EFT. Quite simply you create a specific sentence based on exactly how you are feeling, so relax and just be really honest.

Q **'What can I do if EFT doesn't seem to be producing good results?'**

A Luckily, there are common reasons why it may seem that EFT is not working. These are covered mainly in Chapter 4, although you will find additional tips throughout the book. There is also huge scope for improvement with plenty of practice or by engaging in formal EFT training.

Q **'Why do we set-up with negative phrases? It doesn't seem right.'**

A EFT works best when you focus initially on the negative (see Chapter 4) as you tap on the meridian points. Of course, you can choose to tap for *'I'm happy'*, but if your subconscious says otherwise, it will start to raise objections and progress will be sabotaged. There is little point in introducing positives until your subconscious is ready for change. Listen to the objections or 'tail-enders' and tap for them. EFT Choices Method allows the person applying to identify the outcome that they would truly like to have for the problem at hand, and then put the desired outcome into a set-up incorporating the statement *'I choose...'* Positive statements also have an important part to play in EFT progress when introduced at the right time. More help is provided in Chapter 6.

Q **'How will I feel after doing EFT?'**

A Experiences vary. You can expect anything from elation through to a mild blur or tiredness. You have experienced the equivalent of a full mind–body workout, of acupressure, 'brain gym', neurolinguistic programming and a thorough spring clean of your subconscious. Through releasing energy blocks with EFT, your energy can now flow freely. This can leave you feeling very relaxed or more energised. After a session, pay close attention and respond to what your body is telling you. Rest, exercise, sleep and continue to drink water, according to what your senses tell you.

Q **'If it's so easy to use, why would I engage a qualified EFT practitioner?'**

A Whether or not you would be advised to approach a qualified professional really depends on your issue and your confidence. Many people use tapping very successfully for everyday issues, to rebalance energy and to regain calm in order to make better decisions. More complex issues that are embedded in negative core beliefs may be addressed more successfully by working with a qualified EFT practitioner (see Chapter 5).

Q **'How many sessions do I need to clear my problem?'**

A Compared with most other therapies, the results from EFT are often much faster and are permanent, and in most instances you start to experience improvements immediately. It is always surprising how quickly long-term patterns in attitude and behaviour can change. You need, however, to have realistic expectations and to recognise that it takes longer to deal with some problems than with others. The number of sessions required also depends on your own expectations as well as on the experience of the practitioner. For some issues persistence is a key to success. As a guide, however, in the majority of cases some definite improvement is seen within two to three sessions.

Acknowledge any small or positive changes as they occur. Friends and family will also notice changes. Some changes happen instantly, whereas for others a gradual reorganisation of feelings takes a few days. Nothing works for absolutely everyone and this includes EFT. A very small percentage of people seem not to respond initially to EFT, but with a review of techniques changes can be observed (see Chapter 4).

Q **'How do I know that it's worked for real?'**

A Continuous testing is used in EFT to establish what has happened. In some cases you can test for real; in other cases it can be difficult to recreate the exact negative situation, but there are still accurate ways to test. Testing in EFT was outlined earlier in this chapter. Additionally, the subconscious is very literal and does not recognise the difference between what is real and what is imagined. After testing thoroughly that the negative emotions have been removed, using vividly imagined situations, EFT will work in a real-life situation too.

Q **'I would like help, but I am not keen to reveal some details.'**

A Many people choose to work alone using EFT, sometimes sharing details with others. However, even if you work with an EFT practitioner you can choose to keep information private if this is important to you. Issues can still be treated successfully without the need to verbalise what you are 'tapping' for. This method of using EFT, where confidence is fully respected, has been used with remarkable success in relation to embarrassment, post-traumatic stress disorder, sexual abuse, and other issues where talking can be difficult. You can read more about using codes, objects and other gentle techniques in Chapter 5.

Q **'Can EFT be safely used with children?'**

A EFT is a very safe and successful toolkit to use with children and for children to use by themselves. With a few modifications in the basic procedures, EFT is suitable and highly effective for children for a whole range of issues (see Chapter 14).

Q **'I'd like to help my friend; she's on medication. Are there precautions or limitations to using EFT?'**

A Many people on medication use EFT with great benefit, but always with a medical professional's support. EFT can reduce, or even eliminate, the stress and fears surrounding chronic and serious illness, and often significantly eases symptoms. There are no real drawbacks or side-effects.

Refer again to the section 'Caution, responsibility and abreactions' earlier in this chapter and always heed the golden rule 'Don't go where you don't belong'. It is not advisable to use EFT for the treatment of deep-seated problems except under the guidance of a qualified mental health professional who is experienced with EFT. There is a growing number of such EFT-trained professionals who have a background in psychotherapy or psychiatric issues for specific applications.

Q **'What is the research evidence for EFT?'**

A EFT is gaining recognition from reputable authorities, and programmes of EFT have been offered within education, health and social care sectors in Britain and the US. Its popularity has grown dramatically due to the volume of remarkable results from its practice by clients, therapists, psychologists, health care workers, educators and others. Formal research in specific areas of EFT is beginning to build an evidence base and many studies are in progress via the National EFT Research Programme[7]. A sample of research material is reviewed in Appendix 3.

Chapter 7 also reviews some fascinating emerging perspectives in the field of energy.

Q **'How do I find out more about EFT?'**

A A list of contacts, recommended reading, training sources and information can be found in the resources section at the end of the book.

Despite the deceptively simple techniques in EFT, nothing replaces face-to-face learning from an experienced trainer or formal accredited training body, whether in a session, workshop or retreat.

Opting for professional assistance

Many people use EFT as a simple self-help technique on their own issues. Others choose to work with a friend or a 'tapping buddy' and get good results most of the time. If issues are rather more complex, you will gain great benefit from working with an EFT-trained professional. It is a mistake to expect that knowing the EFT basics will produce advanced results.

There are very great differences between basic EFT and the more artful or intuitive form of EFT offered by an advanced EFT practitioner who has years of experience and training. When the tapping process involves skilled intuition, reflective insight and transformation is arrived at much more easily and quickly. Undertaking basic EFT training for yourself is an excellent way to become more skilled in improving your results.

Most EFT practitioners have a website or literature, and you can choose from a wide variety of specific interests, training and styles. Qualifications and relevant insurance cover are usually clearly stated. Contact details and EFT training options are provided in the resources section of this book. There is no substitute for a high standard of training from an accredited source. EFT practice is covered by ethical and professional boundaries, and these are clearly stated in a practitioner's code of practice.

What happens in an EFT session with a practitioner?

Initially, the practitioner asks about the symptoms, the desired outcome and any relevant history. It is worth finding out whether an individual practitioner taps on the client during a session or whether the client taps on their own points. By tapping on their own points a client learns the basics after minimal practice and gains empowerment more quickly to deal effectively with their own emotional issues.

Consider whether the practitioner has a strict code of practice regarding the choice between tapping on their clients and tapping with their clients. In my own practice I tap with my clients. Together we create the set-ups and the client taps on their energy system while I mirror and tap on my energy system. Clients who tap for themselves are more likely to become accustomed quickly to empowering change for themselves. They learn that the practitioner is there as a guide to healing and not as a healer per se. The only exception to this in my own practice would be where I would obtain permission to tap on someone else during a temporary abreaction, or if they had some physical reason for being unable to tap. Some practitioners tap on their clients as standard, so it is worth checking this at an initial stage.

Before the end of the first session a client will be given full instructions and some suggested set-up statements to try at home. In subsequent sessions progress is discussed and constantly tested. Time between sessions can vary, and might perhaps be between one and two weeks, giving the client time to practise EFT and report back on any noticeable changes.

Broad guidelines for selecting an EFT practitioner

Selection of an EFT practitioner is, of course, a personal choice. You may find the following pointers helpful.

Getting the help you really need

Common sense and instinct will help you decide what is right for you. Good rapport is vital to making progress. You need to feel safe in order to explore difficult areas with a practitioner. If you are concerned that memories of traumatic incidents from the past, or other distressing issues, may cause undue emotional distress, or if you are feeling uncomfortable, the qualified practitioner you select will have on offer a variety of gentle techniques to assist.

Careful listening and questioning

You should feel that the practitioner is attending carefully to what you say. Some questions may surprise you. Astute questioning leads to EFT statements that can target issues effectively. Different approaches will be adopted according to the time-span of problems, varying between issues that are recent and those with a long-standing history. A skilled practitioner will have a well–developed, intuitive ability which will help to highlight crucial moments of insight and change as they happen.

Shining a light on an issue

The right practitioner should add considerably to your own ability to address your issues with EFT. Coming from another perspective, they should be able to help you uncover aspects that you may have missed. These may be feelings about a situation that you have difficulty recognising, or memories of other situations in your life that may have laid the foundation for your present problem. Thus with the practitioner both the origins of your problem and its immediate manifestations will be explored.

Facilitating powerful targeted EFT statements

The formulation of accurate and creative EFT set-up statements adds to the efficacy of EFT. Your aids are the suggestions that focus on specific aspects and reflect outcomes, rather than the practitioner. The practitioner is there as a guide to facilitate the client's natural processing. They are not there to be 'attached' to the client's outcome. If you were to get an impression from a practitioner that they might be thinking along lines such as *'I know how you should resolve this'* or *'It would really please me if you could get over this'*, it should perhaps be taken as a warning sign.

Constant testing

Constant testing is the key to ascertaining whether or not an issue has been dealt with on all levels. Regular testing of your reactions should be made after each round of tapping, and SUD measures are important, although a variety of ways to assess changes is employed. You may be asked to re-run the disturbing scene in your mind or to role-play in order to re-experience the scene, or to engage in an actual real-life test of the issue if this is possible. A skilled practitioner will be helping you to assess your progress continually.

Helping to shift blocks

An important consideration is how the practitioner helps you to handle being stuck on an issue. A skilled practitioner will be creative in helping to unravel and clear blocks to healing using specific targeted strategies. They will also reflect back the participant's responses and reactions as they happen. This practice enhances reflection and the possibility of the participant noticing insightful moments as they occur.

Suggestions outside session time

A skilled practitioner will be able to offer a range of creative and practical suggestions for continuing to tap regularly between sessions to help the EFT process along. Examples include tapping on specific statements, agreeing on some realistic goals, continuing the personal peace procedure and using a daily gratitude journal to record as many positive observations as possible.

Right for you

Trust your intuitive impression of whether or not the selected EFT practitioner has the right skills for you. The kind of challenge the practitioner gives to the individual client must be productive, whether the approach is confrontational, gentle and soothing or conceptual. It should be possible after the first or second session to judge whether a practitioner fits your needs. From this, you can decide whether they are shedding new light on the problem and bringing new vitality to the process or whether you might need to look for another practitioner.

---

1 People new to tapping may confuse the collarbone point with the sore spot. They are two separate points.

2 In most other books this point is called the karate chop point. Working with young people, this description can give an impression that tapping is associated with karate or with hitting things. I use the term 'friendly point' because it refers to the part of the hand used when we shake hands with someone – when we make contact with our fingertips.

3 The friendly point is an alternative to the sore spot. You use one or other in the set-up phase of the tapping routine.

4 About 90 per cent of the time people use the phrase *'Even though …'* to begin the set-up. Alternatives include, *'Although …'*. Younger people may state the issue more simply, without using *'Even though'*, for instance, *'I'm scared in my belly …'*.

5 See www.eftuniverse.com/index.php?option=com_content&view=article&id=2422&Itemid=2020 (accessed April 2011).

6 The Association for the Advancement of Meridian Energy Therapies (AAMET) is UK-based.

7 The National EFT Research Programme, www.eftresearch.co.uk (accessed December 2010).

Part 2

Out on the open road

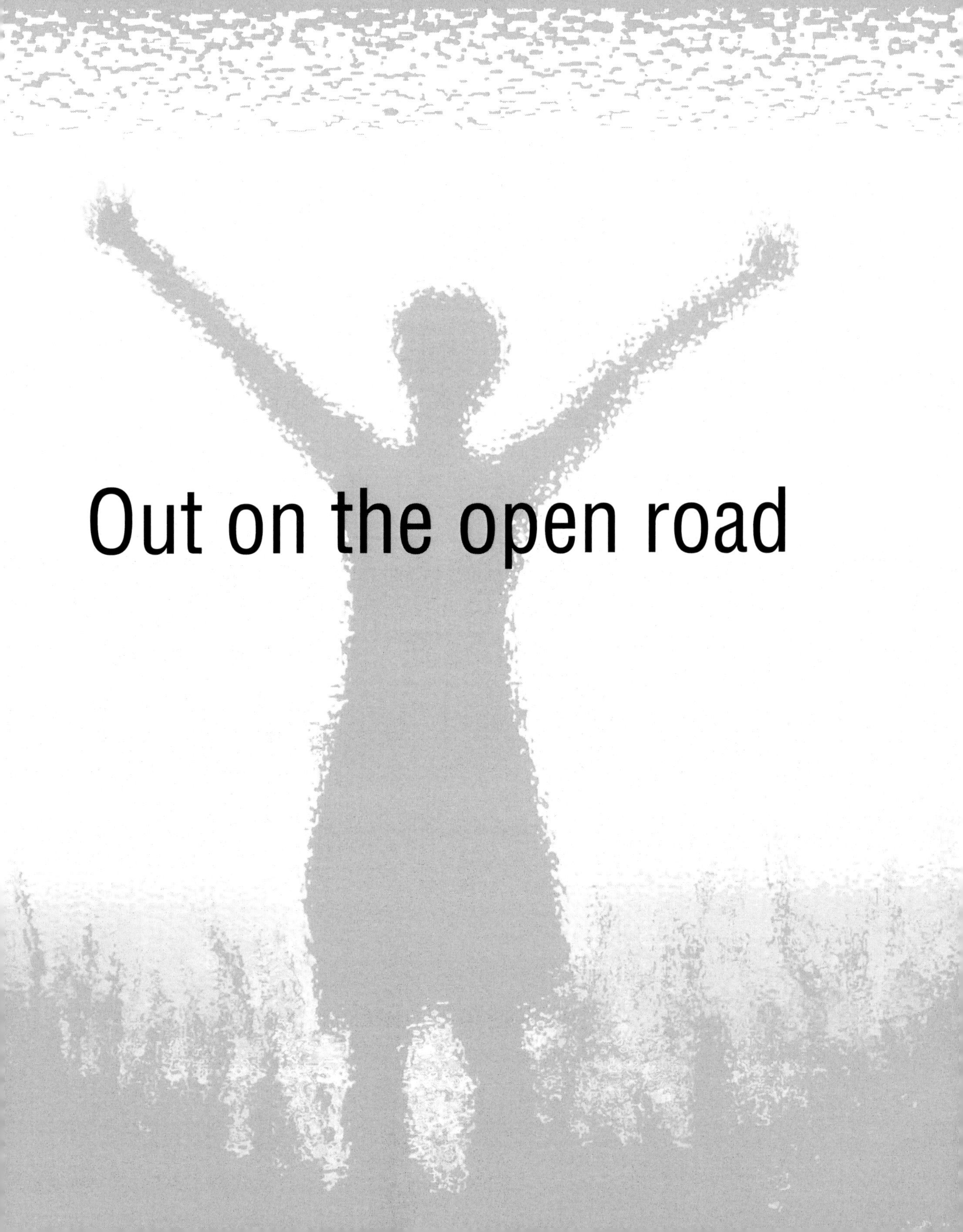

Chapter 4
Advanced map reading

Chapter 4 Advanced map reading

Great results are achieved every day using the basics of EFT, but mastering the art of delivery significantly improves results. This chapter highlights the importance of being specific, responding to individual aspects as they emerge and dealing with core issues.

Choosing your route with EFT

You can start anywhere with EFT and make good progress. If you start tapping on the issue of nail biting, for instance, you may be able to take the edge off the habit and it may even cease. In most circumstances, however, you will need to tackle a variety of aspects of a problem and most probably its root before all energy disruption is removed. Progress is greatly enhanced if the overall or 'global issue' is broken down into specific parts and each part addressed independently. Approaching the problem too globally is a fairly common error on the part of newcomers to EFT. Tapping on a very global problem such as depression, for example, is likely to give temporary or no benefit. Depression, anxiety, problems with self-image, persistent anger and childhood abuse result from numerous specific past events and these underlying issues will be experienced differently by each individual.

Listing aspects

Most of our problems can be broken down into highly specific individual aspects. Fear of flying, for example, might involve elements that are obvious and elements that are not obvious (see Figure 5). Breaking a problem down into specific aspects gives much clearer results and overall progress is quicker.

The metaphor of a table with many legs is used by Gary Craig in the original EFT manual to describe the collapsing of a problem. Imagine a table with lots of legs, where the table top represents the presenting problem – what is troubling you – say fear of flying. A multitude of aspects are supporting the problem – keeping it alive – and these are represented by the many table legs. The problem (or table top) will remain a standing problem for as long as sufficient aspects (or legs) remain. Collapse several of the aspects and the problem will collapse.

You may ask, *'How many aspects do I need to tap on before the problem goes away?'* This will vary. For instance, a person may have listed ten or more aspects. After using EFT with the first few aspects, they may suddenly find that many other aspects (similar to the ones that have already been addressed) have now lost their 'emotional charge'. They seem to have become neutralised by association due to a generalisation effect, which is looked at in more detail at the end of this chapter.

Some aspects of an issue are not obvious, and you will not necessarily see all of an issue's many parts. Similarly, you may not see the origin of an issue, especially if you have had it for a long time. By allowing your intuition to pick up the aspects as you tap, you may find yourself saying, *'Oh that's odd, why has that come to mind? I haven't thought of that for years.'* The aspect that has come to mind is very likely to be a golden nugget of material that is worth tapping on. There is no way of really knowing how many aspects are likely to need attention until thorough testing shows that no more is required, but it is important to remember that persistence pays off. You may end up tapping with numerous aspects or you may collapse the whole problem with the first few aspects.

Addressing aspects

The case study below illustrates how good EFT detective work can help to uncover and clear sufficient aspects of an issue to cause it to collapse. Some of the aspects described in the case study are shown in Figure 5.

Figure 5 **Taking a global issue and examining the aspects**

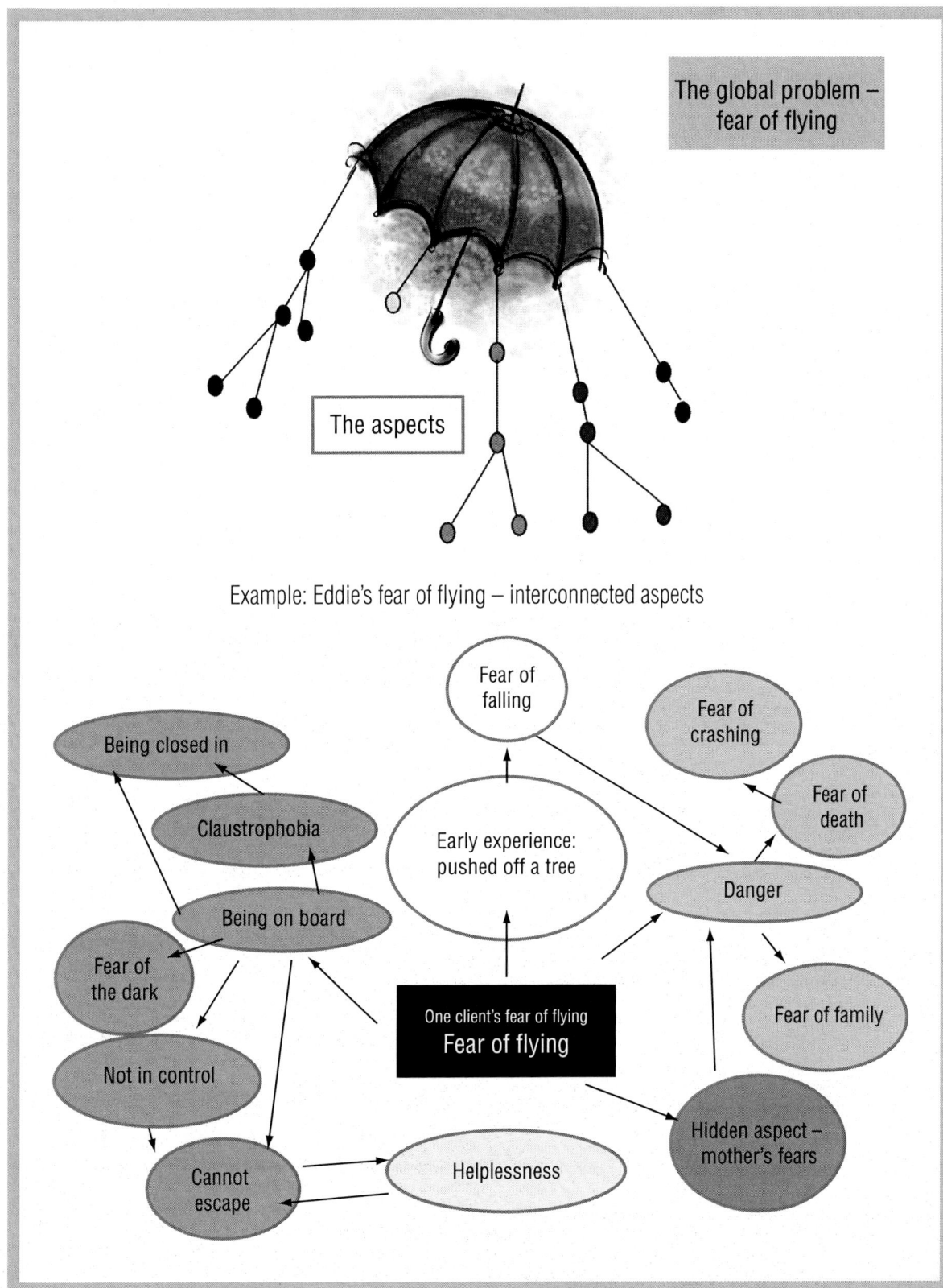

The global problem – fear of flying

The aspects

Example: Eddie's fear of flying – interconnected aspects

Case study

Until four years ago Eddie had a fear of flying. Despite his terror, Eddie had continued to fly because he did not want it to 'beat him'. He had battled with his severe nerves and negative reactions before and during every trip. So intense were his emotions that long bouts of fatigue followed each flight, whether it was for a holiday, for work or to visit family.

Eddie listed all the things that made flying terrifying for him. He had no memory of when the intense feelings had started, because he had flown most of his life. Together, we used EFT on many aspects – emotional, physical and environmental.

In time, an interesting aspect emerged, which was associated with an early incident from Eddie's childhood: his cousin had pushed him off a branch of a tree into a makeshift hammock below. Eddie discovered that the sensation of falling had become linked with his fear of the *'falling out of the sky'* – a feeling he experienced whenever he flew in a plane. Prior to using EFT he had never connected this event with his fear of flying.

Another significant aspect that Eddie identified was physical. The *'gripping feeling right round my upper body'* always occurred when he flew. We tapped on this feeling, although at the time Eddie was unaware of the source.

By the end of a second session, after retesting all the aspects that had been addressed, Eddie was really pleased. He was sure that nothing was now going to stop him from enjoying his forthcoming flight to visit his daughter in Italy. Intuition made me a little hesitant. I asked him to reflect once more at home and to tap while asking himself if there was any other aspect that could hold him back from being free of the fear. He laughingly agreed and left.

A couple of hours later, Eddie called to say that he had thought of one last thing. He had remembered that as a child whenever he had flown with his parents he had sat on his mother's knee and that she used to grip him tightly. He mentioned that probably this had not come to mind when he was making his list because he had not known until about 15 years later that his mother was terrified of flying. She had wanted to keep him safe by hugging him, but she did not want him to know she was scared. Eddie asked me whether this had anything to do with the gripping feeling that had emerged in the session, and if I thought that it was worth tapping on. I agreed that it was and we both tapped over the phone for this aspect and a few connected feelings. Two weeks later I received a surprise postcard from a happy Eddie. Four years later, he continues to have stress-free flights and illness-free periods following them.

Eddie's fear may have been collapsed before we tapped on this last aspect, but sense indicated that it was better to be safe. It just took a few minutes and Eddie now is able to relax and enjoy the skies.

Getting more specific

The effectiveness of EFT improves greatly when you are specific about the feeling you are tapping for. Here are some examples of ways to be specific using EFT.

- Simon had a phobia of spiders. Tapping on *'Even though I am scared of spiders...'* might have had some good effect. But using some of Simon's dialogue, the set-up statement was *'Even though I was gripped with fear when I felt the hairy legs on my arm...'* This was more targeted and more likely to recreate an accurate disruption. You may think that it could take a long time to tap for specific individual memories and aspects, one at a time, but as mentioned earlier, the generalisation effect regularly speeds up the process.

- A set-up such as *'Even though I am sad that he left me...'* sounds very specific and is not a global issue – indeed it is naming a specific feeling. It may possibly even work. But if not, be even more specific about the feeling. What specifically are you sad about? Tapping on *'Even though I can't face seeing my friends since Paul left me...'* tunes into the real feelings. This gives more scope to get to the root and to clear the issue more effectively.

- Often, being more specific in this way using EFT will also provide recollections of similar early experiences in your life. Those early experiences may be the true root of the intensity of your current feelings. It is not uncommon for a person to think that these details are not really relevant; however, addressing those early memories first may not only provide relief from your current upset but also heal the issue completely (see the section later in the chapter on a trip to the core).

- For the purpose of focusing more specifically it may be necessary to make the issue in question as real as possible. For example, a question such as *'What is it about it that makes me feel this way?'* or *'What would it feel like if I were in that situation now?'*, provides a wealth of data to tap on. Becoming skilled at asking specific questions gets you clearly in touch with your perceived experience of the issue, which in turn makes it easier to remove each specific energy disturbance and improve the efficiency of overall healing.

Examples of specifics that have been elicited to tap on:

'the stony silence in the living room.'

'I am stopped by the empty aching in my chest.'

'my head is filled with a cloudy haze since that afternoon.'

'Paul has been my social crutch for the last six years.'

Always remember that common sense needs to be followed when approaching sensitive issues, especially issues such as abuse, phobias and trauma. Making the decision to approach sensitive issues is explored in more detail in Chapter 5.

Getting specific with emotions

The following are some key questions that can help elicit specific events and aspects.

- *How do you feel about having this emotion?*
- *What other emotions are present?*

- *What do you imagine may hold you back from freeing yourself from this emotion?*
- *What physical effects does this emotion have?*
- *What does this emotion remind you of?*
- *When did you first feel this emotion?*
- *How are you experiencing this emotion in your body?*

Some people describe an issue without mentioning an emotion. A prompting question might be:

- *What emotions are felt when thinking about the issue?*

Occasionally applying EFT to feelings about a current upset doesn't seem to help significantly. This usually means that the current feeling or charge is really due to earlier similar formative experiences in the past. It is sensible to apply the techniques to those earlier experiences first. Then the current experience will either already have been cleared up or be amenable to clearing with tapping. You can look for early memories by asking, *'What is it about the current situation that reminds you of the past?'* or *'When can you first recall this ... feeling?'* or *'Who has left you before now with the feeling ...?'* If you are unsure of the answers, a best guess is usually very accurate and should be encouraged.

With tapping, you are always aiming for triggers that cause emotional intensity associated with the memory or event that is being treated. Asking the right questions to identify the core issue can be the key to bringing up to the surface those specifics that trigger the reaction. Listen to the words used to describe the anxiety and use those exact words in the set-up statements. Write words and phrases down, as many emerge once you are tuned in.

When you work with someone else you can help them to become aware of their changes in perception. To do this, draw attention to their current inner experience by asking open and vague questions followed by a long pause. The following are examples of the kinds of question or prompt you might consider.

- *And you can simply take notice of what you are aware of now?*
- *And what do you know about that now?*
- *And what are you experiencing about that now?*
- *And how can you feel differently about ... now?*
- *If that were to happen again, what could you do now that you could not do before?*

A trip to the core

As we saw earlier, if your EFT journey starts with a particular issue the problem is likely to remain until you address the core of the issue. Sometimes the source of the core of an issue is obvious, sometimes it is not, but as the main emotional driver it requires attention. Identifying this driver (or there may be more than one driver) is essential if emotional and physical problems are to be dealt with successfully using EFT.

> ## Case study
>
> Gina had many health issues, and these had escalated since her mother's death. She was painfully aware that grief was an issue for her. However, through EFT she identified that the core issue was to do with safety and particularly with *'losing her safety net'*, which was having a profound, negative impact on her health and emotions. Set-ups included, *'Even though I didn't use it often, my mum was always my safety net...'* and *'Even though I am scared that there's no one there for me now...'*.
>
> Working on the aspects of this core had a very positive impact on Gina's health and outlook in the following months and years.

Other EFT techniques to uncover the core are described below.

Internal scanning

By mentally running an internal scan of the body during a tapping session, vital information emerges which is often connected with the core of the issue. Some questions will access images from the side of the brain that is concerned predominantly with images. Example questions include:

- *Where in your body can you find the deepest pain/feeling/belief?*
- *How does this ... feel?*
- *What does it look like?*
- *How old is this ...?*

Most people are able to elicit rich descriptions such as, *'a bright red knot of spiky rope'*, or *'a grey drawbridge across my throat'* or *'whenever I need to stand up for myself, lead fills up my legs'*, or *'It happened first when I was about five and ...'*.

This type of data forms a vital basis for further EFT set-up statements. For instance; *'Even though I have this bright red knot of spiky rope stuck in my throat when I think about the look on her face, I deeply and completely love and accept myself.'*

Allowing intuition

Further questioning while you are tapping, such as *'If there was a message or meaning, what would you guess it was?'* connects the person to non-verbal processing sectors of the brain. The answers to such questions are seated outside the regular source of information that we all have about ourselves, but if someone is relaxed with tapping they are more likely to access information about a core issue in this way.

If you are working on your own issues do not worry if you think that you cannot find the reason for a particular problem. We try to fathom things out: *'Why can't I get over this? Maybe it's resentment ... or maybe there's a deeper issue, but I don't know what it is.'* The trouble is that everyone has their own 'stories' that they tell themselves, which may cloud the core issue. Also our logical brain gets in the way. Instead of trying to come up with the reasons for your symptoms or for the problem you are struggling with, just tap. The core issues will rise to the surface. You can start tapping on whatever issue or problem you are facing. As you tap and repeat the reminder phrase, just listen for and be sensitive to what comes up. EFT does not have to be complicated: commonsense approaches are usually the most effective. Do not try to force it. Accept whatever comes by the outcome. It is OK not to know how it will turn out. Just be curious and allow yourself to be open: avoid being attached to getting a particular result.

Close observation

If you are working with someone else then close observation of movements and reactions as they focus on an issue will give potential clues about the core of that issue. Notable cues in calibration are explored in the next section, but here we consider some key questions that help to generate response concerning the core issue.

When you ask questions like the ones suggested below, keep tapping and allow quiet thinking time. If you are tapping for another person be aware that they need time to turn over a question in their minds. With practice, it is not that difficult to pick up on tiny cues indicating that real insight has been gained.

Questions you might consider asking include the following.

- *If you could have skipped one experience or one event, or avoided one person in your life, what or who would it have been, and why?*
- *What is your biggest fear?*
- *What makes you really angry about your childhood or your life?*
- *Who will you never forgive and why is this?*
- *Can you remember a time when someone hurt you so deeply that you'll never forget it?*
- *Is there a reaction you have that you wish you didn't have? When was the first time you felt that?*
- *Is there a memory you have that bothers you and that you just can't shake off?*
- *Is there anything about yourself that you don't like or that you would rather were different?*
- *When did you last cry, and why?*
- *Is there a positive side to having this problem?*
- *Is there a remembered sound, voice, smell or vision that might bring this feeling back?*
- *When was the first time you can remember that ... [whatever the issue is]?*
- *If you were to guess why ... [issue] happens, what would you guess?*

Calibration

Calibration in EFT is the key skill of observing and listening for the unconscious cues revealed by someone when they are emotionally connected with the process. Each person will have slightly different patterns and emphases. Some people are naturally proficient at picking up cues, and this can be seen as a form of intuition. Calibration skills can be improved with training and practice. The better you are at calibration the less focus and energy it requires. Table 8 lists some of the common cues.

Table 8 **Unconscious cues**

blink rate/pattern	head position tilt/lean/change heart rate change	pupil dilation/contraction	breathing rate/pattern/shift
smiling/frowning	nostril dilation	upper lip movement	lip biting
eyebrow movement	squinting	touching face or lip	direction of palm/s
body lean	tension in upper body	shoulder move	tonal change during answer
skin tone change	blinking when answering	change in time taken to process answer	sighing

Using calibration we can determine what each set of cues means in terms of change, which adds greatly to the art of EFT. Careful questioning, close attention and practice are essential.

Focusing on the negative and revisiting the past

As discussed in Chapter 3, when EFT is first used on an issue the active focus is on the negative aspects of the issue. This may seem counter-intuitive at first glance. Newcomers to EFT might ask, *'Why do I have to revisit the past? I know it was rubbish and painful at the time'*, or *'Why would I want to focus on the negative? Won't it make things worse? I've left those feelings behind me a long time ago. Actually I don't even think about them now.'*

I offer an analogy of a visit to the dentist to explore this further. A throbbing toothache leads you to the dentist who confirms that you have developed a lot of decay in the tooth. She removes the decay from the top part of your molar, because it seems to be the area that is causing the majority of your pain at this particular time. She notes that you have a lot more old decay down nearer the roots, but she does not want to upset you, so if you are OK now, she will leave it. Sure enough, you do feel a lot better. You have escaped without too much pain. You are, however, a bit confused.

The dentist offers some advice, saying that the rest of the decay could still cause you some difficulty in the future. She suggests that if you do experience more pain you should bear in mind that it all started a long time ago, for some forgotten reason, and you should remind yourself that *'you're a big brave man'*. You are rather puzzled. The dentist thinks again and tells you to return if the toothache comes back and she will scrape decay off the top of the tooth again. She says, *'I can't guarantee that you will be completely cured, but hey, we've all got stuff that causes us pain – I've got my ex-husband.'* She laughs and sends you home, instructing you that one of the best ways to take your mind off persistent pain is to relax and take up a hobby.

This silly analogy illustrates what we all know deep down. Scraping the top off a presenting issue or problem and hoping that the core issue at the roots will just fade away is a folly. The reality is that we all use strategies to get through the day and through life generally, such as distracting ourselves, relaxing, 'being brave', 'facing the music', 'pulling ourselves together', just forgetting about whatever the problem may be, moving on, taking no notice, taking a drink, taking a pill. Indeed, these methods of protection seem necessary and sensible responses; without them life would be too chaotic to manage. Sense tells us that if we stopped the world every time we were upset, in pain, felt angry or disappointed, lacking in confidence, fearful and so on, we would not get much done. Our subconscious also serves to protect us, often burying memories, thoughts and emotions deep within so that often we may not be aware of why we feel the way we do. Early and persistent messages of ill-health caused by negative emotion and stress are too easily ignored as well. All in all we need to check how well we are really serving ourselves.

Further, our emotional health logs a historical record. A current negative emotion that is connected with an unresolved past issue drains our resilience bank. We have explored how subconsciously we continue to gather evidence that backs up our faithful yet limiting beliefs, such as *'I never get anywhere in life'* or *'I am unlucky in love'* and how we allow these beliefs to drain our bank of energy, health, wellbeing and sense of peace. This is exhausting for our energy system. Even though we often do not know what the original 'debt' was for, we still continue to pay the bill every time something similar happens. Unresolved issues have a negative cumulative effect on us.

A throwaway comment made unintentionally in early childhood, such as *'That was a rubbish effort'* or *'You'll never amount to much'*, can have a much larger impact on us than we might imagine. Factors such as our vulnerabilities, personality and support network at that time will determine the impact of any lasting effect on the body's energy system. These risk and resilience factors play a crucial role in how much we are affected positively or negatively by the events around us. The reaction to falling off a bicycle in front of a group of laughing strangers in the playground differs from child to child, and the outcome can range from *'I'll show them'* to *'I'm never going to try something new in front of people again without feeling like an idiot and messing up'*. The life-enhancing decisions we make support us, while the life-limiting decisions can continue to have a negative impact on us for a very long time indeed.

In our attempts to *'carry on'* with life, the belief that we have *'dealt with'* the past is noble, and often essential, as we have already noted. Perhaps, however, it is now time to ask questions such as:

- *Have my strategies to cope, ignore or move on been really effective for me?*

- *Have my strategies given me a peaceful resolution, or am I left with unresolved issues that keep me feeling stuck?*

As we have seen from earlier chapters, EFT gently highlights and addresses the negative strands of how we currently feel about ourselves by making us conscious of factors that may have eluded our understanding until now. Using EFT we can follow the trail of answers and insights as they emerge so that, for even the most stubborn issues, patience and persistent will guide us to a healthier place.

Discarding unhelpful strategies

One would assume that as high-functioning beings we employ rational and effective ways to operate on a daily basis. Thankfully, this is the case most of the time. Being human, however, we can also rely on familiar but unhelpful strategies (as reviewed in the section on 'navigating the journey with blind spots', in Chapter 2). The case below illustrates how, using EFT, Tony the client was able to become gently aware of one strategy that appeared to be affecting his health negatively.

Case study

Tony, a highly successful businessman, told me, *'I don't do emotions'*. He believed that *'showing any sign of emotion'* was a weakness. He was spot on. He did not do emotions, or at least not verbally. It is not my job to judge how a person 'should be', but you may question why Tony had come to see someone who almost exclusively helps people to achieve emotional freedom? Tony had endless problems with his digestive tract that were increasingly preventing him from carrying out a normal life. He was desperate. Medication was not effective and he was facing major surgery.

Tony said that he had read that many digestive problems were linked to unresolved emotional issues. He said that he found this confusing, because he was widely regarded as a *'cold character devoid of emotion'*. Nevertheless, he was willing to try tapping on the physical symptoms of his problems, in order to avoid the need for surgery. We began, and his initial set-up statements were:

'Even though I have a vice-gripping pain in the lower left area of my gut, I accept myself.'

'Even though I have a remaining ball of knots in my left gut, I accept myself.'

'Even though I don't do emotions, this condition does get me angry, I accept myself.'

Measures on the gripping pain and the knots reduced as we proceeded. It was not long however, before Tony found that, much to his surprise, other emotions did emerge while tapping. I had asked him when he first remembered this 'vice-gripping pain'. His face and body sank. As numerous layers arose we began to use an EFT approach called 'softly, softly' (described in more detail in Chapter 5). In brief, what Tony reported was that during his less than ideal childhood – his father was an alcoholic, his mother could not cope, and he suffered beatings – he decided when he was about six years old that, for him, expressing emotions was not going to get him anywhere. He continued to watch his mother suffer, and even though there was a lot of verbal emotion expressed by other members in his family nothing ever got better. As the session continued, we tapped many emerging aspects, including:

>>

Case study continued

'Even though I don't do emotions, it seems like my body does; I deeply and completely accept myself.'

'Even though I saw that emotion didn't help my mum and I decided it was weak, I deeply and completely accept myself.'

'Even though I have buried how I feel all my life and my guts are causing me pain, I deeply and completely accept myself.'

'Even though I see emotion as a weakness, I may choose to find another way to handle things; I don't know how yet, but I am open to exploring.'

By the end of that first session Tony was surprising himself with the vocabulary he was using; he said that he did not know quite where the words were coming from.

Within a couple of months Tony gladly reported to me that he was no longer on heavy medication for his problems, that his then imminent surgery had been postponed indefinitely. We continued sessions and Tony willingly tapped at home and at work. He said 'I still see outward expression of emotion as a weakness' but he added, 'I give my work colleagues and family a bit more understanding'. He joked that 'I even offer the odd smile'. His wife wrote me a letter about her 'changed man'.

Thankfully not too many people experience all that Tony did in his early years, but less significant events can still have sizeable impact in adult life.

The generalisation effect

The generalisation effect is well known among EFT practitioners. It manifests in the most interesting and pleasantly surprising ways. Often in EFT many related problems collapse at the same time without each one having been tapped on individually. In session, for instance, a client may list 30 unpleasant memories all connected with the theme *'Times I have failed in my life'*. It may be necessary to remove the disruption surrounding only a small number of those memories, with EFT, for disruption around the remainder to fade completely without being addressed.

Clients also report that when EFT has eradicated a specific problem, such as a fear of heights, they notice further spontaneous positive changes. They might begin to feel confident enough, for instance, to commit to a relationship or to offer themselves for a leadership programme possibilities they had not generally contemplated before their fear of height was removed. EFT rapidly challenges ways of thinking and provides an opportunity for new neural connections to form without conscious effort.

> **Case study**
>
> Darren, a client, had recently been working through performance issues relating to work. He found himself being uncharacteristically angry and disruptive. After a couple of EFT sessions he was more at ease. He also noted, *'My children have been asking to spend more time with me and most unusually I even noticed a petrol attendant smile at me the other day.'*

'It is great when the world becomes a nicer place because of changes that we make in ourselves!'
client who had worked on anger

The generalisation effect is a common feature in all areas of EFT application and is a very welcome feature in relation to health issues. Collapsing an unhelpful belief can have a huge effect on an aliment or disease, and removing a disruption associated with a memory can extinguish the need for an unhelpful or unhealthy habit.

Improving the success rate: checklist

The basic principles of EFT provide good results even for newcomers, especially for issues that are fairly straightforward. If success is more elusive, the following checklist should help. Potential interferences in EFT can be mastered by considering some of these suggestions. Revisit this section frequently as you build your EFT skills and understanding.

Performing the set-up completely

Even with the best will in the world some issues will not be shifted unless blocks are removed first. Psychological reversal (PR) prevents the whole EFT process from working. PR is discussed in Chapter 6 but in the meantime the main way in which to counteract this is to make sure that the set-up is performed with vigour and that it is spoken (whether aloud or silently), emphatically. Check that the words accurately reflect the feeling and the mood. If you are angry, check what your inner voice would say. If you would normally have sworn, then go ahead. Get to the feeling!

Check the words of the acceptance part of your set-up. You need to be comfortable with the words or they will not work for you. Refer back to the section on creating an EFT set-up phrase, or statement, in Chapter 3 (Step 1 of 'Using EFT: step-by-step procedure'). Instead of saying *'Even though I am annoyed, I deeply and completely accept myself'*, a more appropriate set-up to begin may be *'Even though I am really livid, my blood is boiling, I accept my feelings'*.

Applying EFT to one thing at a time

If your mind is focused on more than one thing at a time your attention will be divided and this will reduce the possibility of recreating accurate energy disturbance. It is a potential difficulty for those who are new to EFT, who may not have yet mastered the skill of concentrating on the issue in question to the exclusion of other thoughts.

It is easy unintentionally to try to apply EFT to more than one issue at a time; for example, a second issue might be activated while you attempt to address the original issue. While using EFT on an issue surrounding anger, for instance, it is common for other emotions such as sadness or guilt to emerge as progression is made. The brain is complex and it constantly seeks connections in our thoughts. It requires practice to know how to handle the messages that emerge within the EFT procedure and to distinguish whether the emerging 'material' should be noted down and approached at a separate time or addressed within the current rounds of tapping. The presence of a second issue may simply be a distraction or it could represent an issue that is in conflict with the original issue. An experienced EFT practitioner is trained to evaluate the developing picture and to guide the client effectively and comfortably.

Avoiding switching aspects during tapping

Sometimes it seems that the subjective units of distress (SUD) level is not changing very much. Commonly, the level has indeed dropped on the aspect in focus and our mind has automatically selected another, now more intense, aspect of the same overall issue. Thus, although the SUD level appears not to have changed, aspects have been 'switched' and the SUD level is representing the 'new' aspect. For instance, a person may be using EFT on the fear of a disturbing memory and reducing the SUD level with progressive rounds of tapping. In doing so, a new aspect, such as *'anger that I was put in that situation'*, may emerge. Without clear and precise testing before and after each round of tapping to measure the status of the aspect in question, there is a danger that a swift global judgement on *'How do I feel now?'* will lend us to believe that we are actually feeling worse than before. The temptation to switch aspects is common. Each specific aspect needs to be addressed until the SUD level is zero, and caution is therefore required to re-check that all aspects are addressed. You can do this by restating the exact wording of the original set-up statement and measuring the SUD. Not exercising caution in this way can mean that some negative aspects will remain and may be triggered again in the future, giving rise to further negative emotions.

Identifying the existence of secondary gains

Secondary gains and reasons for holding on are discussed in more detail in Chapter 6.

Sometimes a secondary gain or hidden benefit interferes with the possibility of letting go of an issue. Examples of secondary gain include *'This issue keeps me safe'*, *'I don't have to risk failure'*, *'I get to avoid doing certain things by having this problem'*, and so on. Once you have identified the secondary gain, you can tap on that directly. Once you have done this the original issue or problem will clear more easily.

Recognising when a limiting belief is interfering

Progress on a current issue will be interfered with when limiting beliefs stand in the way. The interference of a blocking belief is a very common sticking point. By working with someone else using EFT to identify and clear the blocking belief the original issue will fade. Examples of blocking beliefs include *'Nothing will help me'*, *'I'm afraid that I am doing this wrong'*, *'I don't deserve to get over my problems'*, *'I can never get over my problems'*, and so on. As beliefs often operate below our conscious awareness and are interpreted as *'true'*, it is easy to see how progress may be limited (see 'Navigating the journey with blind spots' in Chapter 2).

Acknowledging that your thoughts about your feelings can interfere

Sometimes our feelings (or, really, our thoughts) about the issue on which we are trying to work interfere with making progress.

> ### Case study
>
> I was working with Jennifer, a special educational needs teacher, on her feelings about her own daughter's special needs. Jennifer regularly got very angry at her daughter's excessive demands. Using EFT, the intensity initially reduced from an 8 to a 6, but Jennifer said that she did not think it was possible for it to go much lower. While we tapped, I asked her how she felt about getting angry. Jennifer replied that she was *'really ashamed for not being as patient as I am with other more demanding children at school'*. We then tapped on 'Even though I feel really ashamed for not being more patient …'
>
> While we tapped, I asked her to take a guess about what might hold her back from letting go of the issue. She felt *'embarrassment in my throat that I've let this get on top of me as I'm supposed to be a professional for managing difficult children'*. We tapped on the aspects of Jennifer's embarrassment first, and the beliefs behind why it was embarrassing for her. By addressing the thoughts/feelings of shame and embarrassment cleared the way to enhance the speed of progress of reducing the original presenting issue of anger. After successive EFT rounds Jennifer's anger intensity dropped to a 1.

The existence of an even deeper issue can hold things up

There are many deeper issues that can interfere with a current issue. Larger issues generally arise from upsetting experiences early in life. When an important issue is 'hiding' behind a lesser presenting issue, the whole EFT process seems to falter, because the real issue is not being addressed. In such cases, simply ask, *'If there is a larger emotional issue here, what might it be?'* If the first response is *'I don't know'*, then a guess is usually accurate or will uncover interesting aspects to pursue with tapping. Tapping on the larger emotional issue will begin to clear painful memories associated with it. Finding deeper issues on your own, however, can be hard, and it will help to engage an experienced EFT practitioner to guide you.

When you are too close to the problem

On occasion we are too close to the problem and it can be difficult to see it objectively. In these cases, a person may have achieved very good progress on the outer and presenting layers of an issue using EFT but the core is eluding them. Engaging a skilled EFT practitioner will help the client to unfold the layers, discover patterns and clear the blockages. The supportive presence of another person in this way in order to tackle the deeper layers can make a huge difference.

Tapping assignments between sessions can also help to speed up the healing process.

When the problem has not gone away

Used correctly, the positive changes brought about when using EFT are speedy and lasting. Frustration or discouragement may cause you to give up on using the techniques if progress seems slow. The journey to peace and wellbeing does not always run smoothly, particularly in the face of unhelpful but familiar patterns that have served you for a long time. Persistent and careful checking of progress are essential to track the changes that occur at each tapping round, otherwise our mind can easily help us to switch aspects, to rely on the old patterns or even doubt that any positive change is due to the tapping process. In most cases if progress is not moving at the speed that you would expect, then in addition to the guidelines already offered it is useful to check the following two angles.

See 'Choosing your route with EFT' earlier in this chapter.

- Have all the aspects of the problem been dealt with? Is it possible that a specific aspect either did not appear at the time or was not addressed fully?

- Has the original problem been approached too globally? Identifying a core issue may provide relief in this instance.

Chapter 5
Easing the journey

Chapter 5 Easing the journey

Knowing that EFT works is very encouraging but some newcomers may have a sense of embarrassment, shame or guilt about the issues that they would like to clear, making it difficult to get started at all. Unpleasant memories or disturbing events can be difficult to talk about because of the fear of triggering painful emotions.

Several gentle EFT techniques have been formulated which reduce the need to face too much distress, even when working with the most severe memories and feelings. The techniques described in this chapter will help you to develop skills in handling these sensitive issues and minimise distress. The exercises can be carried out by an individual working on their own issues, by a practitioner with a client or by someone working with an EFT 'tapping buddy'. As with any therapy intervention, specialist EFT practitioners are recommended for people with severe trauma or for more complex cases.

Gentle techniques to add to your EFT toolbox

There are many reasons why people hold back on talking about their issues. Some have been outlined earlier. EFT in general reduces the problem of holding back, as participants can tap without talking as long as they are tuned into the associated feelings. And there are aids to facilitate getting the feeling across with minimum talking, such as the code words and objects introduced in this chapter. Aids such as Access cards, 'PAT Bear' and journals are covered in Chapter 14.

For some people more gentle EFT approaches are necessary. Abreactions are very rare, and EFT is a gentle approach in which an individual is never expected to become over-exposed to intense triggers for painful emotions. The techniques are always step-by-step and can be taken more slowly at any time.

The EFT techniques outlined in this chapter are used in combination with the basic EFT routine. To practise, select a technique to try and then select an annoying problem or issue. At this stage, for safety, opt for an issue with a measure of below 5 on the subjective units of distress (SUD) rating. As always, go only 'where you belong' when approaching issues with friends and family. It must be stressed again that severe conditions, trauma or abuse would be better handled by a professional EFT practitioner than by an individual working on their own issues or by an EFT buddy. Common sense and discretion are imperative.

Generally speaking if you get anxious or blocked when recalling a memory, it might mean that the timing is not right for you to deal with it or that it's not feeling okay to tune into and tap on it by yourself. If you sense that this is the case, then arrange to work with an experienced tapping buddy or a trained EFT practitioner.

If when opening up on a problem, an overwhelming physical or emotional feeling unexpectedly rises quickly before a set-up statement has been created it is a good idea to start tapping all around the meridian points straight away which will help to reduce anxiety without hesitating to formulate the set-up statement. It may be appropriate to add the word or phrase that triggered the reaction. The key is that you are 'tuned into' the problem, it is the ideal opportunity to clear the disruption around the unpleasant memory or negative feeling. It is a mistake to stop, or indeed not to start EFT, when 'in the moment'; just do continuous tapping around the points. Alternatively stay tapping on one point such as the friendly point (FP) or collarbone (CB) if this suits better until the feeling calms, even if that feeling or emotion has not yet been put into words.

If, however it is difficult even to begin to talk about the memory because it creates some negative emotion, a global approach can be used initially and EFT will still work effectively. Using set-up statements such as: *'Even though the thought of talking about this is making my stomach turn, ...'*, *'Even though I am not sure where this will end up, ...'*, *'Even though I am feeling fearful that I might be judged by revealing this, ...'* .Then continue with your chosen EFT technique once the emotional intensity has dropped and the SUD rating falls below 3. This not only minimises the distress but can uncover deeper issues that may otherwise have gone unnoticed. Resolution is reached when the whole event or emotion can be spoken about clearly without intense emotion.

Movie technique

Sensory data (seeing, hearing, taste, touch and smell) is hugely significant in the storage stage of fearful or stressful memories (see Table 13 in Chapter 10). When we recall a fearful memory the material becomes labile again, which means that under certain conditions the sensory data can be restored in a new way (see the section on neurogenesis and plasticity in Chapter 7). For that reason the movie technique, or any EFT approach that encourages replay of the senses, is very powerful for healing as the sensory data of the memory can be reprocessed. After the movie technique has been used, triggers that were previously emotive, for instance – a smell, or a feeling – no longer elicit an energy disruption as they are detached from the original negative response. Used well, the movie technique provides significant permanent changes, creating brainwave energy states that are optimal for healing (see the section on brainwaves in Chapter 7).

This technique is a gentle EFT approach to painful memories. It involves slowly narrating an unpleasant memory as if it were a movie or a film, but then stopping and applying EFT on the minute detailed parts of the movie that give rise to emotional intensity or anxiety. After neutralising the area of intensity in the movie, you rewind the movie a little and narrate that segment again, testing for any remaining intensity. This is done piece by piece until you can run through the whole movie with no intensity arising at all.

An added benefit of the movie technique is that it focuses on specific events, reducing the chance of a participant shifting aspects which can hinder progress (as described in the section 'Improving the success rate of EFT' in Chapter 4).

Movie technique

1 Bring to mind the unpleasant memory and estimate the length of time it would take to replay it. If this is more than a few minutes, select a smaller portion of the memory, perhaps the most intense part. Then create a title for this movie. The title should represent a specific event, for example, *'Blind panic in the crucial staff meeting'*, rather than *'Panic in the meeting'*. The title can be vague, such as 'that conversation', so long as it is accurate for the participant.

2 Start to 'run' the movie very slowly in your mind (using no tapping and no words). When you have run through it once, rate the SUD (the current intensity) on a scale of 0–10.

3 If, after 'running' the movie, the rating is above 7 and therefore quite intense, it would be
   appropriate to create a set-up to suit the current feeling and gently tap with a phrase such as
   'Even though it is just too much to watch it, I am safe and I accept myself'.

   Tapping on this may reduce the SUD sufficiently to enable this technique to continue. If after
   several rounds this has not occurred, discontinue the movie technique and use an alternative
   technique, such as the tearless trauma or the softly, softly techniques listed later in this
   chapter.

   If the SUD rating is 6 or below begin to narrate the movie out loud from the beginning, using
   as much detail as you can. The golden rule is to stop immediately at any intense moment,
   even if it seems tiny, to rate that moment on a scale of 0–10, and then to tap on the emotional
   intensity until it reduces to zero. An example set-up could be, *'Even though all I could feel
   was my head pumping, when I realised I hadn't completed the report...'* When working with
   someone else, monitoring facial expressions and other calibration cues helps to indicate the
   intensity of emotion (see Chapter 4).

   EFT does not expect you to 'brave yourself through the moment' or to stay with the technique
   come what may; quite the opposite, in fact. Techniques are designed to guide you gently from
   distress to calm. In fact, braving yourself through is probably simply going to mean more of the
   same feeling in the future, as skipping over a tiny detail misses the recreated energy disruption
   and this will merely impede successful resolution of the memory.

   A stare, a cobweb, a noise can all be examples of crucial triggers that need attention. Even a
   slight faltering at any point while running the movie needs to be noted and addressed. Taking
   the EFT process even slower and paying more attention to minute and specific details that
   create disruption until the SUD measure of it is zero. In the example set-up *'Even though just
   seeing the doctor's file freezes my chest...'* EFT is used until the negative intensity reduces to
   zero and the specific negative feeling of that segment of the movie is gone.

4 To test, rewind the movie a little and narrate again the segment that previously caused the
   emotion. If any intensity still exists, the last step needs to be repeated. If no further intensity
   exists, continue slowly narrating the movie as before, and repeat EFT at any point where
   emotion surfaces. Take care to attend to all the senses and cues in order to ascertain every
   rise in intensity. The temptation to narrate across the peaks is common as this is what we do
   subconsciously to protect ourselves. Remember, it is during the peak moments of the event
   that the key disruptions were stored in the body's energy system. Clearing the disruptions in
   this piece-by-piece fashion is very effective. Careful guidance by a practitioner helps.

5 When you come to the end of the movie, replay the whole movie again in your mind. Then
   narrate it again verbally as a final check for any remaining specific aspects that hold disruption.
   If any of these aspects still exist, return to Step 4.

6 This technique is complete and successful when the whole unpleasant memory can be
   narrated without any emotional intensity. To test the result thoroughly, exaggerate the sounds,
   colours or details while narrating.

   If you have several specific events that are connected, take time to create several separate
   movies and tap on each of them using this technique.

If there are parts of the movie that feel private and you do not wish to verbalise them, just tap silently on the most intense part of what happened. Alternatively use a code word, as described in the section on 'protection using codes' later in the chapter. You can give a name to the most intense part and then tap on that until it reduces to a low level.

Tearless trauma technique

This technique is another EFT gentle method by which distress can be minimised or eliminated. It is used by EFT practitioners very successfully, particularly when helping clients with trauma or abuse issues. The term 'tearless' refers to minimising distress rather than lack of tears. This method is effective even when the issue being treated is very severe, where there is resistance to approaching the issues or where the participant has little current desire to have insights into past incidents. The technique relies on standing away from the issue initially and 'guessing' its intensity until it is safe to take a step closer. After using this technique clients report, and demonstrate, visible and verbal cognition changes concerning the previously disturbing incident. Properly mastered, this technique adds a useful component to the art of EFT delivery. It works well one-to-one or very occasionally in a group setting, when addressing trauma or abuse. It is recommended in any situation where the client is understandably afraid of the intensity they usually feel when discussing or 'getting into' their incident.

Tearless trauma technique

1 Identify a specific traumatic incident from the past. An example might be, *'My brother pushed me off the high-board when I was seven.'* This keeps the focus on a specific aspect, rather than a global issue such as *'My brother scared me'*, and reduces the chance of switching aspects. Other aspects can be noted throughout the process for attention when appropriate.

2 The question is asked, *'If you were to imagine ... [incident]* now, make a guess at what the emotional intensity would be on a 0–10 SUD scale. Do not start to 'replay' the incident in your mind, but just make a guess right now about what you imagine the intensity would be.' This instruction is essential. The guess needs to be elicited quickly, and this still provides a surprisingly accurate measure. It is a natural inclination to go ahead and begin to replay the incident. This is often indicated by eye direction wandering off into visual field. This is to be avoided as much as possible, as the purpose is to minimise emotional distress. Write the guess down.

3 Create an accurate set-up statement for the EFT process, such as *'Even though I have a deathly falling feeling in my chest just talking about this...'* or *'Even though I guess an intensity of 8 around the high-board event...'*, and proceed with a round of tapping.

4 Guess again what the emotional intensity would be now. Typically, the SUD rating will have reduced. Perform more rounds of EFT until the remaining intensity for that statement falls to zero or very low.

5 Next, do a silent round of tapping. After this round, allow yourself *for the first time* in this exercise vividly to imagine the incident and allocate an actual SUD rating, rather than a guessed rating as previously. All previous ratings have been relatively painless 'arms-length' guesses. SUD ratings at this point have usually dropped considerably, making it possible to continue tapping in the usual way on the specifics of the incident to neutralise remaining disruptions. You can continue using another gentle EFT technique such as the movie technique.

Softly, softly technique

This technique is closely related to the tearless trauma technique. I call it the 'softly, softly technique' as I am not keen on the original title, 'sneaking up on a problem'. With difficult or highly emotional memories, it would be counterproductive and very upsetting to deal with specifics immediately, because this is likely to have a re-traumatising effect.

Softly, softly technique

1 To begin with the memory is introduced gradually, after it has been described very vaguely. This approach and the earless trauma technique differ from most other EFT instructions in which specifics are stressed. In this method, EFT is employed in order gradually to take the edge off increasingly specific details. For instance, if the SUD rating is high, without ever going into any specifics we might begin tapping on *'Even though "that meeting" happened...'.*

2 Once the disruptions around the 'vague' topic have been reduced, one of the other gentle methods outlined in this chapter might be used to address the issue in more detail. As the SUD rating drops, more detailed set-ups can be introduced gradually, such as, *'Even though my world crashed around me that afternoon...',* or *'Even though just thinking about "that afternoon" fills me with a sick feeling in my stomach...'.*

For an extended example of the use of the softly, softly technique, refer to the 'Trauma' section in Chapter 12 and the case study of David who suffered from intense flashbacks. Using EFT in this manner allows gradual healing, moving from the very vague to the specific, and settling energy disruption at each stage. Because the technique removes the need to re-traumatise the participant, it is ideal for trauma and phobia application.

Telling the story technique

In order to resolve an issue with EFT tapping it is necessary to tune into the problem or issue and recreate some disruption in the energy system. Stimulating the energy system is easily done through tapping. However, properly tuning into the issue in order to effectively shift it, can be a real challenge! Especially with more complicated problems. The best ways to tune into our problem is to get as specific as possible. And by identifying and tapping on a negative memory that relates to our problem, we can get very specific. While the movie technique is an excellent method to release negative memories it can be a bit difficult to do the movie technique on your own, especially if new to tapping. The tell a story method or write a letter method is an effective and powerful alternative.

Telling the story technique

1 Pick a quiet and private spot where you can write and do some tapping. Select a specific negative memory or stressful childhood event that you would like work with. If you come up with something that might be too emotionally charged or traumatic, it is best if you work with an experienced tapping buddy or trained EFT practitioner who is familiar with the movie technique.

2 If you are dealing with a particular life theme or core issue i.e. I am defective, flawed, not good enough etc., try to recall a 'key' memory that fits into this theme. For example, select a specific event; during earlier years where you were made to feel not good enough and for the most part, you were ignored or even criticised.

   Note: If you are no longer feeling emotional about a memory but it seems to pop into your mind from time to time, this generally means there is some unprocessed negative emotion attached to it i.e. sadness, guilt, shame, anger, powerlessness, blame etc. The section on focusing on the negative and revisiting the past in Chapter 4 discussed the value of using valuable approaches like tapping to clear unprocessed negative emotions.

3 On a note pad or in a journal, begin to recount this memory like you are telling a story or witting a letter. Some find it helpful to address a letter to caring friend (current or past), family member etc. Of course, it will not be mailed to them.

4 Give it a short but meaningful title like, *'When my parents left town'* or *'When my auntie betrayed me'*. Then get an initial intensity or SUDs level. Close your eyes and say the title to yourself. You might want to try a few different titles and use the one that has the biggest charge. Then focus inward and feel in your body how much emotional intensity this has for you i.e. 0 = no intensity at all and 10 being very intense and emotionally uncomfortable. Make note of the number.

5 Begin to write down the story or memory in detail. Keep to the point and avoid wandering into another memory or event, just make note of any other memories so you can tap on them later. A tapable issue or target only lasts for a few minutes like the crescendo of a movie. If it's longer than five minutes, you are likely being too general or global which will result in poor results or no change at all. Get more specific by breaking it down into smaller clips, scenes or events.

6 Tell/write what happened, what others did, what you did, what you saw (incl. facial expressions of younger you and others), what you heard, what others and you said and especially how the younger you felt. As you write out the memory/story if any emotional intensity arises such as; sadness, shame, blame, guilt, anger, then tap on it to get it down before continuing to write.

7 It can be helpful to give the emotion a colour and sensation i.e. *'Even though I have this hot yellow anger in my stomach when I think about what he said to me, I deeply and completely accept myself'* or *'Even though I have this green burning shame in my throat as I remember this, I accept myself and the feelings I have'* or *'Even though I have this grey sadness in my heart, I love, honour and accept all parts of me right here, right now.'*

8 After the story is completed, read it back to yourself out loud. Stop and tap when any intense emotions that arise before continuing to read. Repeat this process until you can read through the story and remain neutral throughout i.e. you have very little or no emotional intensity.

9 Make sure you test your work and read the letter or story in a few days. Tap on any emotional intensity as well as on any additional aspects or parts of that particular story that come up. And remember to make note of any new memories that come up so you can tap on them as well.

A big advantage of this technique is, that by doing the tell a story or write a letter technique on just a handful of memories related to a particular core issue or life theme, the whole problem will begin to shift for you. Even with dozens of memories attached to one theme it may not be necessary to tap on them all in order to feel a dramatic shift, just a few key ones. The generalisation effect was outlined in Chapter 4.

Protection using codes

How can you progress if you feel that a problem or issue is too embarrassing or personal to reveal, or is hard to put into words? One way to overcome this problem is to employ a key word or code, a colour or a sound. The choice of word or code is irrelevant, as long as it helps you to 'tune into' the problem or issue. The keyword or code is inserted into the set-up statement and the reminder phrase.

Case study

Dawn was sure that she was ready for change, but she did not want to reveal the nature of her problem. To get round the difficulty, she chose a code word. As Dawn was clearly already tuned into her emotions, we started to tap, and said that it was *'the towel business'.* This was all the detail I was going to get, and so we tapped with *'Even though I have this towel business problem ...',* with the reminder phrase as 'this towel business ...'.

Dawn created new code words easily as we worked through the issue bit by bit and applied EFT to each part of the problem that cropped up, until the rating of each went to zero. I tested and retested as we went. I did not and still do not know what the 'towel business problem' was, but this was not important for the method to work. Dawn was delighted with the outcome.

Code words can be silently repeated or hummed. If this technique is not enough to produce a reduction in intensity, a little more may be needed to get to the deeper issue. Suggestions might include putting greater emphasis on the code word or encouraging a more vivid recollection. Rapport between client and practitioner builds essential trust and allows the client to feel more comfortable about any potential barriers to total frankness.

Clients with phobias often adopt a code word to avoid undue upset initially. Thus, spiders may be called *'those things'* for a while until the intensity has been reduced using gentle EFT methods. The set-up statement might be *'Even though I am getting sweaty just mentioning those things...'* It then gradually becomes more possible to approach the triggers associated with the word 'spiders'.

In touch with the issue literally

Many clients bring items or objects to a session so that they are literally in touch with the issue to be treated. Holding or focusing on the item elicits powerful material to tap on. Loss, grief, frustration and any locked emotions are often opened up using this method.

Simple questions such as, *'What does this remind me of?'* or *'What was happening at the time?'* elicits responses and sensations in the body. By noting the location or emotion, the effect of tapping can be strengthened. Examples of statements might be *'Even though this ring holds all those happy memories...'*, *'Even though it hurts to look at this hotel leaflet...'*, *'Even though I hate this photo because she looks like such a nice smiling lady to everyone...'*, *'Even though this certificate was supposed to be my ticket to freedom...'*.

Severe trauma is best left in the hands of a professional (see Caution, responsibility and abreactions' in Chapter 3). In Chapter 12, in the section on 'Post-Traumatic Stress Disorder', you will read the case study of Liz, which illustrates how powerful the method of using objects can be.

Group work can be very powerful and healing but it requires training and experience, especially when approaching sensitive or traumatic incidents. When working in a group setting people might choose to write down their phrase and read it to themselves as they tap, or they might tap on a code word or phrase.

Personal peace procedure

The personal peace procedure is a healing centrepiece of EFT. It can be used as a self-help tool or as a leading tool for helping others. It accelerates and deepens the natural healing process by providing a method to clear out a lifetime of accumulated emotional debris.

In essence, the procedure gives us a framework for addressing every negative specific event by systematically tapping the impact out of existence. The procedure is used for events from the past and the present. It is even suitable for addressing negative thoughts or fears of the future. By removing or collapsing each one, we eliminate major causes of our emotional and physical ailments, easing the path to true peace and harmony.

The personal peace procedure can help to:

- clear the impact of negative life events
- improve self-image
- reduce self-doubt
- improve state of mind
- improve health
- increase a sense of relaxation
- achieve a better sense of freedom.

The procedure can be used as a between-session enhancer, an ongoing daily procedure or for illnesses and pain management. If you do EFT for just a few minutes on all the little incidents that come up in a day you will find your life changing dramatically. The sensitivity that seemed like a burden and a flaw before will begin to appear as the gift it is—a very precise and finely tuned guidance system that lets you know right away when you are getting off the track of your deepest truth.

Below are some basic instructions. My clients write an EFT journal as part of the procedure, which they keep with them and add to as they proceed.

Personal peace procedure

1 Make a list of every specific troubling event that comes to mind. There is no limit to the number – I have seen lists that range from 20 to 100.

2 Nothing is too silly or irrelevant. If it comes to mind, it has a message for you. While making your list you may find that events seem to cause you no current discomfort. List them anyway – the mere fact that you remember them suggests a need for resolution. Time taken at this stage is valuable. Try not to think too deeply at this stage but you can tap as you write. This may be a good idea if writing the items causes any level of emotion. A set-up may be, *'Even though I don't understand why writing this still causes me to be upset, I deeply and completely love and accept myself.'*

3 Give each event a title as though it was a mini movie; for instance, *'Dad didn't come back', 'The moment they told mum that ...', 'the hate in Mark's eyes', 'their laughing faces'.* Take your time doing this.

4 From the completed list attach an SUD rating to each event. You might note themes or recurring patterns. Then begin the process of applying EFT to each event, one by one until the SUD is reduced to zero, before moving to the next. You can start anywhere. Take your time with each item. Sometimes people select to start with the bigger events. As you go, take note of any aspects that come up, add them to your list and apply EFT to each in turn until the SUD rating measures zero.

By addressing each specific item in turn the core issues will also be addressed. Effects will become generalised to other aspects and areas of your life that you have not worked on directly (see Chapter 4). Applying EFT to one 'movie' (specific event) per day will take only a few minutes. As each is resolved, you will notice changes. Your body will feel better. Your 'threshold for getting upset' will be much higher. Relationships will improve and many of the larger issues will not seem to be there any more. By revisiting some of the events you listed originally, you will note how previously intense incidences have faded into nothingness. Items from global themes will also fade by generalisation.

Keep your notes. Consciously notice and retest the items in the weeks and months to come, because the quality healing you will have undergone will seem so subtle that you may not notice it. You may even dismiss it. The saying *'Oh well, it was never much of a problem anyway'* is known in EFT as the apex effect. This is explored in Chapter 6.

As with EFT more generally, for many people the personal peace procedure has been the key to complete cessation of lifelong issues that other methods of therapy have not touched. Professional training or assistance from an EFT practitioner will add to its effectiveness.

Chapter 6
Road blocks and alternative routes

Chapter 6 Road blocks and alternative routes

All the daily positive affirmations and willpower in the world will not be sufficient to help us reach our goals if blocks of self-sabotage exist. Before we can clear these blocks a crucial first step is to become aware of them.

This chapter highlights some of the common blocks that cause emotional difficulty. Alternative EFT routes offered here provide us with safe and effective ways to become aware of our road blocks, and to clear them – to transform our stumbling blocks into stepping stones for the future.

'If you can find a path with no obstacles, it probably doesn't lead anywhere'
Frank A. Clark

Cleaning up graffiti

A central concept in EFT is 'writing on the walls of your mind'. This is a metaphor for our 'self-talk' and refers to the attitudes, opinions and beliefs that we have accumulated over the years, downloaded from our parents, teachers and other strong early influences.

The words that are written on our walls differ for each of us. One person's wall might read *'You are a beautiful person'* or *'You deserve love'*, whereas another person may have *'Don't think too much of yourself'*. Some writing is useful and life giving, and some is not. The 'writing on our walls' is our most prominent adviser and we consult it all day long. It contains our entire 'how-to-do' rule book. It contains our 'cans' and 'cannots', our 'shoulds' and 'should nots' and our 'musts' and 'must nots', as well as our sense of fair play. It contains our version of proper behaviour, and what we consider to be right or wrong. It contains our judgements, our successes and our failures. Everything we hold to be true is written on our walls, and the words tell us about our opportunities as well as our limits. This is why we appear to have different limits in life. Your limits are different from mine partly because the 'writing' reflects differing early experiences. The 'writings' act as a rule book for getting through life. We have been dutifully obeying these guidelines from our earliest days, often without being wholly conscious of them.

We constantly consult the writing on our walls

Interestingly, we may be acutely aware or completely oblivious of different elements of the writing on our walls. Sometimes it is easy to observe other people's writings and sometimes it is not.

Some of the truths that we have learned are useful; take, for instance, a piece of advice from a parent to a child such as *'People will only play with you if you are nice to them'*.. Other written 'truths', however, are not so useful to our health and wellbeing: *'People will let you down, so it's best not to trust anyone'*.

We consult our walls for just about everything. We continue to operate from early 'truths' with alarmingly regularity. *'I won't do that, because teacher might tell me off'*, for example, can have an impact subconsciously in relation to a boss or other authority figure even though years have passed and there is no longer a teacher to *'tell me off''*. Often we are not consciously aware of why we feel like we do in certain situations. Despite trying to be brave or to get through a situation or to ignore it, our energy system registers an imbalance, and our mind and body respond in a feedback loop which is reflected in our emotions, behaviour and health.

Often, the 'truths' conflict with each other and cause confusion. Take your career, for instance: the advice on your wall might be *'Work hard and you will do well'*. But it might also contain contradictory early writings such as:

- *'Don't look for attention'*
- *'Don't think too much of yourself'*
- *'Money is the root of all evil'*
- *'Your brother David is the achiever in our family'*

With such mixed messages it is not hard to imagine in this example that some actions and decisions will cause negative emotions such as disappointment and frustration. Our walls are reflected in our behaviour and in our responses to all aspects of life – relationships, attitude to money and abundance, beliefs about health, beliefs about safety, and the list goes on.

Fortunately EFT makes the process of erasing unhelpful writings much easier to manage. A process known as 'reframing' literally helps us to see a situation from another frame or perspective; it helps us to alter our reactions and to review the significance of feelings by viewing them from an alternative angle.

There is no limit to the writings that EFT can help us to alter. Many of thousands around the world have utilised a method called the EFT Personal Peace Procedure (see Chapter 5) to replace previously unhelpful graffiti from your walls and inspire us to create a more live enhancing existence.

Conflict

Conflict makes us feel threatened. It can come from external sources or from within us. We can learn how to deal with conflict by questioning how we currently perceive it. Through EFT we can do this in a gentle and non-threatening way.

External conflict

Case study

In an EFT session Luke was addressing sadness about his painful marriage separation. He reflected that conflict had been a damaging theme for most of his life. We created several set-up statements as we unfolded and eased layers of conflict pain, measuring SUD ratings as we proceeded.

'Even though lots of conflicts come to mind that make me feel unsafe, I deeply love and accept all parts of myself.'

>>

Case study continued

'Even though I avoid conflict at all costs, I accept my feelings and who I am.'

'Even though I don't stand up for myself when I have conflict, I choose to appreciate who I am and how I feel ...'

Unfolding and progressing through the negative aspects using tapping, calmness and resolution began to emerge. At this stage it was easier for Luke to think about an alternative way to perceive conflict and to create a set-up statement to reflect his current perspective. After several rounds of tapping, he formed the set-up

'Even though I do not feel comfortable with conflict situations, I choose to begin to see them as opportunities for resolution...'

If being assertive is something that has tended to be difficult then allow your skills of imagination to help. Practise vividly imagining being assertive and responding in a way that supports your values. Attending closely to your internal responses and your inner voice will provide you with material for subsequent set-ups (see also to section on tail-enders later in this chapter). By tapping on the feelings as they arise and using all your senses to imagine what are you saying and what it feels like, any blocks will become easier to identify and to clear.

The power of your imagination without any ties is great. You may not be able to affect the outcome of conflict but the way you perceive it will change, and this is significant.

Internal conflict

Case study

Fiona had just been introduced to EFT at a one-day course. For practice, participants were trying out EFT on a minor irritation. She selected a current aspect of conflict with her ex-partner. Fiona reflected that this issue was one in a long list of negatives that had accumulated since their separation. She felt that she could be logical about it and see the 'sense of giving in'. A practitioner might assume that this was the logic side of her brain doing the talking. When we tap we also access the emotional energy, which often tells a different and more resistant story.

As we began to tap using tell the story technique (outlined in Chapter 5) Fiona's internal conflict began to emerge as 'too many feelings are at stake'. She continued, 'I could give in ... but pride and resentment are standing in the way and I refuse to give in.' Using the VOC validity of cognition rating (see chapter 3) her truth was verified. Her belief around

>>

Case study continued

this statement measured 9 on the scale.. We began tapping through the layers of feeling. *'Even though I see the sense of giving in, I refuse to do it ...'*

We continued the round using a negative reminder phrase, *'I refuse to give in'*, and tapping on the top of the head.

During following rounds it felt right for Fiona to begin to alter the reminder phrases as we tapped around the points: *'don't want to see the sense of giving in'*, *'not changing my mind'*, *'not this time'*, *'I refuse to make the first move'*, *'too many feelings at stake'*, *'my pride and resentment stand in the way'*, *'not this time'*, *'not changing my mind'*.

When tested, Fiona's VOC level on the truth of the original set-up had dropped to 4 from a previous 9.

It is interesting to note that Fiona had originally selected this aspect as an example of a minor irritation. It is often the case that talking about an issue in general conversation does not give rise to any real emotional response because we are employing our logical head to cope and rationalise. By starting to approach the specifics of her conflict using EFT Fiona had highlighted the true emotional intensity that she was experiencing. Focusing closely on the disruptions of conflict for her, Fiona began to resolve the conflict. She named and claimed each contributing aspect using EFT, making resolution more possible.

Checking in regularly with Fiona on intensity level, remaining disruptions were identified accurately. Intuition, verbal feedback and close observation of the participant also add vital cues to the best path forward.

Fiona continued, *'I have been resentful but I suppose it would make it easier for all of us if I let it go; it's making me ill anyway'* and *'If I decide to change my plans, it will be my decision'.*

With subsequent rounds of tapping Fiona was now keen to point herself in a healing direction. By combining negative and positive phrases, new choices were created that seemed to fit with her current position: *'Even though I have had good reason to hold on to these resentment feelings, I have perhaps better reasons to let them go. I deeply and completely love and accept myself.'*

The remaining conflict was reflected in the reminder phrases used on alternate points round the body:

'Some resentment stands in the way' (negative) – on top of head

'I may choose to think of my health first' (positive) – on the eyebrow

'Some resentment stands in the way' (negative) – on the side of eye

'It will be easier for everyone to let some of this go' (positive) – under the eye.

We continued with alternate phrasing and finished the round with a positive phrase on the point under the arm: *'I appreciate that I can honour my feelings in a better way; I deeply and completely love and accept myself.'*

>>

Case study continued

Tapping in this way allowed Fiona to self-measure by saying the phrases out loud and using the intensity scale to compare the strength of resentment feelings (at some tapping points) against the strength of willingness to move feelings on (when tapping on the remaining points). The participant is usually able to identify with which *'part'* of them is currently stronger. Resolution of the internal conflict using EFT in this way follows a natural non-threatening path. This can be simplified with alternate phrases such as, *'Part of me feels resentment'* on one point and then, *'Part of me feels like letting the resentment go'.*

As we had continued on subsequent layers of conflict, the phrases brought up several aspects of self-talk (see the section on 'tail-enders' below). Every time this happens we fed the words back into new EFT set-up statements and continued tapping.

So, for example, when Fiona said as she tapped, *'Well it sounds good, but I'm not sure I have the strength'* the new set-up statement became *'Even though I'm not sure that I have the strength ...'*

By continuing to reintroduce combined positive and negative statements when appropriate, and using them in an alternating pattern, Fiona continued to note positive physical and psychological change.

Finally we finished the session on rounds of positive choices only. Moving gently from addressing the negative towards positive healing phrases at the appropriate time enables us to resolve painful feelings permanently.

Fiona reported that her thinking was refreshed and that she felt a lot calmer in general. Obviously, it often takes longer than one session to heal but persistent EFT is an excellent pathway, and tapping between sessions adds to self-healing empowerment.

The apex effect

The rapidity with which EFT can bring about relief sometimes leads people to deny that EFT has been the cause of change. The 'apex effect' is a term used in EFT to describe the tendency of some clients to explain away the results of tapping. In these instances the logical, conscious mind is unable to accept EFT as the source of the relief from even long-standing issues described by clients as *'crippling'*, *'devastating'* or *'wrecking'* their lives. It seems unreal that such painful struggles could be released so simply. Because this falls outside most people's comfort zone they struggle to find an alternative explanation for the changes that have occurred.

Worse still, people can even stop tapping when they begin to feel a little better. Some problems may dissolve immediately with EFT but in most cases persistence is needed. This usually means tracing and dealing with the aspects of the problem, using EFT techniques in several combinations.

Freedom can come within an hour or two, but several hours and additional EFT sessions over a period of days or even weeks might be needed. Persistence and repetition in EFT helps establish new pathways of thinking. It is recommended that EFT should become part of a daily routine, in addition to individual EFT treatments (see the section on new pathways in Chapter 7). This is especially important with issues such as chronic physical disease, depression, addictions and cravings, where the healing process is usually complex and lengthy.

It is not really surprising that people find it difficult to accept that big energy shifts, cognitive reframing and feeling a lot more at ease could be direct results of tapping on a few points and talking out loud. Until the start of the twenty-first century energy psychology in general did not fit with most people's belief system. It was seen as odd and far removed from Western medicine. Holistic approaches, however, look far beyond the symptoms, medication and crisis management of our health and wellbeing. Until recently in Western culture the idea of employing energy balance to maintain health and wellness would have seemed a highly unusual option. Both perception and practice have changed rapidly as energy techniques have grown in popularity.

> *'EFT is destined to be a top healing tool for the 21st Century'*
> **Bruce Lipton, The Biology of Belief**

One way to side-step the apex effect when using EFT with someone else is to encourage the observation of calibration changes in, for example, their language, attitude and symptoms. Often the changes are immediate and quite obvious to the person helping, even if not obvious to the participant. This discrepancy is a potential source of frustration for the helper or practitioner. One of the essential skills of an EFT practitioner is to remain detached from personal outcome desires. The advice of EFT founder Gary Craig is to *'keep yourself out of the picture'*. He stresses that you are a guide and a facilitator of change and healing for another person, and that any positive change is *'through you and not by you'*. (Craig 2011).

Given a little time and space skeptical clients usually do re-evaluate the effects of EFT. Avoid any temptation to try to persuade a participant to agree with your observations. The best advice I can give to newcomers is to be watchful of any changes that occur during tapping, and to be aware that individuals experience the techniques differently. Changes such as SUD intensity, feelings, thoughts and physical sensations might occur 'in the moment' or in the hours following a session or even days later. Subtle changes can easily be overlooked. Recording of language cues, SUD levels and other calibration measures (see Chapter 4) are essential means by which to monitor the shifts closely. If the participant takes an active note of changes as they happen this makes the apex effect less likely to occur.

Tail-enders

By paying close attention when tapping we can pick up on useful information about our own 'self-talk' or hidden objections to statements. In EFT these are called tail-enders and are the *'yes but'* reasons that stand in the way of progress with any self-development or self-acceptance. You may have spent time creating what seems to be an accurate EFT set-up statement only to find that a tail-ender emerges as soon as you start to tap.

We regularly sabotage ourselves. We are aware of some of our tail-enders but totally unaware of others. The more tail-enders we honour the less likely we are to reach our desires. Tail-enders can prevent even the most positive intentions from being realised. The emergence of a tail-ender in an EFT setting, however, provides us with crucial information. Progress can be made in these circumstances using refined EFT skills as long as the participant is encouraged to notice and verbalise tail-enders when they happen. EFT is a natural pain-free way of allowing tail-enders to be highlighted, processed and cleared.

Addressing tail-enders

When someone states an outcome they would like to achieve it can be useful to ask the question *'What would be the downside of achieving that?'* Responses usually include some interesting tail-enders.

Two ways of addressing tail-enders using EFT are by adapting

- standard set-up statements
- alternative choice set-up statements.

Standard set-up statements to address tail-enders

Table 9 provides real examples of EFT standard set-up statements adapted to begin to address tail-enders as they arose in different EFT sessions. With the first participant the question that was asked while tapping on one point was 'How would I feel if I got this promotion?' The response was used to form the set-up statement.

Table 9: **Creating set-ups that address tail-enders**

Positive outcome (How would I feel if ...?)	Tail-ender	Set-up
'I got promotion?'	*'I would have to take a lot more responsibilities'*	*'Even though I'll be expected to take on a lot more responsibility at work when I get promoted...'*
'I changed my career?'	*'It could disappoint my family'*	*'Even though I might disappoint my family if I change my career...'*
'I forgave her actions?'	*'I would feel like I had let myself down'*	*'Even though I would feel that I had let myself down if I forgave her ...'*

After continued rounds of tapping and checking progress belief in the tail-enders eases, leading to calmer and refreshed thinking. Listed below are examples of the resulting acceptance portion of the set-up statements that the same participants formed for themselves towards the end of their sessions.

Details of a method used to assess the truth of a belief are outlined later in this chapter, in the section 'How true is that for you?'.

'... I am willing to trust my inner resource skills to cope well, I accept myself.'

'... I am open to resolving these feelings, I deeply and completely accept myself.'

'... I am finding it easier than I thought, I'm OK for now.'

Creating alternative choice statements to address tail-enders

The choices method of tapping is widely used and involves changing the second half of the set-up statement to include a phrase that begins with, *'I choose ...'*. The method puts the participant back into the driving seat as they are exercising their own will, deciding on and committing to their own course of action. The choice method frequently produces powerful shifts towards the desired outcome.

A choice EFT set-up statement is made by creating an antidote to a tail-ender which combines the negative with the positive. The choice phrase can be utilised in different ways and identifying the right phrase for a specific problem is a skill in itself, but is well worth cultivating because it saves much time and effort in the long run. Table 10 outlines an example of the process to create a new choice set-up statement that addresses an emerging tail-ender. Here a client had originally focused their attention on choosing to keep their finances in good order.

Table 10 **Example of creating a revised choice set-up statement to address a tail-ender**

Original choice set-up	*'Even though I find it difficult, I choose to keep my finances in really good order...'*
Tail-ender	*'But I know that I will get bored doing paperwork all the time!'*
Antidote to tail-ender	*'I choose to find ways to be interested and enjoy keeping my finances in order.'*
Revised choice set-up that incorporates antidote to tail-ender	*'Even though I find it difficult, I choose to notice the interesting and enjoyable aspects of keeping my finances in order ...'*

The revised choice set-up addresses the sticking point of the issue more accurately. It is another illustration of the importance of being specific in EFT to reach healing more speedily and with as little resistance as possible. The 'be true to your feelings' section in this chapter explores the concept in more detail.

Subsequent new set-up phrases might be *'Even though I find that I get bored with my finances easily, I choose to find ways to make cost savings easily...'* or *'Even though I get bored so easily, I choose to release this emotion ...'*

Offering choices within EFT set-up statements generally provides a highly empowering angle as the choices allow you to name and claim the real energy disruptions. It is crucial that we are mindful of what is happening within us at present in order to create new statements that truly reflect our feelings.

'Even though I'm sad she has made the decision, I choose to find peace within myself.'

'Even though I have this throbbing head, I choose to acknowledge that my body is letting me know that it's time to pay attention."

On most occasions a choice phrase is best introduced when any significant SUD intensity (anything above, say, 6) has been reduced. If you attempt to introduce positive choices too early, resistance is likely to remain, keeping you stuck even in circumstances when it is not particularly useful.

How true is that for you?

When an issue requires the core intangible beliefs to be the focus for change rather than a level of distress or disturbance, an alternative to the usual SUD measure is used. For these instances we use the validity of cognition (VOC) scale mentioned briefly in an earlier chapter. This is a measure of 'how true' a belief is for you on a scale from 0 to 10.

Using EFT on limiting beliefs

This EFT technique works well whenever you feel 'stuck', when you are lacking in confidence, or motivation or you are procrastinating for whatever reason. It is best suited for intangible issues such as core beliefs or for the belief elements in any negative issue (see the case study of Peter in 'Going back to the root' in Chapter 12).

EFT on limiting beliefs technique

1 To explore this technique, consider a person saying *'I have a fear of being rejected'*. This is stating their 'belief' in the outcome of a particular situation. Perhaps it would have a VOC measure of 8 (high 'true' rating) as it currently feels quite true.

---

2 Then create a statement about the outcome that you would prefer to feeling rejected, such as *'To feel that my efforts to be accepted are good enough'*. Your belief in this statement asks *'how possible does the desired outcome feel right now?'* The question could be *'How possible does the statement – "my efforts to be accepted are good enough" feel right now?'* Perhaps this VOC currently ranks at 3 – not terribly true. The VOC measure here reflects the relative lack of truth currently being felt.

---

3 To proceed with this example, an EFT set-up statement is created that is based on your current VOC rating of the desired outcome, and tapping begins. The set-up statement might be *'Even though I am a long way off believing that my efforts are good enough...'*, or *'Even though my belief that my efforts are good enough only ranks at a 3 right now...'*, with a reminder phrase such as *'long way off feeling good enough'*.

---

4 After a few rounds of tapping on the negative, follow on with further rounds using feedback on any tail-enders, specific events and positives or whatever comes forward. When negative disruptions begin to fade, a round of tapping using positive phrases can be introduced, such as *'feeling more comfortable that my efforts are good enough'*. Progress can be tested after each round by repeating the set-up statement out loud, for instance *'My efforts to be accepted are good enough'*. By measuring the VOC, this subjective but accurate scale helps you to gauge the need to continue with subsequent rounds.

---

5 If you see little or no movement, check whether fear of success or failure may be getting in the way. Perhaps your subconscious is setting up an objection (see the sections on holding on and reversals later in this chapter). Although on a conscious level you may have a desire to change, your subconscious may put up objections in the form of a tail-ender for a variety of reasons. These objections may sound like excuses, but there are underlying reasons for them. Fear of being rejected is another common suspect and is a result of low self-esteem or of believing that the opinion of other people is more important than our own. Whether the source of 'not moving forward' is due to memories, limiting beliefs or tail-enders, or a combination, EFT can provides an ideal protocol to remove those blocks. Only when the blocks have been removed can true healing to take place.

Be true to your feelings

For some newcomers to EFT trusting the process can be difficult. Doubt can stem from questions about how EFT works, being outside your comfort zone or not trusting your personal ability to progress. Ploughing through and ignoring these tail-enders is a mistake, and doing so is likely to hinder positive change. It is important to be true to just what you are thinking and to tap for it. Creating a fresh set-up statement that acknowledges a feeling as it emerges effectively trades personal sabotage or psychological reversal (see the next section) for more life-enhancing experience.

Examples of 'be true to your feelings' statements

- *'Even though I'm not sure if I will ever get over this ... problem, I accept myself.'*
- *'Even though I don't think I can help myself to get rid of this ..., and I have never been able to help myself in the past, I am willing to be open...'*
- *'Despite the fact that I am finding it hard to progress with tapping, I still love and accept myself.'*
- *'Although I have no belief in EFT working, I will just tap and see what happens...'*

Such set-up statements can be adapted for numerous applications and issues.

Reasons for holding on to negative patterns

As discussed in Chapter 2, we often hold on to patterns of feelings and beliefs that stop us from being at our best. To complicate things, we tend to keep recreating these patterns, often without being aware of what makes change difficult for us. Our subconscious drives us to hold on to some issues because they are familiar and it feels safer to do so, even when they are not particularly useful strategies for us. Figure 6 outlines some of the main reasons we hold on to issues. Unsurprisingly, we frequently cannot recognise or are unwilling to accept these possibilities comfortably. However, while using EFT, the explanations rise to the surface naturally without any feeling of threat. We find that insights are within. We are very resourceful beings: we have all the answers within us, but sometimes we need help to return to a place of calmness before we can make a withdrawal from our bank of inner wisdom.

Figure 6 **Hidden reasons for not letting go of a problem**

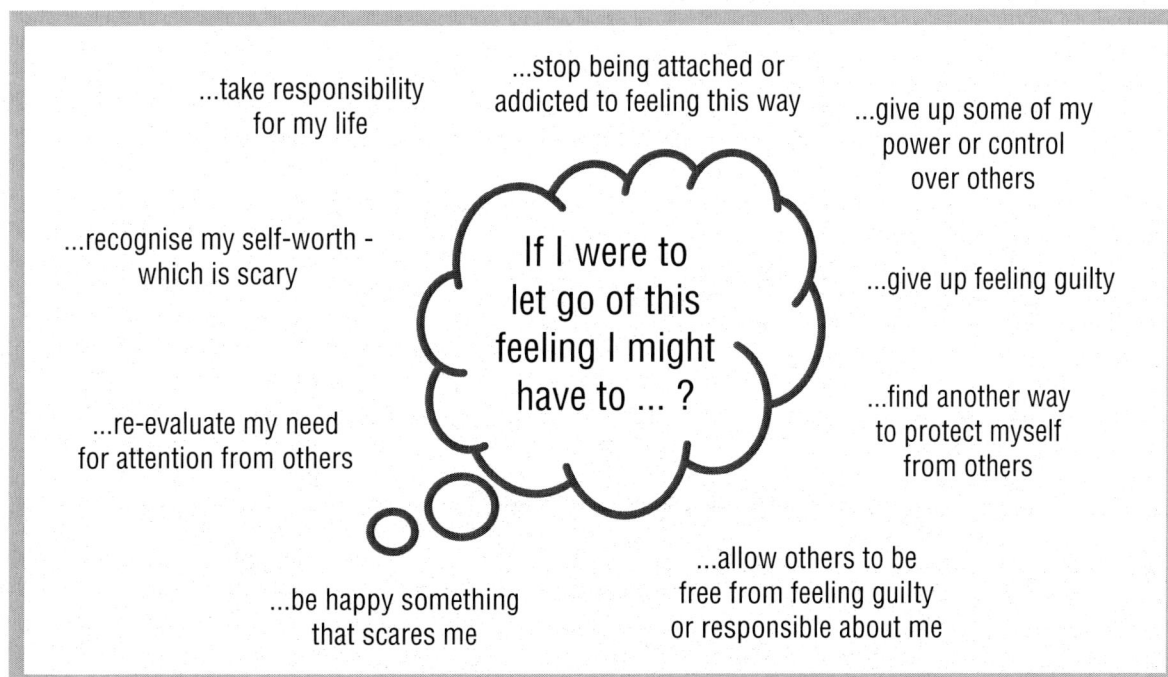

Psychological reversal

Given that EFT is highly effective we can become perplexed if it occasionally appears not to be delivering the outcomes we had hoped for. When this happens it is worth remembering that EFT is not a healing method itself, but a set of techniques which at best acts as a bridge towards a positive outcome. Typically, blocks to positive change (discussed in Chapter 6 – Improving the success rate of EFT) when using EFT include poor-quality EFT delivery, not being specific, not resolving the core issue and not getting to the original emotional cause of the problem. One of the most overlooked obstructions to successful EFT treatment, however, falls into the category of psychological reversals (PR).

It is estimated that psychological reversal is present in approximately 20 per cent of cases. Once PR has been discovered, the solutions for correcting reversals are very simple and highly effective. For chronic or long-lasting problems, complex issues and even serious illnesses, reversals are very common. PRs fall into two basic types: general polarity reversal and secondary benefits.

General polarity reversal

In this type of reversal, energy in the body (or Qi) is considered not to be flowing easily in the natural direction. The polarity is said to be reversed. This can be heightened in the presence of

- negativity: chronic negative thoughts, negative behaviour, or negative events

- addictions: addictive personalities or addictive substances in the body

- dehydration: without hydration the energy system is less conductive and slower

- energy toxins.

Energy toxins, as their name suggests, are toxic to, or weaken, the energy system. The percentage of people affected by energy toxins is unknown although it is thought that it is limited to a small percentage of people. Unlike allergens, energy toxins do not provoke a histamine reaction; allergic antibodies are not present, and skin tests are negative. Potential energy toxins include scented laundry detergent, wheat, corn, dairy products, cigarette smoke, used pillows and mattresses, mould, dry-cleaning fluids, house plants and poor ventilation. Electromagnetic charge from electrical equipment is also a source of energy toxin for some people.

Symptoms are characteristic of the person and may have both physical and psychological aspects: headaches, respiratory problems, sore throats, chronic coughs, frequent colds, eye irritation, fatigue, dizziness, memory lapses, depression, anxiety, agoraphobia, psychosis, mental fogginess, muscle aches and pains, arthritis, digestive problems, lack of focus and concentration, weight gain and hyperactivity.

Fortunately, energy psychology approaches have been shown to neutralise the effects of these substances in a wide variety of cases. In EFT, by performing the standard set-up procedure – rubbing the sore spot (SS) or tapping the friendly point (FP) while saying the set-up statement – will often correct negativity or electrical general polarity reversals. These type of reversals caused by addictions or depression, however, are not usually eliminated in this way and require additional work, as detailed below.

It has been observed in many EFT sessions that resolving an issue is improved as soon as the participant drinks some water. Water is the most fundamental substance for the proper functioning of the human organism and a carrier of electrical messages in the nervous system. It is recommended that you drink plenty lot of water before, during and after an EFT session and that you do not wait for thirst to signal your need for water intake. Of course, this is in addition to your everyday proper hydration, which is essential for maintaining health and recovering from ailments.

Secondary benefit syndrome reversal

This type of reversal occurs when the subconscious mind perceives that it is better or safer to hold on to an issue such as a negative emotion, chronic pain, extra weight or a bad habit than to eliminate it. It is the result of inner conflict between two parts of us that are actually looking for the same outcome but by very different means. Have you ever wanted to achieve a particular goal but found yourself constantly, inexplicably, sabotaging yourself along the way? This is our subconscious being unwilling to 'let go', and our bodies can actually become tied to that negative emotion or issue. After a period of time we may become so accustomed to being angry, hurt, anxious, victimised, and so on, that our body is very reluctant to give up the emotion. The negative condition may be uncomfortable, but the habit begins to feel 'natural' both to the body and to the subconscious mind.

Since SBS is seldom a conscious choice, initially we are naturally resistant to the idea that subconsciously we do not want be rid of the problem or issue. Of course, most people do not consciously want to stay emotionally upset or physically in pain, but the subconscious is a powerful entity, usually exhibiting dominance over our conscious desires. For someone who has carried around a trauma, chronic pain, fear, phobia or other issue for many years the emotion can become a part of their personality, or even their identity. To complicate things further, thoughts can add to the conflict; for instance, *'If I get over this issue ...'*

- 'people might think that I have been a fake.'
- 'it might be scary.'
- 'I may not know who I am anymore.'
- 'it may not be safe to let it go.'
- 'I won't know how to act as a functional "non-victim" person.'
- 'I won't get the attention that I get now.'

EFT can be used very effectively to identify and address secondary benefit reasons for not being able to move forward. Remember though that this does not fix the problem; it simply clears the path forward.

Tried and tested questions that help to uncover secondary benefits include:

'What would be the downside of getting rid of this ... issue?'

'What would be the upside of keeping it?'

'Is it really safe or in your best interest to let this ... issue?'

'Would it harm others? Will you be 'lost' without it? What frightens you about getting over this issue?'

Best guesses are usually very accurate if you allow intuition. Other reasons for holding on were suggested earlier in Figure 6.

The significance of the set-up for secondary benefits

Tapping on the friendly point (FP)

Tapping on friendly point (FP) on the side of the hand for each set-up is regarded as probably the single most important point in EFT. When we tap on the friendly point we are, in terms of Chinese medicine, encouraging balance in the small intestine meridian so that energy flows freely; we are supporting our choices when we are feeling divided or pulled in more than one direction. The functional comparison here is what the small intestine does physiologically in digestion, to separate what is most useful in the food from what will become waste.

Additionally, the small intestine meridian is paired with the heart, and according to Chinese medicine the heart holds the spirit, the totality of life force of a person. The function of the heart network is to propel the blood, enfold the spirit and maintain awareness. The small intestine protects the heart by filtering out negative input, both from food waste and from the effects of damaging energies such as shocking surprise, deep sorrow or even overwhelming joy. When we are under a lot of stress the heart is disturbed and our thinking becomes confused; we become exhausted, breathless and anxious.

The heart meridian is the most important meridian for healing thought, feeling and personality. In balance, heart energy is joyful, radiant, outgoing, loving, generous, optimistic and giving. When it is unbalanced it is careless, forgetful, distracted, restless and may be unrealistically idealistic. It is the location of many emotions, such as, *'a heaviness in my chest'*, *'my heart aches'*, *'my heart feels tight and constricted'*.

By tapping on the side of the hand (along the small intestine meridian) we are balancing the energy to facilitate sorting out what parts of our thinking we want to keep, because they are nourishing, and what parts we want to let go of, because they are toxic to our system. Balancing the energy flow, we let go of what we no longer need, returning to a state in which we foster a generative inner harmony and a peaceful heart.

In summary, when we tap on the side of the hand in EFT, in thought and action, in intention and in energy, we are saying to ourselves inside, *'Even though I have this stressful problem that is upsetting me, I love and accept myself and how I feel anyway. Even though I am having these stressful experiences and I don't know how to move forward, I understand and appreciate myself anyway, and I am doing the best I can'.*

Sore spot

The sore spot (the point used in the original EFT basic recipe) is a neuro-lymphatic reflex point. Performing the set-up procedure here stimulates the lymph system, acting like a switch to turn it on or off. The lymphatic system acts as a drain in the body; it emotionally correlates with clearing and allowing negative emotions to drain away. The sore spot is also close to the lung meridian, which is also emotionally associated with 'letting go'.

Creating EFT set-up statements to address secondary benefit reversals

When tapping on the friendly point (FP) select a set-up statement that matches the current feeling, such as *'Even though,...'*.

'... I don't know if I really want to get over this [depression/trauma/chronic pain, etc.], *I deeply and completely accept myself.'*

'... It may not be safe to get over my.[insert issue]...'

'... I may not deserve to get over this issue...'

'... I won't know how to act if I get well...'

'... I would have to sort out my messed up life...'

'... I don't want to forgive the people that ruined my life...'

'... I don't want to be "normal"...'

'... I'm afraid this won't work and I'll never be well...'

'... For whatever reason, I don't want to overcome this problem...'

Reversals can present huge road blocks but they can be effectively remedied using accurate EFT. Careful listening and measuring helps enormously to identify an accurate set-up that hits the target. As already mentioned, fixing a reversal does not fix the issue; it gets rid of the impediment to fixing the issue. Continued EFT is usually required to address layers and aspects of an issue. This is not always the case, however, as I have often witnessed a client clear on an issue immediately once a significant secondary benefit reversal has been eased, purely by performing a set-up procedure on the side of the hand.

Correcting secondary benefit reversals using EFT is rewarding, as benefits are often immediate. This is particularly beneficial for anyone who has negative patterns they seem unable to break – habits such as smoking, overeating or procrastinating, and indeed any sabotage pattern. New participants in EFT may have been trying to change their attitudes and actions for weeks, months or even years without success, and they blame themselves for their failures. However, once secondary benefit reversals is corrected, tapping opens up a whole new world. They report feeling lighter and having more energy. The *'lack of motivation and will power'* and *'self-sabotage'* they have been living with no longer have power over them and they start to make progress where once there was only the feeling of failure. It is very exciting to watch this happen. Correcting secondary benefit reversals and tapping aids relief with both emotional and health issues, as described above. The effects of permanently erasing psychological reversal also include benefits in areas such as performance in sports, at school, at work, in creative endeavours such as writing, painting and playing musical instruments.

Happy holding on thanks

Although EFT is very helpful in uncovering issues and helping to clear blockages that prevent a person from moving forward, it is easy to overlook the fact that some people are not ready or are unwilling to make changes, even when they know that changes would make life better. This is different from not knowing how to move on, or being sceptical about EFT. Without a desire to change, positive change is simply not possible. When attempting to help someone else the choice not to change must be respected. Whether you are a professional practitioner or helping as a friend or family member, with the person's best interests in mind you need to remain strictly unattached to the outcome.

As earlier chapters have stressed, however, as long as someone wants to change, EFT can work for them. If someone is feeling negative yet desires to feel differently then anything is possible. This is even the case with those who are unable to express their feelings or frustrations in words. Many people find it difficult to talk about their feelings, and with EFT this does not matter. It is the energy disruption that is addressed, and adult, academic or clinical descriptions of an issue is irrelevant. Clients with autism or young babies, for example, regularly benefit as a result of shifts to more positive, calm emotions and behaviour despite the fact that no words are exchanged.

Permission, forgiveness and persistence

Permission is a powerful feature in EFT. Permission to accept what is happening, to hold on to a feeling or to let go all play a part in self-acceptance, which is a major contributor to healing. Below are suggestions for EFT set-up statements that you can adapt to your own words:

'Even though I have [problem], *I give myself permission to deal with this* [problem] *...'*

'Even though I can't [negative], *I accept myself and allow myself to believe that I can* [positive] *...'*

'Even though I don't [negative action], *I give myself permission to* [positive action] *...'*

Fortunately, as part of the natural process of EFT willingness to forgive often arises even when a session starts with anger, rage and resentment. Layers of energy disruption emerge and clear with successive tapping rounds. Obviously forgiveness can still be a source of conflict for an individual, and acknowledgement that this is acceptable can be built into a set-up:

'Even though I'm not ready to forgive yet, I am ready to explore the possibility in the future...'

The importance of persistence with stubborn issues (the ones that prove hard to shift) cannot be underestimated. Resist the urge to give up on tapping if it does not seem to be working quickly enough. Chapter 4 in general and particularly the section on improving the success rate will certainly help. Always check your SUDS level, keep tapping successive rounds, re-checking your SUDS level. If you get stuck try saying *'Even though I'm stuck on this (insert details of issue) at a 4 (insert your number), I deeply and completely accept myself and choose to easily be a 0'.* Step outside your current way of thinking and tune into the emotions that are coming through, for example, anger or frustration if things are not moving as quickly as you would like. Tap on them and also tap for the issue being more complicated than you expected.

Nature's medicine

The benefits of humour for the immune system are well documented. Published studies have shown that laughter lowers blood pressure, reduces stress hormones, increases muscle flexion, and boosts immune function by raising levels of infection-fighting T-cells (the disease-fighting proteins) and the levels of B-cells, the disease-destroying antibodies. Laughter also triggers the release of endorphins, the body's natural painkillers, and produces a general sense of wellbeing.

Building humour into EFT sessions can:

- relax a client who is tense or perhaps unsure of the process

- help to re-process powerful emotional states once negative disruptions have begun to clear; at key moments humour can provide an effective 'break-state', moving us from one emotional 'state' to an alternative 'neutral state'

- be used to help to address the 'weirdness aspect' of EFT; for example, we might tap *'Even though I have no idea why I am sitting here doing this nutty tapping, I am here now so I might as well give it a go...'* This use might sound a bit feeble but in my experience acknowledging any 'comfort zone' issues by going ahead and tapping anyway has a powerful transformational effect

- help to uncover truth and insights; the proverbial truth known for centuries that 'Many a true word is spoken in jest', is very apt – humour commonly disarms the truth which may otherwise be too painful or too likely to evoke negative reaction.

Case study

Sean was fed up with his habitual pattern of questioning his own decisions which regularly prevented him from moving forward with his plans. While using tapping, he began to explain. Despite the upsetting details at one point, humour helped Sean to reflect on the conflict and to gain useful insight.

We were tapping on conflicting feelings and a set-up statement was *'Even though the one thing I can be really sure about is that I am always unsure ...'* Sean's VOC belief measure in this statement was a 9.

After a few rounds of tapping Sean altered the statement to *'Even though I am sure about my unsure-ness, I may choose to become surer about being sure ..."*

Realising our mutual Irish origins, and only because I knew he trusted me, I took a chance and offered a further set-up statement on the next round: *'Even though I'm not sure to be sure, I may choose to be sure to be sure ...'* (*'to be sure'* is a phrase associated with Irish stereotyping).

We laughed lots as we continued tapping, and when we measured again on VOC scale Sean was satisfied that he was more comfortable with his decision-making skills. We finished the session tapping on all the things that Sean felt *'sure that I am sure about.'*

Joking aside, Sean continued tapping on further aspects of this issue at home. He slowly gained more insights and confidence in his new-found and more helpful pattern for trusting his decisions.

Humour can be included in EFT practice in many ways. A further example was with an EFT client who was moving away from an upsetting negative position about a relationship. The new set-up was *'Even though I am/have been really mad with myself that I didn't see what he was doing and I should have really gone to the opticians...'* Humour in EFT, as in any therapy, should be treated with care. As a newcomer to EFT it is probably good practice to avoid it until a very firm grounding of the techniques has been mastered. Even with considerable EFT practice, joking and laughing should be used only where appropriate, and essentially in circumstances where there is already good rapport.

Chapter 7
Exploring the emerging map on EFT perspectives

Chapter 7 Exploring the emerging map on EFT perspectives

For many people EFT and other forms of energy psychology rest comfortably within their understanding and way of living. But it is hardly surprising that for others, for whom EFT is unfamiliar, it appears to be frankly quite strange. We are naturally inclined to ask 'how does that work?' We require the hard facts and especially when considering a subject outside our comfort zone. Whatever your current comfort zone, you are invited in this chapter to review your perspective of EFT from the point of view of your personal 'map' of wellness.

EFT is a unique mix of fascinating influences, historic and new, Western and Eastern. The selection of perspectives and findings offered in this chapter is by no means a complete picture of EFT. Evidence-based research in EFT has built up gradually. Our understanding is rapidly developing in relation to related fields of research such as neuroscience (see Appendix 3). The National EFT Research Programme was launched in the UK in 2009 and more reliable data from controlled trials has begun to accumulate (Feinstein et al, 2006).

'Education is when you read the fine print.
Experience is what you get if you don't'
Pete Seeger, singer and activist

Unwrapping a deceptively simple set of techniques

The basics of EFT are simple. So simple, in fact, that for the last several years I have regularly taught EFT to very young children. It is easy to imagine that simple techniques cannot possibly be effective, especially in the treatment of complex and chronic issues.

You may be of the opinion that a solid theory base and practice solely by professionals are prerequisites for a therapeutic practice to be valuable? My educational background is psychology and so I have studied many therapies, their applications and their success rates. I am accustomed to expecting to research a theoretical background, even though many therapies and approaches still fall sadly short of delivering practical, cost-effective results. EFT emerged from a relatively non-traditional source and like so many others I began to explore this 'weird stuff' with a good dose of healthy scepticism.

What I found was that EFT worked despite the fact that I did not understand how. It worked for me as a self-help tool, and for my family, and then later, after various levels of training, as a therapeutic professional. It continues to be a most effective lifestyle choice for tens of thousands, and is the most efficient yet simple approach that I know. Used correctly, it works for any issue that has emotional content, provided there is some intention to change. The future of EFT and energy psychology in health care and wellbeing for all is extremely promising. Just to set the record straight – I did not remain a sceptic, but I still welcome scepticism about EFT from newcomers as a sign of a healthy inquiring mind.

In EFT workshops and sessions throughout the world people usually look and feel calmer within a few rounds of tapping, as emotions or memories emerge and clear. They gain a fresh cognitive perspective on previously troubling issues. The experience of tapping is satisfying, but the question *'What's just been happening?'* usually follows. Reasons for asking the question include a mixture of interest, curiosity about the process and scepticism about positive shifts. I have to admit that EFT looks and sounds a bit strange when you first come across it. The truth is that we are still learning to explain EFTs fascinating results and it would be a foolhardy to try to offer a comprehensive viewpoint. Instead of focusing on how EFT works, it is more beneficial to reflect on our current observation of what changes occur when we use it and to consider some exciting emerging perspectives in related fields.

Energy and electricity

'In every culture and in every medical tradition before ours, healing was accomplished by moving energy'
Albert Szent-Gyorgyi, Nobel laureate in medicine

Although factors such as positive intention, insight and support play a part in therapeutic change, especially in more complex issues with a practitioner, the success rate of EFT in comparison to other interventions is accredited to the combination of stimulation of acupressure points to encourage the flow of *qi* (energy of life force), while mentally focusing on an issue and verbally making a statement that reflects our current state.

In accordance with the principles of Eastern medicine, when we are well, resilient, calm and open our energy or 'life force' flows in a clear direction around the energy meridian system. When we are not doing well that flow is halted or sluggish, and the energy is regarded as being out of balance in our body. EFT restores the balance and stimulates better flow in the meridian system, the energy block around an issue is released and emotions shift into more positive states. EFT is truly holistic; its mind body effect is all-encompassing and with great efficiency.

EFT uses tapping on meridian points to achieve its results, we need to look further than models of the brain and biochemistry to explain the effects of EFT. The tips of our fingers have electric and magnetic qualities (Church, 2008). When we use our fingertips to tap on acupoints in a sequence on the body a high concentration of mechano-receptors and free nerve endings in the skin are stimulated. The receptors generate a signal, or a piezoelectric[1] charge (an electric charge resulting from pressure). Our whole body is actually a piezoelectric generator, and some organs have a primary function to conduct this energy from one part of the body to another. The network of connective tissue throughout the body provides perfect semi-conductive conditions (see also the section on removing trauma with EFT in Chapter 12). The electrical signals are carried though the entire body within connective tissue and via organs at a much faster rate than through neural or brain-signalling transmission.

The route that the electrical signal follows is a path of least electrical resistance that we name the meridian energy system. It has the same flow and pattern in all humans (see Figure 1). The signals and pathways can be measured by instrument, yet these channels or meridians are invisible to the eye.

Any form of mechanical stimulation to our body causes a minor electrical charge whether it is pleasant such as a cuddle, touch or massage or a negative experience such as shutting your foot in a door. Focused tapping in EFT recreates negative energy or charge in the body specific to an issue before dissipating it. The vital difference between touch and EFT is that when we tap we consciously focus on a specific issue and access the locations that have the closest connection with energy flow. The combination of specific techniques performed within EFT has a direct and profound effect on the mind–body connection.

Biochemical changes

The well-known effects of the stress response are outlined in Chapter 12. EFT studies (see Appendix 3) regularly replicate the same feedback loop of stress reduction and subsequent release of emotional intensity (see Figure 7).

Figure 7 **Physical and emotional release in EFT**

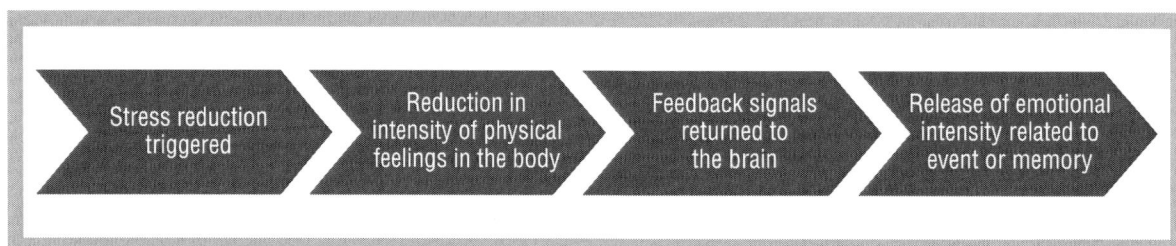

Stress reduction triggered → Reduction in intensity of physical feelings in the body → Feedback signals returned to the brain → Release of emotional intensity related to event or memory

Emotional states are dependent on a balancing interaction between neurotransmitters and hormones. The release of serotonin, one of the 'feel-good' hormones, is increased during EFT sessions and correlates with tapping on specific points (Feinstein et al, 2005; see Appendix 3). Lane (2009) describes the neurological and physiological effects when acupoints are stimulated. Opiataes are produced, serotonin and gamma-amniobutyric acid (GABA) and cortisol is regulated. The neurochemical changes reduce pain, slow the heart rate, decease anxiety, shut off the flight/fight/ freeze response, regulates the autonomic nervous system and creates a sense of calm. The relaxation reponse reciprocally inhibits anxiety and creates a rapid desensitisation to traumatic stimuli.

Brainwaves and emotional states

Attention has been devoted to observing and monitoring the brainwave changes that occur when using EFT. Biofeedback technology is used to monitor the balance and intensity of the four brainwaves that each contributes to recognisable patterns of our consciousness and emotional state:

- beta waves – faster – thinking, worry and anxiety; regular – alert, engaged thinking
- alpha waves – sensory experience and relaxation
- theta waves – slow – subconscious emotion
- delta waves – very slow – signs of healing and spiritual connection.

When we are calm and alert, all of these four ranges are present to a greater or lesser extent and they are also balanced between left and right hemispheres (see Table 11). The intensities and balance of our brainwaves change according to the emotional state we are in.

Neurofeedback experts Gary Groesbeck and Donna Bach (2008) have facilitated many EFT sessions where brainwave frequencies, heart-rate variability and hemispheric integration is monitored and displayed. In 2008 they assisted at the Exploring Consciousness EFT international event in the UK.[2] Biofeedback monitoring begins as a participant is seated and invited to bring to mind a worry or distress-related issue. The fascinating changes in brainwave patterning is reliably recorded by electroencephalography (EEG). A record of the electrical brain activity along the scalp produced by the firing of neurons within the brain is displayed for others to see on a large screen.

Table 11 **Observed brain waves and integration changes during EFT**

Brain wave ranges and levels of consciousness	Recorded changes as EFT session progresses
Beta (14-35 hertz) **Faster Beta** – Uneasy, tense, worry, anxiety, stress and emotional intensity. Brain lateralisation 'out of sync' **Regular Beta** – Alert, active, engaged thinking, concentrating.	As an issue is brought to mind, the participant typically shows thinking in the faster Beta range. The brain function is lateralised – 'out of sync' thinking is recorded when participant is emotionally intense, anxious or stressed. Beta waves continue to remerge in a session as new issues or layers emerge. As the participant continues to use EFT, the beta level is again reduced to a new healthy level.
Alpha (8-13 hertz) State of light meditation, like daydreaming. Open to sensory experience, visualisation and relaxation. Super learning and memory retention Increased health benefits. Alpha provides a bridge between the conscious and the subscious mind.	As tapping starts, the calm of Alpha begins and this is followed by bursts of Theta as memories and emotions emerge into consciousness. Emotional intensity, anxiety, stress reduces for the participant as emotional issues of the moment are released during EFT. Alpha provides the bridge to the theta 'experience'.
Theta (4-7 hertz) Increased creative inspiration. Spiritual connection! subconscious awareness, gives us the ah-ha moment. Longterm memory, storehouse of repressed emotions and memory. Deep healing of body. Retention of learned material. Theta provides optimal peak experience.	Additional theta brain wave spikes occur, even when the person may not be conscious of the emotional connection to what they are saving. During the session access to theta enhances internal focus and the emergence of memories. The theta range allow us to connect with the issues that need to be resolved by accessing the pertinent emotional memories. During this stage a participant is in optimal state for transforming emotional blocks, clearing limiting beliefs, and healing physical ailments. Core issues begin to be resolved.

>>

Brain wave ranges and levels of consciousness	Recorded changes as EFT session progresses
Delta (1.5-3 hertz) When delta is present with other waves in waking state, Delta acts as a radar to seek information that is not available to us on a conscious level. Accesses deep unconscious level. Provides intuition, state of empathy, physical healing, boosted immune system, instinctual insight and energy healing. 	Delta wave sometimes occur, especially when the person is connecting to deeper or spiritual healing. It brings moments of emotional, personal, creative, and spiritual insight. EFT resolves long term emotional issues and tunes the brain to its highest levels of performance, corresponding to a more balanced pattern of healthy thinking and feeling. Overall, with progression, the brain wave pattern stabilises and becomes more balanced or synchrorised between hemispheres. This hemispheric integration is also known as whole brain functioning.

A summary of the similar pattern of results are outlined in Appendix 3 and discussed in the GAD section of Chapter 10.

Other extensive trials have been conducted with thousands of anxiety patients who have had their brain-frequency patterns analysed by Dr Joaquin Andrade while undergoing energy therapy.

Heart rhythms and coherence

When you experience stressful emotions such as tension, anxiety, irritation or anger, your heart-rhythm pattern becomes irregular and incoherent which negatively affects your health, brain function, performance and sense of wellbeing (see Figure 8). Fatigue, sickness and disease, heart problems and ailments are more likely among people with incoherent heart-rhythms.

Figure 8 **Heart rhythms when stressed and when feeling positive**

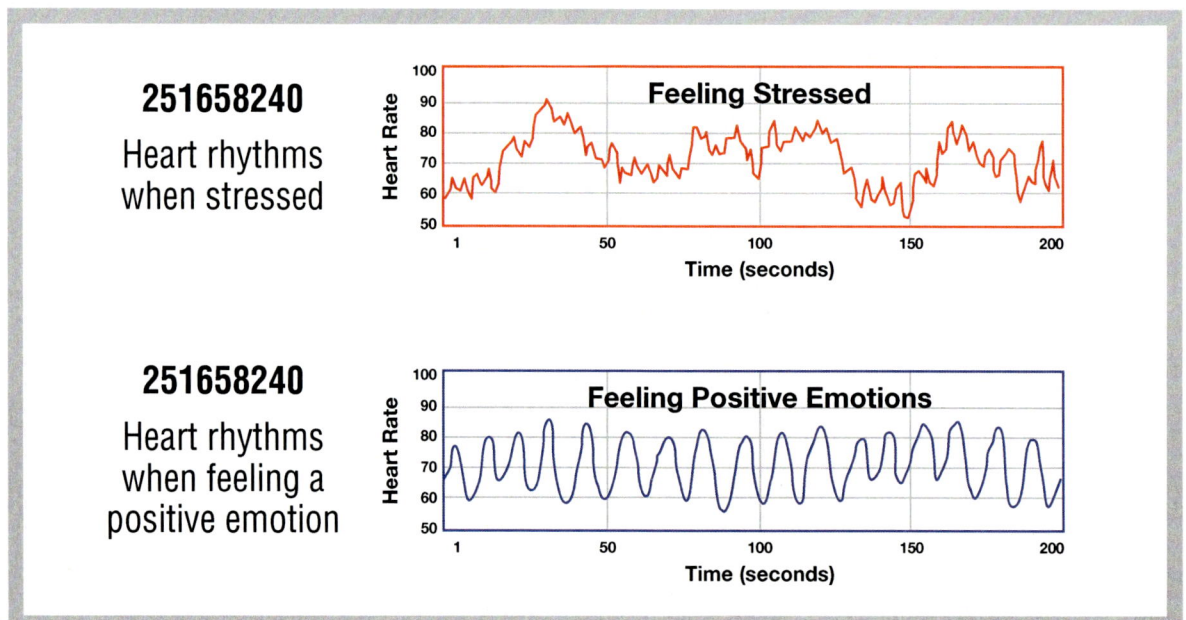

In contrast, when you experience positive emotions such as appreciation, care, joy and love your heart-rhythm pattern is more ordered and coherent. Ordered and harmonious heart rhythms are an indicator of what is known as your 'coherence level'. High coherence is a state associated with positive emotional attitudes. These send signals to the brain that reduce stress and improve brain cognitive function, hormonal balance, immune response, coordination, reaction times and overall sense of wellbeing. Heart-rate coherence indicates a stress reduction and enhances intuition. This helps you to have better focus, more energy and improved mental clarity.

When heart-rate variability patterns are monitored during EFT sessions they correlate with movement to healthier responses, indicating that EFT brings resolution to emotionally charged information (Groesbeck and Bach, 2008).

Hemispheric integration

When we experience any event in our lives we record two separate memory representations, one in each brain hemisphere, each of which has a unique function and perspective. In simple terms, the logic hemisphere (usually on the left side) deals with the details, the parts and processes of language and linear analysis. By contrast, the gestalt – meaning 'whole processing' or global, rather than linear – hemisphere (usually on the right side) deals with images, rhythm, emotion, spatial relationships, intuition and personal safety.

The corpus callosum at the rear of the brain allows quick access to both linear detail in the logic hemisphere and the overall image in the gestalt hemisphere. When there is good communication between the two spheres, the result is integrated thought. By filtering and scanning the perspectives of factual perspectives with emotional feelings, mental clutter is cleared and we are opened to rounded thinking and recall. The more that both hemispheres are activated by use, the more connections form across the corpus callosum, which in turn results in faster processing between the hemispheres and more integrated function.

In emotional balance, the two hemispheres are primed to exchange new information and learning for the brain, allowing us to bring about immediate changes in our thoughts, actions and beliefs.

We all have a degree of hemispheric dominance (a natural preference) to taking in information and for making decisions but this dominance is further extended in times of stress or in situations of new learning. We tend to rely on the side that serves us best. Negative emotions generally have the overall effect on brain functioning of reducing our hemispheric integration. When we are negative, consciously or not, we are at a distinct disadvantage as we have less access to all the intelligent data.

Over the course of EFT sessions, hemispheric integration naturally improves as the client moves towards positive shifts. An increase in brain symmetry during EFT enables both sides of the brain, the hemispheres, to begin to work together in a more balanced manner. This opens up our choices, which in turn aids resolving issues.

Any tapping (and particularly the full EFT recipe) encourages multi-sensory processing as standard, and increases hemispheric integration. In addition, the nine gamut exercise in the original version of EFT helps participants neurologically to cross the 'visual midline', thereby activating both right and left eyes, integrating the right and left visual fields and increasing hemispheric integration. So, apart from any other motivations to include EFT in your life, you may appreciate more positive reasons to tap every day.

You can read more about potential applications of EFT to help improve neural connections for young people in Chapter 14.

The opportunity for hemispheric integration when using EFT has important implications for children and for anyone with learning challenges or sensory integration disorders. EFT helps to rebuild weakened pathways in the nervous system. When used on a regular basis, integration is optimised.

The amygdala and emotional memories

Our emotional state considerably affects the way in which we retain information and the accuracy with which retention occurs. The amygdala is the most notable brain structure involved in emotional responses and in the formation of emotional memories (see Figure 9 in Chapter 10). Distinctive to other memory formation, the hippocampus and the amygdala act in a synergistic way to consolidate long-term emotionally based memories (Richter-Levin 2004). We know from experience how memories formed at emotional moments can have powerful and long-lasting effects.

As a memory is recalled, the brain structures involved cause a series of neurons to activate or 'fire'. A coordinated and repetitive activity among any combination of neurons strengthens their synaptic connections – neurons that actively fire together (at approximately 270 miles per hour). Each time you think and re-think about an event the memory is strengthened, which is why traumatic memory, obsessions and depression can be so debilitating and can appear to be inescapable.

Interestingly, research has shown that when any behaviour is driven by the amygdala (primarily fear and stress memories) it is possible to unlink the thought from the emotional response so that we become less emotionally affected. Stimulation on acupuncture points decreases activation signals in the amygdala (Hui et al., 2000). This also corresponds with the observation that tapping appears rapidly to decrease elevated emotional responses in stressful situations by settling the disrupted energy patterns (Feinstein 2008a). It is also worth noting that electrical signals (produced by tapping) reach specific locations in the brain, such as the amygdala, hippocampus and other structures associated with emotions, much quicker than any biochemical response would.

EFT practice shows that positive changes occurs once energy disruptions are rebalanced in the body's energy system around a specific issue. New information arriving to the brain for analysis will no longer match the component with previously stored related memory elements residing on an existing neural network. A new message of safety is introduced to the body as a result of the mismatch of what we have been used to – the older, emotive-arousing memory. Our brain notes this discrepancy and further brain processing is instigated to unhook the memory of the stress response. Tapping provides optimum conditions for positive change and this is not limited to the short term.

Research suggests that our emotional condition affects the induction of long-term neural plasticity – our ability to build new connections in the brain structure (see the section on plasticity later in this chapter). Loosely speaking, any two cells or systems of cells in the brain that are repeatedly active at the same time will tend to become 'associated' so that activity in one facilitates activity in the other. Interrelations between the amygdala and brain regions, such as the hippocampus, may be not static but dynamic. This means in effect that with the help of techniques such as EFT we can not only tackle blocks, limiting beliefs and emotional memories but we can also begin to build new, healthier neural networks to represent our refreshed outlook.

The reticular activating system

I strongly regard EFT as the most versatile and effective set of techniques available for providing the 'missing link' – bridging the gap – between what we say we want and what we end up getting. Why then, even with good basic EFT skills is it not always straightforward for us to reach our goals and desires? Why do we find ourselves getting tied up with unhelpful details? It is worth delving a bit deeper here to explore how we tend to prevent ourselves from achieving the passions and goals that we talk about. In this section we look at the functioning of a specific small part of the brain and consider how EFT can be employed to retune our 'antennae'.

Located within the brain stem lies the reticular activating system (RAS), an arousal mechanism that keeps the brain alert and awake. This primitive brain function for survival acts as our scanning device (like antennae) to 'tune into' the parts of our external environment that are regarded as most important at any particular time.

At any one moment we are exposed to millions of pieces of sensory information through our sensory organs – sight, hearing, smell, taste and touch. We focus on the sensory information that we judge to be relevant. Without this filtering, our experiences would be too chaotic and unmanageable. The RAS filters the huge bank of sensory information available to us at any moment to about 130 pieces per second in the conscious mind, about the maximum our nervous system can handle at one time. The filtered incoming sensory information is then transferred to the active cortex of the brain, so that we remain in prime alert to act quickly.

Retuning your antennae

As explored in Chapter 2, our filters can work for us or against us and this depends on the quality of those filters that we created early on in our lives. For example, we might have given ourselves a permanent underlying instruction such as *'listen for my name being called'*, with the subtext *'as that means it's my turn or my opportunity to be/do something positive'*. Alternatively we might hold underlying instructions that are not so helpful and that we may or may not be aware of. A simple example might be, *'Listen out for anyone who questions me'*, with a subtext *'that must mean that they are criticising me personally'*. Based on our past experiences, our RAS makes constant reference to our core beliefs in order to filter 'relevant' sensory data. This processing is very fast and largely out of our conscious awareness. Our 'perceived' experience, good or bad, is further influenced by the autonomic nervous system which automatically regulates basic functions such as digestion, salivation, perspiration, and so on. Very easily you can find yourself in a sweat as a result of an encounter you were hardly aware of.

EFT can help us to establish knowledge about our current RAS preferences. This is extremely useful as we can then review any negative thoughts and limiting beliefs, fine-tuning our attention and freeing up our goals and desires by using further EFT. This is not limited to the present as we can also use this powerful set of techniques for reviewing our past (refer to the section on cleaning up graffiti in Chapter 6).

Exploring two further features of our RAS helps to explain how EFT is used to review and clear issues:

New patterns, new pathways

The brain has around 100 billion neurons with more potential connections between them than there are atoms in the universe. EFT allows us to fine-tune what is attracting our attention and emotion on a moment-by-moment basis. When we make positive progress by tapping we are helping our RAS to review what we would like it to attend to, and we naturally begin to filter for more positive stimuli from the outside world.

Using EFT we commonly reach a point when the 'fog clears' around the blocks we are focusing on, our emotions make sense and we begin to gain insight and answers. These moments coincide with the creation of brainwave patterns that are optimal to creating new thinking.

As we begin to gain progress with EFT, whether with a belief or a fear or any other negative emotion, it is crucial to bank the benefit from these golden moments of insight and learning to give the best chance for them to be 'hardwired' permanently into our brain processing. I regard insights in a session as just the beginning. For me, they often represent cracks of daylight through a door that is being opened. For many, these doors (and there may be many doors) to lighter living have been closed for a long time and the negative or limiting patterns may have been in existence for many years.

So, EFT begins the process as we have already said. For permanent lasting effect new patterns of thinking and feeling need to be reinforced in the mind and in the body. I always strongly recommend a short session of daily tapping over the coming days and weeks to build permanence. A period of 21 days is often quoted as sufficient to make a new habit. Continuing to use positive choice tapping, and tapping on any new negative aspects or layers that emerge, will help considerably to build on these new neural networks.

The pathways of negative thinking are actual physical neural pathways that have been strengthened over time with repeated firing between synapses. Hebbian theory which is commonly quoted as 'cells that fire together wire together' describes a basic mechanism for synaptic plasticity. Each time you think and re-think about an event the memory is strengthened as the wiring of neurons strengthens.

This hardwiring process is speeded up and strengthened if we are persistent with EFT for the issue being addressed in the early days. The RAS will serve us by attending to what we have instructed it to do. EFT gives us the ideal opportunity to switch from focusing on unhelpful data to attending to more positive data. The less useful underlying drivers will fade and we can get closer to our goals. Long-standing limiting beliefs, even though they are much less 'life giving' ways of thinking, are nevertheless familiar and therefore too easy to fall back on in the early days. Once you are truly congruent with refreshed thinking, persistent tapping helps to strengthen the new neural connections physically. At the same time the neural connections that represented the previously limited thinking weaken physically.

Real and synthetic reality

Another interesting feature of our RAS is that there is no distinction between 'real events' and 'synthetic' reality – real or imagined. The RAS processes whatever message it is given, and under the right circumstances this feature can work very well for us in helping us to achieve our goal or desires. So, if our imagination can work wonders for us, then why does imagining our goals not always work? Unfortunately, no goal, vivid or otherwise, has a chance when our limiting beliefs are handing out their undercover instructions – *'Not me', 'I'll get found out', 'It will happen again', 'I'm no good at...'*. *'This makes me feel unsafe'*, and so on.

The good news is that EFT is one of the successful techniques for permanently reviewing our limiting beliefs. Unlike other techniques where we merely gain a new sense of logical reasoning or a new strategy to cope, EFT helps us remove negative disruptions around the things that make us feel stuck and at the same time guides us toward positive solutions. From a position of congruence we are best suited vividly to imagine what we desire, and to make that goal achievable. Without the obstacles anything is possible.

> *'Life is like a mirror, and what you see out there, you must first see inside you.'*
> **Wally Amos (writer and business entrepreneur)**

Neurogenesis and plasticity

Until around two decades ago it was the general view that we are born with a fixed number of brain cells and that our total brain cell count declines with age. That view has now been totally revamped following captivating neuroscience research showing that in fact the brain never stops changing and adjusting. New research shows that we can rearrange brain cell connections (neuroplasticity) as well as produce new brain cells (neurogenesis) throughout our lives. In other words, by creating new experiences consistently, we can generate new neuronal pathways and neural networks. We are seeing that the brain has capabilities beyond our wildest dreams as we begin to understand that we are not hardwired for life but instead are very capable to re-programme or shift to more adaptive and successful modes.

Neurogenesis, the birth and development of new neuronal cells, was thought to occur only in developing organisms. However, recent research has demonstrated that neurogenesis does indeed continue into and throughout adult life (Gage, 2002). This amazing capacity of neurogenesis is an important mechanism underlying neuronal plasticity, which enables the brain to adapt. Various types of plasticity dominate during different periods of our lifespan.

Alongside these processes throughout our lives synaptic pruning eliminates weaker synaptic contacts while stronger connections are kept and strengthened. Experience determines which connections will be strengthened and which will be pruned; connections that have been activated most frequently are preserved. Inactive or weak neurons die through a process called apoptosis. Plasticity enables the process of developing and pruning connections, allowing the brain to adapt itself to its environment.

As an illustration, consider the fear response. Neural connections between an anxiety-producing image and the emotional response may be increased or decreased using intervention, and the stress response therefore becomes either stronger or weaker the next time the trigger is encountered (Nader et al., 2000). EFT gives us a chance to ease the fear response, and neurogenesis and neuroplasticity provide us with an opportunity to rewire. As explored earlier, EFT provides a perfect 'window of opportunity' to influence neural connectivity. In summary, when a stimulus that has previously produced anxiety is recreated the emotional response has been unhooked; it no longer has the disruptive effect on the energy system enabling the neural connectivity to alter.

This function has obvious survival value where the primal reactions of the brain – fight, flight or freeze – (the freeze response is explored in more detail in Chapter 12) can be updated in terms of threat or non-threat, based on new data that is received. Any time a fearful memory is brought to mind, the memory becomes 'labile' – susceptible to being stored in a new way. It seems that energy intervention such as EFT provides optimal circumstances to calm response and an opportunity for revised learning by enhancing the processes of neurogenesis and neuroplasticity. We do not need to think that we will be stuck – we are primed for change.

Our fresh understanding is that our neural pathways mould, change and grow constantly according to what we focus on. We constantly acquire new knowledge and skills through instruction or experience which leads to persistent functional changes in the brain. Repeated experience strengthens the pathways which in turn has profound effects our body. Individually we have far more of an effect on our mental and physical health than has ever traditionally been understood.

My favourite mantra is *'Your constant thoughts become your reality'*. The key questions are *'What are you thinking about?'* and *'What are you focusing on?'*. We all know that old habits and accustomed behaviours are repetitive and familiar. To change means entering uncharted territory with no reassuring landmarks. This is literally what is happening in the brain when we move away from our default mode toward new experience. We may feel lost and tempted to end the discomfort of uncertainty by returning to the familiar – the old story. You are not alone if you feel uncomfortable as you begin to proceed through new territory, but I encourage persistence.

By adopting a more regular focus on things that you love, admire or are grateful for, new neural connections are created between brain cells. With regular attention an entirely new network connecting brain cells or neurons can begin to develop. These neural networks are created constantly according to what we choose to give our attention to although in practical terms it is evident in EFT practice that positive focus is only really internalised once our negative emotions have been calmed. Before then, our subconscious tends to reject best intentions to be grateful or positive as they are not in line with our current true feelings (see section on Law of Attraction in chapter 8).

Using EFT, you learn to nurture and develop a greater control over what you give your attention to. From the toolkit of techniques being put into action using EFT, your attentiveness and consciousness is also actively developed as negative disruptions are systematically removed. Using focused tapping we experience issues fading in importance, and the emergence of clearer thinking. New neural connections are being created and it is up to us to strengthen them into permanent superhighways. When we change our minds and write a new story, we change our brains, and persistent EFT provides a perfect catalyst.

Epigenetics

Some remarkable new research shows that consistently repeating new experiences even alters gene expression. Bruce Lipton, an internationally recognised authority of the new biology known as epigenetics, began his groundbreaking work in 1982. His research at Stanford University's School of Medicine revealed that the environment or non-genetics factors operating though the cell membrane can control the behaviour and physiology of the cell, turning genes on and off. His discoveries ran counter to the established scientific view of the time, according to which life is solely controlled at gene level. The hugely significant finding has lead to the emerging field of epigenetics, ' the study of the molecular mechanisms by which environment controls gene activity' (Lipton, 2005, pg 26). The science describes in effect the malleability of our genes as they are activated or deactivated by many factors originating outside the cell and even outside the body. Moreover, gene expression can literally change from moment to moment according to our thoughts and feelings. Thanks to Bruce Lipton and other leading voices, the power of the mind is finally gaining the attention it deserves. The concept of changing our DNA and hence cells with our emotions is outlined in Lipton's book *The Biology of Belief* (2005). In short, change your beliefs and you will change your genetic make-up to live the life you want.

Epigenetic medical research is benefiting from the latest advances in gene theory, as well as other leading edge concepts concerning the electrical systems of the body and cell membrane conductivity to throw light on previously inexplicable results such as those obtained from energy psychology techniques including EFT.

Your DNA is not your destiny

Traditionally it was believed that what is encoded in DNA is unchangeable. We commonly hear that certain conditions are genetic suggesting that it there is nothing we can do about them, except perhaps medication or surgery. Epigenetics, however, offers alternative evidence as it focuses on the switching on and off of gene activity. So, for example, although you may have a gene for high cholesterol this might or might not become expressed. While we are born with a certain code, we are also born with switches that tell the code what to do. Environmental input and lifestyle choices influence the epigenes to turn on or off the genes activity in our system. Changes in gene expression may remain through cell divisions for the remainder of the cell's life and may also last for multiple generations. The underlying DNA sequence of the organism remains but non-genetic factors cause the organism's genes to behave (or 'express themselves') differently.

Epigenetics is probably the most important biological discovery since DNA as understanding that our fate is not sealed at the gene level opens a whole new world of possibilities. There are things we can do to change our gene expression and therefore our health daily, by our food intake, the air we breathe, and particularly by the thoughts we think. We are the 'caretakers' of our genetic roadmaps.

Ground-breaking research Candace Pert (1997) and Deepak Chopra (1990) has shown that when we suppress our emotions our DNA mutates and these mutations can then lead to disease. Likewise, when we welcome and free our negative emotions and start to relax we can naturally heal. This evidence matches the reported effects produced when EFT is practised as we gain freedom from negative emotions, creating a foundation for health, healing and vitality.

Candace Pert, a neuroscientist, pioneered research on how chemicals inside our bodies form a dynamic network of communication between mind and body. She identified the opiate receptor and tiny proteins in the body called neuropeptides which are responsible for our emotions as they regulate our mood, behaviour and our health. As a result of these types of study it seems no longer useful to consider the mind and body as separate entities, and many researchers now speak of the *'bodymind'*.

A scientific study conducted by the Heartmath Institute in California demonstrated that when study participants evoked strong positive emotions such as love and appreciation their DNA unwound and increased in length. However, when these same individuals experienced strong negative emotions their DNA became shorter. The processes were reversed when the individuals switched back to experiencing strong positive emotions. Emotions influence our DNA and positive emotions have a positive effect on our genetic blueprint.

Poor environmental influences and lifestyle choices also affects our offspring. Changes in gene expression may remain through cell divisions for the remainder of the life of the cell and epigenetic changes can be passed down for many generations. The underlying DNA sequence of the organism remains but non-genetic factors cause the organism's genes to behave (or 'express themselves') differently. We need to acknowledge our choices and responsibility more readily than we ever previously imagined.

Your genetics are malleable

Epigenetic 'malleability' helps to explain why identical twins become distinct as they age. Your genome does not change with age *but the epigenetic state changes dramatically*, especially during critical periods of life such as adolescence. It is largely influenced by our responses to physical and emotional stresses.

When a gene is turned off epigenetically, the response of genes has been inhibited. You do not manifest disease merely by a defective gene but by how your genome is being directed to express itself. Epigenetic medicine research and practice has begun in earnest – the curing of disease by epigenetic manipulation, by changing the instructions to cells to reactivating desirable genes and deactivating undesirable ones. This exciting field may well represent our future medicine.

Attitude is everything

Just as your epigenome controls the expression of disease, your mind controls your epigenome, and *therefore your mind controls your healing*. The science of epigenetics can be used to explain things like the placebo effect and spontaneous healing, which until now lacked a scientific basis. Your mind has the power to create or cure disease because your thoughts affect the expression of your genes. Epigenetic study overlaps consciousness science and quantum physics, showing us that we have masterful control over our own lives.

Advances in our understanding of epigenetics dovetail with mind–body medicine and spiritual principles, of which EFT is one, in which working with your body's electromagnetic system produces healing. Epigenetics supports an explanation of why using EFT *through your body's energy field has an effect on a cellular level*. By altering the signals to your energy meridians you can directly influence your cells affecting their genetic expression. As genes are so mutable that they can change from moment to moment in response to your thoughts and feelings, then anything you can do to create a positive feeling state can profoundly, and immediately, improve your health.

Science is helping to explain the link between your body's energy field and disease. More research is certainly needed into the connections between thought, quantum physics, energy, and consciousness theory and healing. Since we now understand that genetics is intimately linked to mind and consciousness, the key to healing lies in controlling your beliefs and emotions. Mind your thoughts, because beliefs and emotions are what trigger the expression of specific DNA.

> *'The code imprinted in our DNA, the one thing we thought was for certain,*
> *is just waiting for direction by us to change, creating a civilization that*
> *brings health, happiness, and vibrancy in ways in which the current*
> *medical establishment only dreams of'*
> **Dawson Church**

Dawson Church, in his book *The Genie in your Genes* (2008), has provided a thoroughly inspiring read and an exciting pointer to the future possibilities of epigenetic medicine. He cites some three hundred medical scientific studies to illustrate how beliefs and emotions can trigger the expression of DNA. Many of the studies cited are related to factors that affect our wellbeing, including childhood nurturing, belief, spirituality, prayer, visualisation and the quality of our social networks.

By keeping the quality of emotions and thoughts and the nature of intentions in check we create a positive advantage for ourselves. It is refreshing to learn that despite our genes we can significantly influence the outcome of our own health. EFT and other energy psychology techniques can therefore be viewed as important epigenetic medical therapies. Dawson suggests a direct connection between the act of tapping on meridian points combined with the use of carefully chosen words and immediate changes in the body on a deep cellular level. The class of genes called immediate early genes, or IEGs, are of central importance. Over one hundred genes in the body are activated by our thoughts, feelings and experiences to influence our immune system and hormones every day. They can be turned off or on intentionally (within as little as 3 seconds) through chosen thoughts, beliefs, emotional responses and experiences.

It is indeed enlightening to realise that you are truly in the driving seat. By actively taking control of our consciousness and using it to influence our genetic expression, we are in effect performing continuous genetic engineering on our own bodies and having immediate effects on emotional and physical issues. It seems that advancing research in epigenetic medicine is truly helping us to explain at least in part how EFT brings us better health and wellbeing.

Psychoneuroimmunology

Psychoneuroimmunology (PNI) is a rapidly developing field of study and practice concerning the interaction between psychological processes and the nervous and immune systems of the human body. PNI takes a multidisciplinary field spanning immunology, psychology and neuro-endocrinology.

PNI studies include: the physiological functioning of the neuroimmune system in health and disease; disorders of the neuroimmune system (autoimmune diseases; hypersensitivities; immune deficiency); and the physical, chemical and physiological characteristics of the components of the neuroimmune system.

What the field of PNI tells us is that every part of our immune system is connected to the brain in some way, whether via a direct nervous tissue connection or by the common chemical language of neuropeptides and hormones. This suggests that the immune system (which keeps us free from external invaders and also maintains our internal homoeostasis) is sensitive to outside influences such as the chemicals secreted in the brain in response to our mental–emotional processing (moods and feelings).

PNI research continues to investigate the connections between the mind, neuroendocrine (nervous and hormonal) and immune systems, and the disciplines of behavioural and mind–body medicine strive to apply this knowledge within a therapeutic framework. By gaining understanding of the interactions between mental and emotional states, immune system functioning and health, it could be said that we are passing from the surgical revolution through the chemical revolution and have entered into the behavioural revolution (de Kooker 2001).

We can see that what happens in our minds at the level of our perception and our emotional reaction (to perception) can have real effects on our physiology (our physical response) and, more specifically, our immune system. Recent research in PNI (Psychoneuroimmunology) has clearly identified how positive thoughts and emotions enhance the immune system and the healing process. The brain converts expectations and feelings into biochemical messengers. Over seventy secretions are produced or activated by the brain as a result of positive emotions. This concept is not new at all, and ancient wisdom has always encouraged a focus on maintaining a 'healthy' mind in order to maintain a healthy body. It is only now that we are beginning to piece together the connections.

What is important is not whether we have emotional ups and downs, but rather the fact that lingering unresolved emotions and inflexible ways of coping can become the source of chronic low-grade stress, which can undermine immune system functioning.

> *'We are not talking about causation of disease, but the interaction between psychosocial events, coping and pre-existing biologic conditions'*
> **Ader et al (1991)[3]**

Mind–body medicine gives us understanding of how states of mind can affect our health; it offers us an opportunity to respond with a sense of control to the psychosocial factors in our lives. Research in the field of mind–body medicine has revealed a collection of 'immune power' traits. These 'healthy habits' can be developed by individuals to serve as buffers against immune system breakdown and disease progression. They include: being aware of your mind–body feedback; learning how to view life with a sense of commitment, control and challenge; developing strengths to fall back on in the wake of loss.

The emphasis in PNI on searching beyond the traditional therapies and concepts of allopathic medicine (the biological based approach to medicine) without excluding them has made the art and science of healing more whole and also more complex.

Our consciousness toolbox – mindfulness and positive intention

> *'Assessing life through the lens of everyday experience is like gazing at a van Gogh through an empty coke bottle'*
> **Green (2005)**

We are complex beings of mind–body interaction. In attempting to unscramble the effects and influences of EFT, the quality of our consciousness tools is without doubt of prime significance.

We have seen that individual thoughts change the structure of our brains, causing chemicals to be sent throughout the body, where they interface with cells and influence our DNA. Every thought and feeling changes something in the body. We have underlined the benefits of positive states of mind on the rates of illness recovery, bodily rhythms and the immune system. Having a positive attitude can protect us from illness, and the power is within us to create healing.

In placebo studies it has been reliably shown that if we have the intention to heal then even an inert medicine can work to heal us and a clinical effective medicine can be rendered inert if we have the belief that it will not work. Numerous fascinating studies are provided by David R Hamilton in his book

How your Mind Can Heal your Body (2008). The power of our intentions and attitudes is far greater than we could ever have imagined.

Becoming consciously aware of the location and features of an emotional feeling can improve the rate of EFT progress significantly. One important way this is practised in EFT is by focusing on sub-modalities. This neuro linguistic term refers to distinctions of form or structure rather than content within a sensory representational system. Tapping on identified features, such as *'hot, tight, grinding*, red knot of rope in my knee', brings about speedier change than using a phrase such as; 'pain in my *knee'.*

Positive intention is central to EFT still when EFT is used in pairs, groups or within an EFT 'borrowed benefits' session (a very successful method where you keep your own issue 'in the background' while tapping for someone, and still resolve your own issue). Under optimum conditions of positive intention, even without realising it, participants within a group report significant shifts in physical and emotional issues that have occurred when their mental intention has been focused not on themselves but on the person in focus within the group at the time. It appears that in using EFT in groups we are able to clear energetically and absorb beneficial learning for ourselves on issues parallel to those for the client in focus. Surrogate EFT brings about similar positive effects (see Chapter 14). It seems that when we clearly resonate or 'vibrate' our own intentions within ourselves or with others, similar thoughts are returned. The concept of similar vibrations being attracted is the underlying notion in the 'law of attraction' (see Chapter 8).

A common human trait is to spend too much time and energy dwelling on what we have not achieved. When we focus on how a goal does not seem to be possible, the goal is repelled. Just as energy flows to wherever your attention goes inside the body, so too your experience flows in the direction of whatever you pay attention to in your life. The truth is that we continually allow ourselves to be in a state of energy flow or disruption by the quality of our thoughts.

To get maximum effect from EFT when focusing on an intention, goal or shift, check that attention is focused on the positive, in a positive way. In EFT we usually begin focusing on the negative, but once negative disruptions fade we move intention to what is wanted. So, for instance, moving from, *'feeling despair that I'll never get rid of these feelings'*, to *'noticing the moments when I feel lighter and more energised'.* Moving from negative to positive tapping, using choice statements and installing new beliefs are all examples of positive intention that work beautifully once the negative disruptions have been reduced sufficiently.

The benefit of focused positive intention between two people, a group or even at a distance is often striking. Beyond EFT, everyone has experienced the positive effects of good intentions and best wishes from others in everyday life. Being pleasant and having positive intentions create genuine positive physiological and psychological effects for all concerned. This type of unconscious mental assistance provides powerful possibilities when it is given focused direction within the EFT process.

Research has also shown that kind acts cause changes in the chemistry of the brain (Hamilton, 2010). Endogenous opiates (the body's natural version of morphine) and dopamine (a neurotransmitter linked with the brain's complex system of motivation and reward) flood the brain and make you feel good about yourself, life and the universe. Kind acts also significantly alter physiology, for example, you produce nitric oxide in your arteries, dilating them to reduce blood pressure. Levels of free radicals (organic molecules responsible for ageing, tissue damage and possibly some diseases) circulating around your bloodstream also drop significantly. Internal inflammation, which has now been found to play a key role in just about every serious medical condition, is also substantially reduced. Regeneration of cells in your heart also speeds up, and if you have any injuries wound healing also accelerates.

All these findings add weight to the idea that you get back what you give out. You give kindness and you receive multiple benefits. We are genetically wired for kindness, and our nervous systems are at their healthiest when we are being kind. Lack of kindness, compassion, gratitude or forgiveness stresses the nervous system and, long term, can make us sick.

> *'Only when you truly inhabit your body can you begin the healing journey'*
> **Gabrielle Roth**

The power of reflection, and learning to stay with a feeling, even a threatening one, in EFT allows us to begin the healing process in a gentle and unthreatening way. These features generated in EFT help us to begin the discovery that any emotion is just a set of neural firings in our brain which can be altered permanently. EFT reflects findings in neuroscience, energy healing and mindfulness. Our brains are plastic and can grow and change through properly guided mental activity. We gain a better understand of ourselves, we change our minds, brains, relationships and we improve our health.

---

1 Piezoelectric energy is the type of electricity generated by mechanical means, when pressure is applied to certain structures.

2 Exploring Consciousness with EFT, International EFT Event, April 2008, Ilkley, West Yorkshire, http://www.eftevents.com/events2008.htm (accessed 8 December 2010).

3 Electroencephalography (EEG) records electrical brain activity along the scalp produced by the firing of neurons within the brain.

Part 3

Your wellbeing journey

Chapter 8
In the driving seat

Chapter 8 In the driving seat

Being able to accept yourself for who you are is a key component to good emotional health and wellbeing. Self-acceptance is inherently connected with a healthy self-esteem, being aware of your strengths and being able to accept positive compliments graciously. Accepting yourself for who you are also means being able to handle positively the areas in life that are more of a challenge, being open to development and feeling comfortable along the route. In this chapter you are invited to explore how EFT can be employed to service your resilience and self-esteem.

Who is driving the bus?

Imagine that your life is like being on a bus. Do you always feel you are in control of your journey or does it feel very random? Perhaps other people find ways to run your journey for you? Instead of being a captive chained to the last seat of the bus with someone else driving, going through life having experiences you do not want, EFT can help you regain direction. Using EFT can help you to get firmly back into your own driving seat. By replacing worn-out negative thinking and nurturing a more positive mental attitude, you can rediscover your true potential.

Who are you pleasing?

It is great to be pleasant and supportive of others around you, but patterns of behaviour around 'people pleasing' can be limiting, or occasionally severely limiting. Patterns such as those shown in Table 12 are often absorbed subconsciously through experience. People pleasing patterns operate through the need to be loved, accepted or through a fear of abandonment. Next time you catch yourself in a people pleasing pattern that is not working for you, agreeing to something you just do not want to, ask a few questions to yourself. *'What am I trying to avoid here?'* or *'Where do I feel it in my body?'* Uncovering the background motives of these patterns to clear them and discovering healthier patterns is made easier using EFT. Through tapping layers of; core issues, limiting beliefs, fears and motives, the behaviour patterns are reprocessed naturally.

Table 12 **Common reasons for pleasing behaviour**

'I am … *'I have …*	*scared/in the way/a bother'* *the need to do it right/to appear blameless to survive/to appear perfect to survive.'*
'I am not OK as I am …	*not as good as another/don't fit in/don't belong/if they really knew me they would not like me/people won't like me.'*
'I am scared that if I am myself I …	*won't be accepted/will be put down/might not get their love/make someone angry/won't be good enough/fail, so I alter my truth to fit in/not get my needs met so I deny my truth/let people down/disappoint/can't trust myself/someone else may be unhappy and it must be my fault'*
'I need …	*others to validate me/to jump through hoops for love'*

An example set-up statement to address a people-pleasing pattern could be 'Even though I feel that if they really knew me they wouldn't like me, I accept myself right now.'

While using EFT to address limiting beliefs and core issues, natural insights and reframes (discussed in more detail in Chapter 6) typically come to the surface in a matter of time, such as:

'I am OK as I am'

'I am doing the best I can'

'I am open to change'

'I am open to new freedom and joy'

'I am true to myself'

'I take care of myself'

'I end relationships that cannot be healthy'

'I change only myself'

'I am wanted'

'I choose to notice'

Continue tapping using statements that feel comfortable. For instance, 'Even though I have felt tense with people for so long, I choose to notice moments when I feel at ease...'

Too perfect even to get started

It can be severely limiting to be driven to do things perfectly. This is different from having high standards. Perfectionism exists as a defence or a protection mechanism. Whether we have taken on this pattern of thinking from over-keen parents, from teachers or from our own high standards, the belief that we have to do everything perfectly can lead to problems. For some people the toxic combination of self-value based on the approval of others, and self-esteem that needs constant external validation, creates a vulnerability which is at the mercy of opinions and criticism of others. The inner voice can go into overdrive, leading to a range of potential negative emotions. If doing something perfectly is the minimum-standard that is acceptable then this can become procrastination, where fear of not doing something perfectly results in not starting at all.

How forgiving of yourself are you when trying something new? Do you give yourself permission to do it badly at first? What measure do you use to judge your progress? Next time you find yourself avoiding trying out a new situation or feeling a bit stuck while learning something new, use EFT on your feelings about yourself, the situation and similar feelings from the past. Set-up statements need to reflect the responses, but may be similar to:

'Even though I feel like I have to do this perfectly, I completely love and accept myself.'

'Even though I don't know how to do this and in the past ... has happened when ..., I give myself permission to make mistakes as I learn.'

'Even though I haven't started ... because I am afraid of making mistakes, I completely love and accept myself.'

Reminder phrases could be: 'afraid of doing this badly', 'churning in my stomach', 'I have to do this perfectly or ...', 'I forgive myself for making mistakes', 'what if I do this wrong?', 'feeling bad in my head when I was about five years old.'

Insights and memories of specific situations can be addressed with further rounds of tapping. Trust yourself to recall times when you were punished for not being perfect or for decisions you made in order to be valued. By noting your 'new learning' and the times you made mistakes, you can progressively use EFT to ease both the past and current aspects of the issue.

Starting on a new task

If getting started is a problem, some basic steps make it easier to succeed:

- commit to a definite outcome
- think realistically how long it will take you to complete the goal
- break down each day into daily tasks (and subtasks if necessary) that need to be done to take you closer to your goal.

Take your time. Listen and attend to your feelings and thoughts at each stage, and create accurate EFT set-up statements to reflect any negative disruptions.

'Even though I don't want to fail again, I deeply and completely love and accept myself.'

'Even though I can hear my dad's voice telling me "don't bother trying", I want to be able to do this; I love and accept myself.'

As the negative gives way to a more positive healing path, further rounds of tapping can introduce positive statements, for instance:

'Even though I have been hard on myself, I choose to notice my moments of confidence.'

'Even though my critical voice often nags me, I choose to praise myself for committing to this goal.'

Self-esteem and worth

Low self-esteem holds many people back from leading a happy and fulfilling life. EFT can help to uncover the core issues that underpin low self-esteem. It can expose the connecting negative beliefs and remove their emotional charge. People then typically report that the 'belief' now seems ridiculous and that it no longer holds any power over them.

Case study

Louise was the first to admit that she was self-effacing. She often heard herself saying to her children things like *'Oh I am a rubbish Mummy'* when she made a simple mistake and *'Oh, empty head is back in town'*, when she forgot something. Louise wanted to show her children that she was *'human and able to apologise'*. Faith in her parenting skills was dampened one day when her younger daughter came out of her nursery one afternoon saying, *'I am a rubbish girl, I can't draw like Sarah can'*. Louise did her best to boost her daughter's feelings of self-worth, but a week later, to add insult to injury, Louise's elder daughter said to her mum in an angry moment, *'You're a rubbish mum'*.

>>

Case study continued

Louise had all the best intentions but decided that she needed to find a better way to communicate. She came to EFT sessions to try to get a better understanding of why she found it too easy to put herself down. After a short period of tapping, Louise was surprised at the memories that showed up.

'Even though Dad never said sorry ever, I don't have to be wrong anymore...'

'Even though I have been apologising for lots of things all my life that weren't my fault...'

'Even though I have been hurt in the past, I'm open to finding other ways to teach my girls to be strong...'

After a handful of sessions Louise reported that she felt that she had rediscovered how to communicate with her children and other adults assertively and confidently. She was surprised with the levels of guilt and anger that had been buried for so many years that had been having a damaging effect on her self-esteem and her relationships.

EFT provides ideal opportunities to review limiting beliefs and unhelpful patterns of behaviour concerning self-worth and respect. First, acknowledgement the problem with accurate set-up statements such as:

'Even though I can't bear it when my boss...'

'Even though I know that it won't be long before...'

'Even though it doesn't matter about my health, as my family are more important,'

Any of the above can be altered to individual needs and followed with an acceptance phrase such as the ones below:

'... I accept myself as a peaceful person and that ....'s behaviour is not my responsibility.'

'... I deeply and completely accept myself and I accept my fear and choose to feel calm.'

'.... I accept my humbleness and I am opening to the idea that I am just as important as others.'

Feelings around not being good enough are all too common even from a young age.

Case study

Laura's catch phrase was *'I'm no good at anything'*. This was not very inspiring for her, considering she was only eight years old. This week she had decided that she was not good enough for her class play. When we sat together she reluctantly admitted that she was a good friend, but she put this down to luck. Holding her script, Laura turned her head sideways so that it was at an angle, and said, *'I can't read it'* and *'the teacher only picked me because she felt sorry for me'*.

Nevertheless, Laura was keen to feel different and she positively engaged in tapping. Set-up statements we used included:

'Even though I'm no good at anything...'

'Even though I don't want to do the play, it's sooo hard...'

'Even though I sometimes cry when everyone else seems to get it and I don't...'

Ideally, every child's pattern of thinking would be more positive. Unlike adults who may have already experienced decades of less-than-ideal patterns of thinking, young people are still just making up their minds. The challenge for parenting programmes and the school curriculum is to nurture young people so that developing patterns are as healthy as possible. EFT is easily placed in the hands of teachers, parents and caretakers of young people's wellbeing so that they can pass on these simple empowering and effective techniques. You can catch up with Laura's progress in Chapter 14 in the section on EFT in schools.

Abandonment

Feelings of abandonment, fear of being left alone or feeling unsure that those you love will remain in your life can stem from a variety of different causes. The feeling can happen at any age to anyone. It can be very traumatic and is often similar to grief. Triggers can include:

- feelings of isolation within a relationship
- break-up of a relationship
- childhood incidents
- loss of job and professional status
- children growing up and leaving home.

Early abandonment is often responsible for attachment issues that can have ongoing consequences in adult life. If you were abandoned emotionally, or physically neglected as a child, it is not unusual to find that you are fearful of commitment as you grow older. Being attracted to, or frequently being involved in, the wrong type of relationship can be an indicator of abandonment issues.

Case study

Peter was in a caring relationship with a strong and supportive partner. He could not understand why he slid into a sense of panic every time Rita arranged to do anything without him. It had got worse recently and now Peter was on medication for a recurring stomach problem. Despite efforts from Rita to assure him that everything was OK, Peter was getting really upset with his reactions. They did not seem to make sense. After tapping using a few set-up statements, he said, *'The thing is, this is the longest relationship I've ever had and I am scared of losing Rita because of what I say and do, I just can't make sense of what I am doing.'*

We continued tapping, *'Even though I get this aching pain in my stomach when Rita steps out of the room...'*, with the reminder statement, *'this aching pain in my stomach'*.

After a few rounds we reached the under eye (UE) point (which happens to be the stomach meridian point) and I asked, *'When do you remember this aching pain for first time?'* Peter tapped silently and thought for just a moment and then his head dropped slightly and he said in a low voice *'Sitting on the doorstep locked out of my house. I think that I was about three or four.'* Peter was back 'in the moment'. We continued tapping silently for a few minutes until the SUDs had dropped. We then continued by using the telling the story technique (described in Chapter 5). Peter explained that mum often left him on his own without explanation. I asked what was happening for him on that step. He said, *'What will happen to me if Mummy doesn't come back for me?'* His SUD level rose back up to 9.

The set-up became *'Even though I never knew what would happen to me if Mummy didn't come back for me, I was a good son.'*

We continued tapping on all the aspects of this memory slowly, using the movie technique: *'I see myself just sitting there alone'*, *'I see a little me not knowing what to do'*, *'What if Mummy doesn't come back?'*, *'She hasn't told me if she is coming back'*, *'What will happen to me?'*, *'I feel empty'*, *'I don't like feeling alone'*, *'It must mean she doesn't care about me'*, *'Even though my stomach aches...'*

In further EFT sessions Peter and I tapped for many specific events where Peter had been left in early life without explanation, including being left at the gates of a busy building without explanation. It was his first day at school.

He had been unaware of the depression that his mother suffered, until he was an adult, at which point other relatives filled him in. It was clear that she had been unable to cope and she was not able to give him the comfort and relationship that he needed. As an adult he understood these things on a logical level and he had believed that he did not dwell on them. His energetic body and mind were, however, understandably holding on to these disturbed patterns and they had affected him in all subsequent relationships. *In the next few sessions* we continued to address the patterns of *'expecting to be left without explanation'*.

A year later Peter emailed to say that *'life is sweet'*, that he had *'stopped pushing his beloved Rita away'* and that his *'professional relationships were much smoother now'*, *'no longer have "that doorstop feeling" as I am engaging with life'* and *'I now see commitment in a totally new light.'*

Jealousy

The perceived threat of jealousy can cause real pain and a wide range of emotions including embarrassment, fear, resentment and anger. Jealous thoughts can quickly destroy a relationship through blame, insecurity or self-pity. Fighting jealousy internally can mean going to extreme lengths to avoid the fear of being hurt or disappointed, which often results in further negative thoughts, feelings and behaviour.

You can begin to tackle jealous thoughts using EFT to help you address all the layers of feelings such as, *'the picture of that note in my head', 'she told me she cared', 'why doesn't he ...?'*. As with most emotions, careful testing and calibration is needed to track progress. Switching aspects is common here, as other emotions, events and beliefs are also likely to rise to the surface.

The steps listed below are an alternative way into healing, while still using the standard EFT procedure at each stage to begin the process of releasing jealous feelings. This process is a small step in the personal peace procedure. The time needed for the procedure, in order to complete resolution, varies from person to person. It could be a few minutes or hours, or it could be weeks or months. Avoid rushing; it is worth pursuing all aspects to ensure a permanent and pleasing resolution.

Letting go of negative feelings

This exercise is adapted from the personal peace procedure. Take notes of emerging aspects and feelings as you proceed.

1 Visualise vividly the relationship without negative thoughts in order to gain a different perspective. Notice as much detail as you can about what this alternative perspective looks like, what it feels like, what is being said. Listen out for tail-enders. Tap on the positive and negative aspects.

2 Ask about or search for the first time when 'feeling safe' was threatened. Safety is very often the base for jealousy and initial events are important. Be prepared to take the 'best guess' if memory fails you. Tap on the emerging data and responses.

3 Record the situations that trigger jealous feelings and systematically apply EFT on each of these until no negative emotion remains. This can be tested by vividly imagining being in those situations again.

4 Perform EFT rounds on forgiving yourself or anyone who may have caused this negative emotion, if it feels appropriate.

The steps above can be adapted to easing any negative emotion and especially to those around relationships.

Comforting the younger you

It is not difficult to appreciate that the experience of being neglected, traumatised or unloved as a child can remain with you in some form as you grow up. The range of negative emotions is wide and can include inner sadness, loneliness, anger and fear. Depending on the personality and circumstances of the adult, the emotions may be clearly on show or they may be buried deeper. Either way, emotional anguish from the past (and this does not have to be hugely traumatic to have a lasting impact) can have a core negative effect on ongoing health and wellbeing.

Because a high proportion of adult issues are a reflection of early experiences from childhood, many EFT practitioners use a variety of skills to help the client to connect with events that affected them in their childhood in order to begin the healing process. When this is done professionally, the client is provided with a safe and comfortable pathway to explore and clear negative disruptions rooted back in time. Gentle EFT processing leads to resolution. Balancing and clearing early trauma makes the task of clearing present-day issues a whole lot easier.

Case study

Ash wanted to improve relationship issues. He suspected that he had 'always had a problem' and he felt this stemmed from events of his childhood. In an EFT session we had reached a point where he had connected with the emotions and physical feelings that he had experienced in an unpleasant event at the age of 6. He chose to tap while addressing *'young Ash'*. The effect of the *'adult Ash'* validating *'young Ash's'* position across a whole series of tapping rounds had a very powerful effect.

'Even though young Ash couldn't stop Mum and Dad from hurting each other...'

'Even though I can tell that little boy that he did his best and it wasn't his job be responsible for his brothers and sisters...'

'Even though I would like young Ash to know that he eventually became a dad himself and he makes better decisions about how children should be treated...'

'Even though Ash never had an apology himself and that has been hard, it is time to start letting go of some of the hurt, and...'

Reviewing limiting beliefs

Using EFT often guides us back on to the natural pathway of who we really are. When the masking effect of limiting beliefs and negative patterns are eased, our mind and body reboot and refresh, like a computer. We are reminded of who we truly are and how we need to behave to honour ourselves. With the cobwebs clearing, fresh insights are easier to recognise and this new learning encourages enhanced neural connectivity in the brain. Continued and persistent tapping may be required to encourage lasting effect with some issues and to strengthen the new neural pathways.

Sometimes, however, some focused tapping can make positive changes happen quickly.

Case study

Julie labelled herself as a sensitive person, which she saw as both a positive and a negative attribute. She was proud that she was compassionate and had natural empathy, but at work there was no time for compassion. Julie said, *'I take things personally, but I hide it, otherwise it gets me into trouble.'*

Julie reported that while tapping her inner voice went something like this: *'No one takes things as personally as me; it's unacceptable to show my emotions; it's not safe to show my emotions; I need to act like I have thick skin when I'm in public.'* Your 'inner critic' (that negative inner voice) works hard in an effort to serve your beliefs even when they are not useful. Holding beliefs like these can feel constricting and is exhausting on the body. Julie was keen to continue to use EFT to address the negatives.

'Even though I take things personally, I deeply and profoundly love and accept myself.'

'Even though I feel that it is unacceptable to show my emotions...'

'Even though I don't seem to have a sense of humour about myself, I deeply and completely love and accept myself.'

'Even though I try to act like words don't hurt me, even though they do, I deeply and completely love and accept myself without judgement.'

EFT helps you to name, claim and then let go of the energy-sapping inner criticisms.

By reducing the negative disruptions around each aspect, one at a time, it became easier for Julie to focus on attracting the abundance she desired. In time, she was keen to try out some more positive choices in her pool of beliefs. We created some new set-up statements to practise at home.

'I'm willing to let go of beating myself up for taking things personally ...'

'I choose to notice that other people are taking care of their own things in the best way they can ...'

'I am open to see that other people's responses are a reflection their own needs...'

Installing new beliefs or life changes

The following EFT exercise helps to check your readiness to take on a new belief or life change. It uses the approach of viewing the degree of readiness in the context of logical levels of processing, one at a time. The descriptions of the logical levels of processing are taken from neurolinguistic programming (NLP); they are: environment, behaviour, capabilities and skills, beliefs and values, identity and something known as 'spiritual/greater system', which refers to our connection with a greater good or purpose. Using this schema, a belief can be tested at each level of processing, thus leaving no stone unturned. By paying particular attention to feelings – both physical and emotional – thoughts and sensations via all the senses at each stage, a great deal of data can be calibrated and tapped on.

Lots of positive insights and shifts can occur while following this exercise, often through the exposure of tail-enders (the 'yes-buts'). Whereas objections, resistances or fears would usually stop us from achieving what we think we would like, EFT provides a way to begin to clear these blocks. Continue using successive rounds of tapping at each stage before moving on to the next.

Exercise to assess readiness for a new belief

1 Choose a statement that expresses a desired new choice for how you want to be, or for what you want to be more of, and repeat the statement out loud; for instance, *'I am feeling strong'* or *'I am ready to give up my fear'*. Note the response that your mind and body return. It could be positive or negative or a mixture. If the response is all positive, then complete a round of tapping using that feedback; for instance, *'Yes, I am feeling strong.'*

---

2 If negative tail-enders arose in response to saying the statement initially, for instance, *'I am scared'*, *'I've never been strong enough'*, *'Only if I can stop myself from thinking ...'* Proceed by creating an appropriate set-up statement to address the tail-ender, for instance, 'Even though I have never been strong enough... When this statement is tested for validity (how true does this feel?) prior to tapping, the VOC rating is likely to be high as it feels very true. Continued tapping using this set-up statement allows the VOC (the perceived truth) to fall and reframing occurs.

---

3 To address the belief at the first level of processing – the environment – ask in turn, *'Where, when and with whom are you ...* [insert desired new choice]*?'* The feelings, images, thoughts and sensations that arise from each of these questions provide more tapping material. Any further tail-enders that arise throw light on objections or resistance or fears or areas where clarification is needed. An example EFT set-up statement could be, *'Even though I feel that I am not able to be strong in this job ...'* Again, these tail-enders need to be addressed before the new choice can be acceptable at the environment level of processing.

---

4 To address the belief at the level of behaviour ask, *'What specific behaviours or actions show you are capable of being ...(strong)?'* As before, the responses and tail-enders at each level can be addressed with tapping. An example set-up could be, *'Even though I get annoyed with myself because I leave it too long...'* With these settled, the belief becomes acceptable at the behavioural level of processing.

---

5 To address the belief at the level of capabilities and skills ask, *'What mental states or abilities are you using when you are capable of being ... strong?'* Continue using the 'yes but' tail-enders in EFT statements. An example set-up statement could be, *'Even though I don't know if I can be assertive like I used to be...'* With these settled, the belief becomes acceptable at the capabilities level of processing.

6 To address the belief at the level of beliefs and values ask, *'What values and beliefs are you using when you are capable of being strong?'* An example set-up could be, *'Even though I was not encouraged to be assertive...'* With these settled, the belief can be accepted at the beliefs and values level of processing.

7 To address the belief at the level of identity ask, 'What kind of person are you when you are capable of being ... (strong)?' An example set up could be, *'Even though I don't know if my children would like it...'* Settled, the belief can be accepted at the identity level of processing.

8 To address the belief at the level of the spiritual/greater system ask *'Who else does this serve, or what greater mission or vision does it serve when you are capable of being ... strong?'* An example set-up statement could be, *'Even though I don't know how that would change my life...'*

Blocks to peak performance

The greatest obstacles between you and your goal are usually your fears, self-limiting beliefs or low self-esteem. The subtle mental programming we run subconsciously serves to block our efforts and positive intentions, reducing our peak potential. Self-defeating barriers to success need to be identified and cleared. Below are five common fears that hold us back. They are all work-related examples, but the effects of EFT are equally powerful in any performance setting – exams, public speaking, sports, arts.

EFT is being put to good use across the world every day in extensive performance arenas to help uncover the cunning subconscious scripts that we are afraid to deviate from. Tapping allows us gently to untangle those blocks to success and to process them into beliefs that work better for us.

Fear of failure

Failure can be more than just not getting the result you want; it is also about not being the person you want to be. When our self-esteem is at risk it is tempting to avoid risk in fear of failure. To have success in performance we need freedom from this type of block, and the resilience and confidence to explore the many alternative paths ahead of us. On a daily basis some strategies will work and some will not, and when a mistake is made the actions need to be reviewed. With blocks in place it is easy to assign failure to ourselves; EFT helps you to clear the fog when this occurs.

'Even though I am sad as I often think "not you Tom", I am willing to find alternative ways to protect myself, and...'

Fear of rejection

Many people fear rejection at home and at work without even realising it. It is easy to become sensitive and to see 'signs of rejection' that may not really exist. A common coping strategy is to avoid getting rejected by not engaging, just in case. The rejection becomes painfully personal. Under-performing hurts, but for many the hurt of rejection is greater. EFT can skilfully peel away and heal layers of fears around rejection, allowing clearer thinking to emerge.

'Even though my stomach hurts because I've let yet another chance pass me by...'

Fear of criticism

When people are hurt by criticism they become scared to take any risk that might subject them to further scrutiny. Avoiding criticism can inevitably lead to avoiding opportunity. The pain of criticism can hurt so much that it is easier to suffer the frustration of feeling stuck. This fear holds many people back and they perform far below their potential in order to remain comfortable.

'Even though I get annoyed with myself for not putting myself forward...'

Fear of competition

Competition is inevitable in work, home and relationships. If it is viewed in an unhealthy manner there is a risk that you may become limited to the belief that unless you can be the 'best', or close to the best, you are worthless. Typically people may use self-to-other comparisons to determine if they are *'better than'* or *'less than'* another. Being *'less than'* is a painful reminder of feeling inferior; it can be a limiting belief from the past. By not joining in, painful associations are avoided but so is the chance for success. Engaging an EFT practitioner can help to explore the true source of the competition fear and help to guide forward.

'Even though I spend so much time judging myself...'

Fear of success

This can seem like a strange fear, but it is not uncommon. Many people progress with their lives, work, sports, qualifications and then somehow sabotage themselves unknowingly when they get to a certain level. Often this can be about not wanting to out-perform and stepping outside your comfort zone. Many people have their own glass ceiling when it comes to performance and abundance. Early influences that are the basis of limiting beliefs can be addressed by creating appropriate set-ups:

'Even though I was always told not to think too much of myself...'

'Even though I am a long way off believing that I deserve success, I choose to be open to the possibility, and...'

When the emotional layers of limiting beliefs concerning performance have been lifted with EFT, then more positive choices are created spontaneously or can be introduced. Additional methods to invite reviewed thinking include:

- choice statements (see Chapter 6)
- 'how true is that for you' exercise (see Chapter 6)
- installing a new belief (earlier in this chapter).

Open your intuition with EFT

Intuition is our inner knowing about how to honour our own truth and take care of ourselves. It occurs as a natural extension of our normal senses and is a powerful innate wisdom, usually associated with right brain activity. To gain real access to our intuitive intelligence we need real ways to bypass our traditionally taught intellect, ego, analysis and judgement, and to get clear of our own filters and biases.

We are born with natural intuition. Children use this extremely well most of the time, but by the time we reach school age we are taught to rely much more on logic to make decisions; this can devalue our instinct and allow it to fade. We can, however, encourage and trust our instinct more if we actively practise. The problem for most of us is that intuitive thought is very rapid and therefore easy to miss. For many, intuition has neither felt natural nor been encouraged in adult life. In addition we can block our knowing or insights with our beliefs and critical judgements, often without realising we are doing so. Fear of failure, or striving, or the need to succeed, or having something to prove, or feeling responsible for an outcome, or keeping busy, or analysing, or worrying, hurrying and judging can all get in the way of our intuition.

Undoubtedly logic still has an important role in our human experience. Intuition, however, offers guidance and direction. Logic simply helps rationalise our decisions on a daily basis, but it is only when the mind is quiet of logic and chatter that the intuitive voice can be heard. Learning to cultivate this passive receptive mode allows us to be truly with ourselves. If you are doing EFT with someone else, less energy is needed to find the answer or to solve a problem if intuition is accessed. True intuition is effortless.

EFT gives us all a wonderful opportunity to access and use intuition. I have learned to trust my intuition and my willingness to share it, without being attached to 'being right'. To become truly proficient with EFT, the ability to access your intuitive process is essential. Ironically, you are best equipped when you trust in the knowing, even though you 'don't know how you know'. EFT lends itself to using intuition since the set-up statements can be formed as you go along, without much forethought. This gets easier with practice. Supervised training will also help to highlight any confusion between natural intuition and giving advice – beware thinking that you 'know' what another person 'needs'. Logic and continual careful checking both help in EFT. Effective balancing of the complementary skills of logic and intuition develops through EFT experience and practice. In the meantime open up your intuition. Trust it and act on it.

The law of attraction

Our busy lives might lead us to think that we are not able to influence the quality of our days, or our lives, very much. But the concept of the 'law of attraction' disagrees. Think about which events and connections are attracted to you when you are having a negative day.

'Your consistent thoughts become your reality.
The question is what are you thinking about?'

Moment by moment, in order to attract desired experiences in our lives, it is not what we say about our desires that is important but what we spend our time feeling and thinking. In energy terms it is what we are 'vibrating' that counts. Whatever we are feeling or vibrating is what we communicate as our 'energetic position' to the universe (everything outside us). According to the law of attraction the universe matches the vibration we are emitting and returns similar experiences to produce more of the same feeling and vibration.

For instance, if you tend to notice beauty as the day passes, more evidence of beauty is delivered in all corners of life. If, however, you tend to note or 'vibrate' fear, you are regularly delivered more experiences that cause fear. If you vibrate life in a sense of joy, you will 'bump into' more experiences that enhance your joy. The law of attraction is therefore always operating with your vibration or energy, not your words.

You have constant control over your vibration because of the choices you make about your thoughts and focus. Negative habits such as gossiping, moaning, talking too much of ill-health or poor finance, comparing your situation with others and even spending too much time in the company of these will drain your energy reserves and create negative energy vibration. Negative thoughts inhabit many of our waking hours (see 'It starts with a thought' in Chapter 2). Because negative patterns of vibration are habitual they can seem hard to shift, but EFT can act as one of the fastest and easiest ways permanently to change your vibration. The techniques can help to identify and put at ease the tail-enders and doubts that originate from any inner-voice which would otherwise sabotage even the most consciously positive plans. The overall effect of the law of attraction is cumulative, and returns the vibration in most interesting and surprising ways. As we have seen, the brainwave patterning changes that are observed during EFT illustrate key opportunities to choose how we think and feel, as the patterns that are created are ideal for refreshed learning (see Chapter 7).

Attitude of gratitude

Another crucial way to enhance positive vibration in your life is to focus on the appreciation you already feel you have in your life. We just do not do this enough! There are many ways to note or record gratitude, but a solid record that you can refer back to is surprisingly powerful. One of my top recommendations to clients is a gratitude list written into a journal every day for the tiniest things that you notice to appreciate. Make the list absolutely personal to you. The items of gratitude can be anything that you have taken the time to appreciate: beautiful raindrops on the window, an unexpected smile from a stranger, a phone call that went better than you expected, freedom in your limbs, a tasty orange, and so on. Tune into different senses – sight, hearing, touch, taste, sound – to gather a diverse catalogue of gratitude.

I recommend that you record gratitude items that are brief moments rather than hours or days long. Wayne Dyer, international motivational speaker and author of *The Power of Intention* (2004), recommends cultivating an *'attitude to gratitude'*, as he calls it, which allows you to harvest an abundance of moments. Cumulatively they can expand your positive experience at an exponential rate.

Chapter 9
Taking charge of anger

Chapter 9 Taking charge of anger

Anger takes many forms, from irritation to blind rage, but the emotion that always underpins anger is fear. Among available anger management techniques EFT stands out as it provides rapid, flexible relief for any age and delivers long-term emotional and physical health benefits.

EFT can be used on all aspects of anger in self-help, in groups or with a practitioner. Tapping provides valuable 'in the moment' assistance to reduce the negative effects of anger quickly. Underlying patterns of thinking and limiting beliefs around the expression of anger are also gently challenged using specific EFT procedures. The benefits for the person with issues around anger are empowering both for them and for those around them. Clearing the negative disruptions around anger, the cumulative effects of EFT include enabling people to achieve better mental and physical health, to feel more positive about achieving their goals, to solve problems and to enjoy relationships.

Anger

Anger is a powerful emotional state. It is a physical and mental response to a threat or to harm. The mind and the body get ready for action, the nervous system is aroused, and this increases the heart rate, blood pressure, blood flow to muscles and blood sugar level, and causes sweating. The perceived threat also sharpens the senses and increases the production of adrenalin.

Anger can be expressed in many forms. In a mild form, anger can be felt as disgust or dismay; at a moderate level it can be a feeling of being offended or exasperated, and at an intense level it can be felt as instant rage or resentment that festers over many years.

When was the last time you really got angry? Was it when you witnessed an injustice, or when someone elbowed you out of the way to get on the bus, or was it when you were rejected for a job you thought you deserved to get?

'For every minute you remain angry, you give up sixty seconds' peace'
Ralph Waldo Emerson

Patterns of anger

People deal with the effects of anger in different ways.

• Some express anger when it is still small.

• Some suppress it deep inside, fighting to maintain control of it, too scared to express it; longer term this can be damaging for health.

• Others bottle it until it bursts, shocking others with its intensity because there had been not even a hint that anything was wrong.

Before you can effectively deal with problems and move on it is essential to release the pressure of anger.

'I never get angry – I just grow a tumor instead'
Woody Allen

If anger is not expressed in a healthy way or you get angry too frequently, it can have a significant effect on your daily life, relationships, achievements and mental and physical wellbeing.

No time to check in

'I get this bubble of rage. I go wild. I feel like crying. I don't know how to control myself. It happens too quickly'

young EFT client

The heightened emotion of anger entices us quickly to translate complex information into simple terms – 'right' or 'wrong', for instance. This can be useful in an emergency as it saves crucial time. However, anger is expressed from the more primitive reptilian or limbic part of the brain, and a speedy reaction may not always be for the best. The greater the level of anger, the less likely it is that you will check in with the frontal cortex areas of the brain to access reason and logic. Quick and 'irrational' decisions typically include shouting, getting even, and even lashing out physically or verbally.

With a little practice many people use EFT when anger is building so that they can quickly regain some calmness; the reasoning frontal cortex is accessed, allowing us to direct our energy to rational decisions and in turn increasing our chances of achieving a better solution. The 'tapping tune' (the song and action created by young teens) sums up the effect of tapping nicely, *'I choose to be calm it's a better plan.'*

'Loving people live in a loving world. Hostile people live in a hostile world. Same world, how come?'
Wayne Dyer

Healthy expression of anger

Healthy expression of anger involves facing what makes you angry and setting boundaries for yourself by determining what you will do in response to what makes you angry. An EFT session offers opportunities to gain insight into these boundaries.

After clearing through some of the negative layers of anger using EFT, one strategy is to express your feelings in an assertive way by filling in the gaps of the following statement:

'When you ... I feel ... and to protect myself I will ...'

For instance, *'When you shout at me like that I feel frightened and to protect myself I will walk away.'*

By using an assertive phrase to express how you feel you are taking ownership of your feelings. Tail enders that emerge as a result of making such a phrase can be erased with further tapping.

Healthy anger is not used to punish, it is not violent, and it is not used to intimidate, control or manipulate another. It is expressed, discussed and moved through, not stuffed down and ignored. It can be a force for good when expressed assertively. Anger becomes a problem, however, when it harms us or other people.

Unhealthy expression of anger

Anger is often immediate, but it can arise again after the event as we recall a situation. It can surface years later from childhood roots, and can stubbornly hang around inside us for decades because it was not acknowledged sufficiently at the time.

Patterns of unhealthy expression of anger have a very negative impact on our emotional and physical health. Typical patterns include: a willingness to blame others for mistakes; choosing to be in the company of anger and aggression; holding on to anger excessively; hiding or holding on to emotions that we feel express weakness; taking out anger on ourselves, others or the world because we feel bad, guilty or a failure.

'I attacked the specialist when he told me that
my mum would probably not get better'
EFT client

People's responses are affected by gender, age, social factors, peer group, ethnicity, religion, social position and family history. The expectations of the people close to us, or of society in general, can influence how we act. Throughout our lives we get used to behaving in certain ways, having set responses to situations, and these 'learned behaviours' can form a pattern which is naturally difficult to break.

Patterns of unhealthy expression

Abuse

Unhealthy expression of anger is a component of abusive relationships. This kind of anger can be experienced with great intensity and can be expressed by screaming and yelling, physical violence or threat of violence, sulking, manipulation, emotional blackmail and silent smouldering.

The relief that EFT can bring to abuse victims is explored in more detail in Chapter 12.

Unexpressed anger related to childhood abuses can result in addictive problems later in life. Many people stuff down negative feelings of shame, anger, isolation, fear, sadness or loss. By pushing feelings down we make it impossible to work through them or move past them, which keeps us trapped in a downward spiral.

Rage

Strong emotions such as fear, sadness, shame, inadequacy, guilt or loss can be easily converted and expressed as rage. Rage is often linked to early experiences of shame or punishment. Expressing rage gives the angry person a feeling of power, offsetting feelings of shame and inadequacy. You can read about how Darius used EFT to uncover the hidden source of his rage in Chapter 9.

Aggression

Aggressive behaviour can be physical or verbal and it often emerges when people act on their instinct to protect themselves or others. Shouting, threats, physical attack, hostile questioning and exaggeration are some of the by-products. Common expressions of aggressive behaviour include people getting their own way by making other people feel guilty and playing on that guilt, or developing a cynical attitude and constantly criticising everything without addressing problems constructively.

Self-harm

Self-harm is a terrible consequence of finding it hard to deal with internal emotions or intense feelings. Relieving anger is one of the motivators for self-harm as many self-injurers have enormous amounts of rage within. Afraid to express it outwardly, they injure themselves as a way of venting these feelings although any release from anger brings only temporary relief. Like many more obvious ways of expressing anger, self-harming does not solve problems long term. In my experience, EFT has been an excellent aid for addressing a huge variety of psychological drivers in individual cases of self-harm and in group settings.

'EFT is by far the most powerful and empowering tool in my psychotherapy toolbox. After one session one client recently said " I don't need to think of harming myself any more when things get bad, I have now got something I can use instead'
George Brooks, psychotherapist and trainer

Long-term effects of unhealthy anger

Long-term effects include:

- problems in relationships
- poor decision making and more risk-taking behaviour
- mental health problems, including depression, anxiety and self-harm
- poorer overall physical health and conditions such as high blood pressure, colds and flu, coronary heart disease, stroke, cancer and gastro-intestinal problems.

People experiencing difficulties with anger often fail to identify their anger or to see it as a problem. They may not seek support and may be more likely to see other people as the problem. Changing behaviour takes effort, and tapping techniques can bridge the gap between acceptance and moving forward, making positive shifts easier.

'Now I can express my anger more openly and constructively. I didn't realise how much feeling I was hiding and how much hurt I had been carrying'
EFT client

Uncovering the triggers of anger

If anger is a defensive reaction to a perceived threat, loss or stressor, and it all happens so quickly, how can we possibly help ourselves? Through EFT it becomes easier to establish the underlying triggers to anger. Triggers may be focused on external factors and people or on internal factors including beliefs. Understanding your own triggers is a move in the right direction to releasing the destructive nature of anger. Shortcuts to dealing with anger, even hiding it away, feed anger. If you feel overwhelmed by your anger or are losing control, you need to manage it before it manages you.

Each layer of negative disruption can be addressed with EFT to ease current feelings, past experiences and future worries about anger. Underneath anger there is almost always fear, although anxiety, sadness and hurt are often connected. When EFT is applied to anger resistance can arise. More anger may emerge because another underlying emotion is continuing to drive the angry feelings. But anger can rapidly subside with EFT once the aspects of the underlying disruptions have been cleared.

Feeling powerless

Negative core beliefs can lead to feelings connected with blame – about not being good enough or feeling unreliable, bad or unlovable (see Chapter 2). When others tell you that you cannot be trusted or that you are stupid or you let them down, this further reinforces your beliefs about yourself. These feelings lead to shame and a defence mechanism builds. You cope and respond the best way you know how – for some it is with anger. The traits that we do not like in others are sometimes a reflection of ourselves. Falsely blaming or accusing others takes the spotlight off our own behaviour.

Testing the evidence of a negative thought/belief

A good way to employ EFT to reduce the hold of a negative belief or thought is to check out what evidence exists to support it, using tapping.

Case study

Phil has been turned down for promotion. His boss confides that there is an even better opportunity in the pipeline in a year or so. Phil thinks *'That's it, he's just trying to let me down gently; he sees that I haven't got what it takes. I'll leave now before they really find me out.'* Phil hides his anger but within weeks he has had to go back on to blood pressure medication.

Checking out the real evidence that exists to support your current negative thinking is an excellent way to challenge anger in an assertive way. To do this successively you can tap on your inner dialogue to clear the disrupted feeling.

In the session with Phil one of the initial set-up statements used to test evidence was '
Even though he favours others ahead of me – as he didn't ask me on to the project team...'

After spending time reducing the initial negative feelings we kept tapping and introduced the open-ended statement:

'Even though the evidence that tells me he favours others over me is ...' We continued using testing and feedback:

'Even though he chose Owen, who doesn't even know the account...' We continued tapping using each piece of evidence until Phil decided *'Actually, I'd prefer to wait for promotion anyway because our first baby is due and I want to be around as much as I can.'*

>>

Case study continued

He then said, *'Um, I like the sound of that even better, I must go back to him and find out more.'*

Anger cleared and, back in a calm place, Phil was able to re-negotiate a considerable promotion that suited his needs within the next couple of weeks. He had previously considered resigning from the company mainly out of embarrassment and misunderstanding.

Tapping is a gift for dealing with anger. Used correctly instant results are commonplace. EFT works when you are in the moment, getting angry or already angry. The effects of EFT are not merely a result of convincing yourself to feel a bit more positive, or being distracted from an issue. Cognitive shifts settle and new thinking emerges. These effects are often permanent when re-tested in the following months and years.

What's the fear?

Because anger is fear-based, it evokes the same physiological reaction (see Chapter 10). Emotionally it is a feeling of not being in control, being found out, ignored, unsafe or unloved. EFT helps to uncover and release the basis of fears and helps to resolve threats so that the stress response reduces and the anger fades.

A simple way to start working with anger using EFT is by tapping using set-up statements that suit you. It is best to begin practice in peaceful times when you feel calm. Benefits can be gained immediately.

'Even though anger doesn't serve me well, it protects me from ...

* *having to take responsibility*
* *other people*
* *feeling scared*

... I accept my feelings with calmness and understanding.'

'Even though I feel that if I stop my anger...

* *will have to forgive others*
* *will be admitting to it*
* *will lose my identity*
* *won't be safe*
* *won't be in control*
* *will let others take advantage and walk all over me,*

... I am willing to accept my feeling without judgement.'

Sooner or later, when the source of fear has begun to dissolve through using EFT, you can introduce set-up statements that have a more positive base.

'Even though I don't want to let others think I'm weak, I am open to the possibility of being strong in a different way.

Additional reasons for holding on/letting go are listed in Figure 6 in Chapter 6.

'Although I need this anger to remind me of the hurt I experienced, I accept my feelings with calmness and understanding.'

'Even though it's early days, I am willing to see this differently.'

Got the T-shirt

Case study

'That's the way we sort things out', Jamie told me. *'My mum, my brothers, my sister, my nan and uncles, we all fight and yell.'* At 13 he was in constant trouble at school for getting angry with his mates and 'losing it', as he called it, with the teachers. He admitted that he liked the power and control that he felt in the first moments of being angry. *'They really notice me.'* The year head had certainly taken notice again, as Jamie was in isolation for the fourth time this term. But today he was sitting (voluntarily) in the Teen Rage workshop that I was running in the school as part of their personal, social, health and economic (PSHE) education programme. He was not alone, there are always lots of young angry pupils. I learn a lot about life, and about fears, from them.

A while into the workshop Jamie said, *'My mates think of me as hard. I've got a reputation. I don't know how else to be now.'* This is the sort of thing that Jamie was known to say frequently, but today was different as he decided he wanted to lose that chain of responsibility.

Shortly afterwards, Jamie did work out a different way for himself using EFT. Over the following weeks he discovered how to notice what made him angry, what to do about it, where he felt the anger and how to replace it with more positive emotions: Not bad for a young lad who was used to losing it!

Jamie also decided that actually he had other more positive ways to influence his mates. He used his wicked sense of humour and natural charm. During the next term he told me that he felt he was now the real Jamie instead of *'some stupid tough nut'. He was really pleased with himself and was totally inspired. 'I've been helping my mates to grow up too'*, he said. 'Quite a few of my mates have been tapping and changing themselves as well.'

Resentment

'Resentment is like drinking poison and hoping that it will kill the enemies'
Nelson Mandela

Making the decision to hold on to resentment, hurt or injustices can be desperately damaging to your health and wellbeing. The decision to battle against the world and people with anger is an unwise choice. Ugly consequences are too easy to create. Holding on to anger or a grudge takes a lot of negative energy and it hurts. Trying to comprehend forgiving someone when holding tightly on to a grudge is almost impossible.

Case study

Paul had hit a core target. Both his parents had put huge pressure on him when he was a child and a teenager. Being the older brother it was always down to him to sort things out as his parents were busy running the family business. As we tapped, Paul listed a number of frustrations and events. His brother had *'got away with murder as a child'* but it was *'always me who got the blame'.*

Paul had not thought these details relevant before, but he was convinced by the SUD ratings and the reactions in his body. There was a lot to tap on: all the aspects of the incidents in his youth and in the present, his feelings about what was expected of him, and the resentment that all his life any disagreement between himself and his brother was somehow his fault. We tapped on conflicting feelings as Paul put his words into the set-up statements:

'Even though part of me wants to apologise for being such an idiot, part of me has not wanted to be sorry...'

'I accept the part of me that doesn't want to say sorry.'

Within another couple of rounds Paul was comfortable and offered the statement
'Even though part of me has been reluctant to make the first move, I am open to letting some of this feeling go ...'

Paul continued to tap for a variety of aspects and specific events until he was content that he was calm enough to approach his brother and talk. In a following session he took a closer look at his relationship with his parents.

A few months later Paul emailed to tell me that he was doing fine and had started to mend relationships. He was no longer getting anger in his chest and when he did experience any negative feelings of anger he found that they subsided when he tapped on the side of the eye point. (The eye point is linked to rage when out of balance, although Paul was not aware of this at the time – see Appendix 2). He had also noted that *'Relationships at work seem easier now ... at first I thought other people had changed, but I realised it was in fact me that had changed!'* The generalisation effect is often a surprising side-effect for clients, but is always welcome (see Chapter 4).

EFT strategies for anger

Exercise on letting go of angry feelings

Using your own words give yourself permission to feel angry and to release it with EFT. The 'letting go' feeling is really rather good as it increases the release of 'feel-good' brain chemicals that flow round the body. This type of empowering and physiological EFT effect is common. Users of EFT get into a calm zone, feel better and act at their best once more.

Letting go of angry feelings exercise

You can try this on your own or with a friend. First recall a low-grade event (SUD measure less than 6) that annoyed you. To begin it would be best to highlight a specific event and perhaps not the person that you have the most trouble with. Choose something like the rude service in a shop that caused you anger, a one-off. When you feel more confident you can use the exercise for something more annoying or anger-inducing.

1 While thinking about the annoyance, notice the thoughts and feelings that go with it. List them and give the overall annoyance a number between 0 and 10, with 10 being the highest intensity. Give the annoyance a description and include any feelings that go with it. For example, *'Really fuming about the rude cashier'*. Create your set-up statement to incorporate your description; for instance, *'Even though I was fuming at being spoken to like that, I love and accept myself.'* Start using EFT.

2 Check the intensity as you go. Always keep tapping using the same phrase until the SUD rating is very low or zero. As the initial feelings change, alter the reminder phrase to suit as you tap, *'He shouldn't have said ...'*, *'He shouldn't speak to anyone like that'*, *'It made me feel like an idiot'*.

3 If you find the overall feeling of anger has reduced enough, then I encourage you to introduce some positive phrases. Do not attempt to introduce these too early as they will be too easily rejected by your subconscious. So when appropriate, a suitable set-up can be introduced, such as *'Even though I was fuming at the time, I accept I have this anger, I forgive myself.'*

4 If appropriate you might choose to tap further rounds on any insights you have gained during the process. These may include thoughts or memories such as *'He was trying to explain'*, *'I did get the wrong end of the stick'*, *'He got a big reaction from me'*, *I was on edge about a work issue at the time'*. A new set-up could be:

'Even though I was in too much of a hurry to listen and I got the wrong end of the stick ...'
'Even though I was really fuming, I can see the benefit for me of letting go of my anger now...'

Accepting the powerful feelings of anger

'Even though I have this anger at [insert problem], I am open to find a different way to express myself...'

'Although I can't seem to stop my anger, I choose to take notice before I act ...'

'Even though I feel that I can't help my anger, I am willing to make good choices about how to express it ...'

Tuning into triggers of anger

'Even though I'm getting angry just thinking about going to see her ...'

'Even though she really gets my blood boiling...'

'Even though he always seems to get a reaction out of me ...'

'Even though I don't agree with him, I choose to remain calm ...'

'Even though we don't ever seem to see eye-to-eye ...'

Exploring the background

The reasons why you get angry are not always clear. By tapping continuously around the points, asking questions and really tuning in, you are supplied with good material to start off a tapping routine. Included below are suggestions that work, but it is your choice. Keep any questions open ended.

'Who or what causes you to feel anger?'

'Why do you think you react this way?' This provides reasons, and you can talk these through as you tap along.

Getting to grips about describing the feelings of anger pinpoints what actually happens in the body; it specifies the experience. The response *'I get a flashing warning in my head, but it's usually too late'* highlights key words to use in the set-up statement.

'Do you respond to this feeling?' This question, again, will elicit material for tapping.

'Where do you get these feelings?' Describing the location of this anger – where you feel it – is helpful in aiming EFT in the right direction. An example of a set-up might be:

'Even though I have a dagger feeling in my head ...'

By asking, *'When do you feel the anger?* or *'What reminds you of your anger?'*, helps you with the trigger, as discussed earlier in this section; for instance:

'Even though I'm reminded of this anger when I see him in that photo...'

'What is it about the situation that makes you most angry?' This question establishes who or what is causing the anger. Feeling that someone is forcing you to do something, for example, can cause you to feel powerless. The set-up statement can then be *'Even though I feel powerless when ...'*

see the section 'Reasons for holding on to negative patterns' in Chapter 6

'*Why do you need to hold on to this anger?*' This invites reasoning and logic to help. This question helps you create the set-up statement '*Even though I need to hold on to this anger because ...*'.

'*What benefits exist to letting go of this anger?*' This question highlights the positive effects of letting go, and at the same time steers you towards where you want to be. The set-up statement might be '*I accept myself and choose to let it go because ...* [insert the benefits here]...'

Anger from other people

Being on the receiving end of anger or simply witnessing it can be tough. Many people put up with regular displays of anger from people close to them, because they love them, fear them or feel that they deserve no better. If you get angry as well, things can quickly escalate. Staying calm yourself is obviously good for both of you but it can be difficult.

As described earlier, EFT can be used 'in the moment' and it is really surprising how swiftly you can regain calmness – a very empowering position. Surrogate tapping for another person is also an excellent option as long as you are calm and have their best intention in mind; it is strictly not a fixing tool!

Future-proof tapping

Longer term, it can be really helpful to work out what usually makes you angry and how this makes you behave. Think about it when you are not feeling angry and make a list. Use a method like the personal peace procedure to ease each item on the list one at a time (see Chapter 5).

- What triggers your anger?
- What signs tell you that you are on the brink of uncontrolled anger?
- Can you recognise any unhelpful patterns of behaviour?
- What have the consequences been?
- What works to calm you down?
- Are there any triggers in your daily routine or your environment that you could change?

By sharpening your talent in identifying the sources of anger for yourself you can help to ease any 'victim feelings' when something does not go well. This allows calmer and better choices. Ultimately there are always some problems beyond your power to change. EFT allows you to concentrate on working out what you can change and to gain true acceptance about those you cannot.
The techniques will guide you calmly to review your reactions to situations, by providing a natural way to handle feelings, relax and accept who you are.

Chapter 10
Fears, phobias and anxieties

Chapter 10 Fears, phobias and anxieties

We all experience some level of fear in our daily lives, and in moderation it is a good thing as it helps us to remain alert and safe. Many of us live with a host of fears, some so small that we do not even notice them.

For some, however, fears are so great that life becomes limited to an impractical extent. Fear is the root cause of all anxiety, including phobias, anxiety disorders and panic attacks and even anger. Whatever the intensity of the fear and however long ago it was initiated, EFT can be profoundly helpful. Applications can be applied on past events, current symptoms and adapted to clearing negative disruption around the thought of future anxiety. The practice of future proof tapping means that you are able to make permanent shifts in thoughts and behaviour without being in a real panic situation.

Fear

Fear is a chain-reaction in the brain that starts with a stressful stimulus and ends with a number of responses including the release of chemicals that cause a racing heart, fast breathing and energised muscles. This is also known as the stress response or the fight, flight or freeze response (the freeze response is explored in more detail in the section on trauma in Chapter 12). The stimulus could be a spider, a knife at your throat, a waiting audience or a set of footsteps behind you.

The brain is a profoundly complex organ with more than 100 billion nerve cells comprising an intricate network of communications that is the starting point of everything we sense, think and do. Some of these communications lead to conscious thought and action, while others produce automatic or autonomic responses. The fear response is almost entirely autonomic, and this means that we do not consciously trigger it or even know what is going on until we feel the symptoms. The areas of the brain involved in creating the fear response are outlined in Figure 9 and Table 13.

EFT can be applied to all levels of fear that are current or recent. If relief does not come easily then unresolved issues from the past may require attention before permanent positive progress can happen.

Figure 9 **Areas of the brain involved in the fear response**

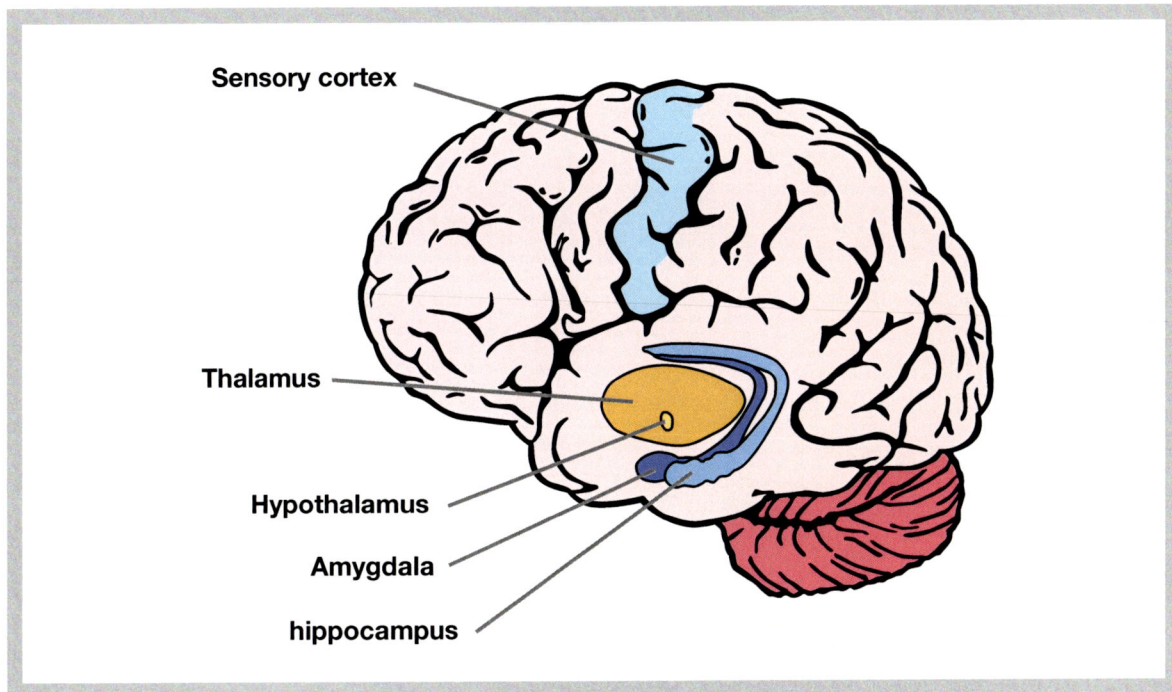

Table 13 **Areas of the brain associated with the fear response**

Area of brain	Function in the fear process
Thalamus	Sensory input of sights, smells, touch and sound is channelled through this area. If the input causes an unconditioned fear stimulus (a perceived threat to safety) the thalamus branches part of this signal directly to the amygdala which is involved in producing the fear response. The remaining input is sent to the sensory cortex.
Amygdala	Decodes emotions, determines possible threat, stores fear memories. Creates fear response quickly and sustains it until signalled to stop.
Hypothalamus	Under stress the hypothalamus produces the adrenocorticotropic hormone (ACTH) which stimulates production of adrena line and cortisol. The 'fight, flight or freeze' response becomes activated.
Sensory cortex	Input is interpreted and evaluated, but this process takes a few seconds longer than the time for a fear response to be triggered, so fear can be experienced before it has been assessed properly. Asignal is then sent from the cortex that can either inhibit the a mygdala from continuing the fear response or sustain it.
Hippocampus	Acts like a filing system. Stores and retrieves conscious memories, and processes sets of stimuli to establish the context of the current experience.

Anxiety

Anxiety is a generalised mood condition that can be distinguished from fear in three ways, as outlined in Table 14.

Table 14 **Differences between fear and anxiety**

Fear	Anxiety
Occurs in the presence of an observed threat	Occurs without an identifiable triggering stimulus
Related to the specific behaviours of escape and avoidance	The result of threats that are perceived to be uncontrollable or unavoidable
State as a result of current or present circumstances	Future-oriented mood state in which one is ready or prepared to attempt to cope with upcoming negative events

All types of anxiety are regularly eased using EFT, whether 'in the moment' or little-by-little, through individuals applying EFT for themselves or working with a practitioner.

'I've suffered from anxiety for over three-quarters of my life and at the time when I met Christine, I felt locked in a cage with no key. Gradually over many sessions, I realised I wasn't allowing myself to be happy for various reasons, and using EFT Christine helped me to see that I was "allowed" to be happy. I could learn techniques to cope with the panic and allow myself to have a life. I began to believe in myself, which I had never really done before.'

'Yes, I do have the odd relapse, but my panic and anxiety is so reduced that I can get on with things. Yes, I'm doing the best I can.'

EFT client

Anxiety disorders

When anxiety becomes excessive it can be classified as an anxiety disorder. These disorders are often debilitating, chronic conditions and they can be present from an early age or can begin suddenly following a triggering event. They can flare up at times of high stress and are frequently accompanied by symptoms such as headache, sweating, muscle spasms, palpitations and hypertension, which in some cases lead to fatigue and even exhaustion.

Anxiety disorders include panic attacks, obsessive compulsive behaviour, generalised anxiety and phobias. EFT is very effective for addressing all anxiety disorders and can be approached from a variety of angles. It can be used to:

- ease physiological symptoms
- explore beliefs about the anxiety

- examine issues of personal safety
- address emotions around inability to function well.

Many people opt for help from a skilled EFT practitioner and this is wise if the anxiety is intense. Self-help EFT is still effective for addressing less intense aspects of an issue.

Using EFT on an anxiety

1 Name the anxiety and give it an overall SUD rating.

2 Track back to establish when the fear or anxiety first started. Remembering life events will help to provide information about the source.

3 Tap for specific events and memories slowly, in turn, rating and testing on each aspect as progress is made. If no specific detail about the past comes to mind, try to visualise yourself in the present, confronting your fear or whatever it is that causes you anxiety. As you slowly recreate the situation or object of your anxiety as best you can, increase the sub-modalities (make your senses more vivid) to make the images more intense. Increase the volume, bring the picture nearer. Take note of what is happening in your body or any emotions that emerge. Feelings in relation to beliefs, physical symptoms and behaviours that are associated with the anxiety may also come to mind. Continue to use EFT on each aspect that comes up.

4 When SUD ratings have reduced significantly, recall a situation that includes elements of the anxiety and measure the SUD rating. If necessary, make the image bolder, brighter and louder to test more accurately. Use EFT on any remaining anxiety feelings again, until the intensity goes to zero.

You may wonder how long this process takes. It can sometimes take just minutes for you to see a noticeable difference. Or the process could take days or weeks, depending on the intensity of the issue and other blocks such as those outlined in Chapter 6. Tapping several times a day is often recommended for all anxiety-based problems, at least in the initial stages. The tapping in itself provides comfort and reduces the anxiety symptoms. Regular practice habitualises the body and mind to calmer response and elicits permanent shifts, as discussed in chapter 7.

More gentle approaches are needed for anxieties that bring extreme discomfort. A number of methods, such as 'softly, softly', 'telling the story' and the 'movie technique' are outlined in Chapter 5.

For severe or complex anxieties you might want to consider seeking advice from an EFT trained practitioner.

Generalised anxiety disorder (GAD)

Generalised anxiety disorder (GAD) is a common chronic disorder characterised by long-lasting anxiety that is not focused on any one object or situation. Those suffering from GAD experience non-specific, persistent fear and worry. Physical symptoms can include tightness in the muscles, headaches or a pain in the back of the neck, shortness of breath, a racing heart, pins and needles, dizziness, sweating, restlessness, difficulty concentrating, irritability and abnormal tiredness. Ordinary worrying does not bring on symptoms like these, but for someone with GAD the anxieties trigger ever-new rounds of painful soul-searching.

People with GAD worry about almost everything, which bothers them further, but they are unable to stop. They are aware that their perception about worry is out of proportion and the cycle of worry continues. When sufferers reflect on their situation they can see that it does not make sense but they cannot put their anxiety to rest as it has become an established disorder.

Some GAD sufferers can function perfectly well in their jobs when they are busy and focused but, perform excessive mental processing when they are outside work. In severe cases this can lead to people being unable to live a normal life. They may fear they are about to crash the car if they drive, that they are going to let everyone down or they get caught up in worrying and feeling anxious about everyday regular situations.

As you can imagine, GAD can has been regarded traditionally as a difficult issue to treat with therapy because in calming one set of anxieties an alternative set appears as a replacement. EFT, however, has been shown to be very effective in the treatment of GAD. A large-scale pilot study on the treatment of GAD patients was carried out by Joaquin Andrade, a medical doctor in South America over a 14-year period. Patients established marked improvement in brainwave functioning within 12 sessions of meridian energy techniques. These beneficial results were achieved within fewer sessions and were more permanent than results from groups who were given other conventional talk therapies including cognitive behavioural therapy (CBT) (see Appendix 3).

Phobias

The single largest category of anxiety disorder is phobia. Sufferers typically anticipate terrifying consequences from encountering the object of their fear, which can be virtually anything. Phobias are among the most intense and extreme emotional and physiological reactions a person ever experiences. A phobic response is largely out of control and tremendously frightening, and each occurrence can be accompanied by painful physiological side-effects and residual stress.

The speed with which EFT can remove phobias is usually dependent on the complexity of underlying issues, not the intensity of the fear. EFT treatment of phobia is gentle and does not require an individual to 'push through the fear'. Instead the intense fear gradually reduces until it is gone. Treatment for real phobias requires a clear understanding of the principles of EFT. With intense phobias, opting to work with an experienced EFT practitioner will be sensible.

In the majority of cases when it is used skilfully EFT eradicates any phobia. In some cases the problem will vanish in a few minutes, and even when it does not relief is usually a few brief sessions away – dental phobia, spiders, rats, heights or crowds – it really does not matter. If enough of the aspects are addressed to collapse the phobia, it will be gone, forever. Interestingly, in many cases people even begin to like or to enjoy what they once dreaded (see Table 22 in Chapter 14). It is important to stress that common sense is not affected when a phobia is removed using EFT. For instance, removing a client's intense fear of heights does not affect their sense that standing at the edge of a tall ledge can be dangerous.

Types of phobia

Phobias can be classified in two types.

- A simple phobia is focused on a single object, situation or activity. Common examples are a fear of spiders, dogs, vomit, enclosed spaces or flying. Phobias that appear initially to have a single focus sometimes do not. Careful questioning while using EFT will help to uncover and address the sources and aspects.

- A complex phobia involves several anxieties. Agoraphobia is an example of a complex phobia. The anxieties involved in agoraphobia will vary from person to person but may include several of the following: fear of entering shops, crowds and public places, or of travelling in trains, buses or planes. There can also be the anxiety of being unable to escape to a place of safety, usually home.

What may present as a simple phobia may not always be so, and when this is the case it is less straightforward to clear. EFT nevertheless can tackle complex patterns and connections to clear the most resilient phobias.

Case study

Billy had an extremely intense phobia of mice. He had tried several methods of therapy prior to EFT, but he was still having severe phobic reactions several times a week. Despite really *'trying to be brave'* and *'get on with life'*, Billy was becoming increasingly limited in what he could do and where he could go.

We used EFT for several sessions using code words (see Chapter 5) before Billy could mention the word *'mice'*. He reacted intensely to anything at all connected with mice, including the letters M I C E or words including these letters. He avoiding watching television in case an image of a mouse appeared and he avoided opening a magazine, again to avoid exposure. Lately Billy had started to avoid almost any outing just in case there might be a mouse or a trigger to remind him. In time, I learned that he regretted not being able to walk into the local shopping centre which had a Disney store. He knew that his daughter wanted a stuffed version of the famous mouse and this filled him with intense fear too.

Recently, then, Billy avoided *'going out if at all possible'* because *'what is out there is out of my control'*. He had virtually become a prisoner in his own home.

Persistence was needed. We used EFT on every stimulus, event and belief using gentle EFT techniques. Each time the SUD rating reduced Billy was pleased with his immediate fears but the phobia was still proving stubborn to eradicate. It seemed as if there were no specific past events that were connected directly to exposure to a mouse.

During one session, several sessions after we had started, we were tapping and Billy began to describe a time when he was about 8 years old and was waiting in a car park for his dad. He saw a mouse. As we tapped, I noted that Billy had used the word 'mouse' quite easily. We were using the 'softly, softly' technique. Billy described *'the mean look in its eyes'*, the look that *'is just so evil ... It just looks at you right in the eyes'*, and *'you don't know what it will do'*. Billy reported a *'fear feeling rising in his chest'*. He also turned his head very

>>

Case study continued

slightly – a slight flinch. (I had noticed Billy do this gesture in a previous session when we had touched on another area about his past.) He had no idea where the phrases he used came from because he said that the animal had been too far away for him to see its features, and as far as he could remember he had not been scared of mice at the time.

We carried on tapping and questioning until the fear in his chest reduced, and then we began to emphasise the phrase *'It looks right at you'*. I asked, *'Who looks right at you?'*, and without a thought Billy replied, *'Dad'*.

This, it turned out, was the first of many beatings that Billy suffered from his alcoholic father. The evil eyes that could not be trusted were his father's. The deeper issue of abuse was at the root of the phobia, and that mouse had been a bystander when Billy had been beaten by his father. Billy held a phobia of mice for 37 years. After this stage we did not really mention mice and spent time on other memories that Billy had stored.

Within a few more sessions Billy had dispensed with most of his avoidance behaviours and was getting no phobic reaction at any level. A month afterwards, he telephoned me to let me know that he had his two pet mice in his lap!

I received a note from a lady called Karen one month after she had attended an introductory EFT training day. She asked me to share part of the note to encourage anyone else who suffered as she had, with becoming *'frozen to the spot'*.

Case study

I had a severe phobia of dogs. My phobia was so severe I would sweat and shake and always be frozen to the spot. Although I work, I was avoiding so many things in life. My family were supportive but completely exhausted with having to protect me. I was very sceptical about EFT but it did work. I had forgotten the demo you did on my phobia, in the training, until a neighbour's dog got into my garden.

'Normally, I would have been frozen to the spot with fear but I was amazed to find that I felt no fear or anxiety at all. My curiosity got the better of me and I went out into the garden to test myself. Again, I felt no fear or apprehension. It was then I realised the EFT did work. As you know, I have been tapping every day for other aspects on my list about dogs but had not tested it at all.

'I have just returned from the park. In the past, I would have never dared to go, and I hadn't been for nearly 10 years. It was lovely to feel that free again. I would highly recommend that anyone should try EFT for their fears.

Social phobia

Social phobia is another complex phobia. It is based on extreme fear of people or social situations. Although common, it is one of the most under-reported conditions. Individuals' symptoms stem from a persistent fear of embarrassing themselves or being humiliated in public and can involve excessive fear of scrutiny by others, of using a public place, or when participating in any performance, sports event or presentation. People become very vulnerable. Commonly, an intense fear of being negatively judged leads them to avoid meeting people in social situations or doing presentations for their work. This can be a debilitating emotional conflict that sticks for decades. The stress response symptoms of social phobia, also known as social anxiety disorder, can include the usual array of rapid heartbeat, sweating, tremors, nausea, diarrhoea, muscle tension, muscle cramps, blushing, confusion and dizziness. Feelings of shyness or unease in social environments are not social phobia unless accompanied by extreme anxiety and a sense of dread.

To add pressure, social phobia is often one of those hidden problems that results in the individual bearing the weight of a terrible secret. An increasing number of young sufferers are reported as being school phobic. Social anxiety can lead to panic disorders, obsessive compulsive disorder and depression. In extreme cases, some people develop agoraphobia and are too afraid to leave their home. Some sufferers become unemployable and there is an increased incidence of drug or alcohol abuse, suicidal thoughts and other devastating results.

Typical roots and features of social phobias:

- often begin in childhood and can become intense in teens
- higher incidence in females than males, and appear to run in families
- linked to judgemental environments and absence of encouragement
- threat of being embarrassed by someone perceived as powerful
- related to issues of esteem
- belief that small mistakes are more important than they really are
- fear of public speaking and a general fear of all social situations.

EFT can bring effective relief to those with social phobia and can be applied to aspects such as physical symptoms, specific events, specific people and early memories as well as limiting beliefs and the core issue around feelings in each case. I have worked with many cases in which EFT has helped to reverse the need for people to remove themselves from work situations, performances, examinations, sporting events and social occasions. By making quite simple tasks less stressful, people have been able to enjoy their lives.

'Even though I am scared of ...'

'Even though my hands are sweating so much...'

'Even though I fear situations that are out of my control...'

'Even though I am afraid of being embarrassed/ awkward in a social situation...'

By recalling a past situation that involved a feeling of awkwardness or embarrassment in a social setting EFT can be used to clear all the negatives, reducing the SUD rating of each aspect in turn. By focusing and tapping on as many different aspects of the past situation as possible, the memory can be recalled in full details without any negative feelings about it. Once this has been done move on to any other memory or belief that you still feel discomfort with.

> Choice statements (see Chapter 6) and assessing readiness for a new belief (see Chapter 8) can both be very useful to explore with EFT once negative disruptions have begun to fade.

Panic attacks

Life can be extremely tough for those who suffer with severe panic attacks, and these types of anxiety problem can be difficult to shift using other interventions. I am moved by the courage shown by people who try to get on with their lives while daily carrying inside them the most debilitating fear. Many end up in hospital accident and emergency departments with real symptoms that appear to be those of a heart attack or hyperventilation, only to find that the symptoms subside in time. People are dismissed and often embarrassed as tests confirm that they are generally healthy but have had a panic attack.

Thankfully, gentle EFT does work for even the most severe panic attack cases when applied skilfully and safely.

Table 15 **Common symptoms of panic attacks**

Intense fear	Sweating	Nausea
Sense of doom	Shaking	Fear of losing control
Feeling of unreality	Flushing	Tingling or numbness in hands
Racing or pounding heart	Chest pains	Fear of dying of heart attack
Difficulty breathing	Dizziness	Fearing the worst
Choking	Light-headiness	Fear of dying

EFT can be applied to the symptoms of panic attacks and sufferers begin to gain relief quickly. Further EFT on the state of hypervigilance in the body will help to reduce the heightened anxiety that is responsible for frequent panic attacks.

> *'Members are so grateful to have a tool that they can use themselves when they need to and so many are making permanent changes toward being panic free'*
> **Ian Browne, psychotherapist in Re-lease, an anxiety support group**

Panic attacks are usually triggered by a specific event but the seeds may have been sown some time earlier. As stress has become a common currency in western society these attacks are becoming ever more frequent and some people develop panic disorder as a result of having regular attacks.

'I suffered for 16 years with panic attacks, post-traumatic stress disorder and depression. I barely existed. I had been visiting a therapist for years and although I got some comfort, I still always ended up feeling the same way. Nothing was helping. Every day I felt sad and depressed until I tried EFT. At that point, I had been about to give up and stick with the chaotic life that I had got used to.

In the last nine months, after six EFT sessions and practising a bit every day, I feel so much stronger, lighter and more hopeful as a person than for as long as I can remember. I reduced my long-term medication and have now have finished it. My life feels like it is finally beginning again. Thank you. You helped me to allow myself to live again'

Joanne, EFT client

EFT can address several of the underlying issues of panic.

Fear of the fear

As a panic attack is scary, the more you have them the more you live in fear of having another one. The basic fear response from a minor occurrence may be enough to trigger a cycle of 'fear of the fear' panic.

With EFT, a good place to start is to address the 'fear' of a potential panic attack. It is this fear that can keep you prisoner in your home, just waiting for that next attack to come. This fear can stop you from making plans to enjoy your life. Here are examples of EFT set-ups that can reduce fear of the fear:

'Even though I have this fear of the fear...'

'Even though I think this time I will die...'

'Even though I don't understand this fear...'

'Even though I sit and wait for this fear...'

'Even though I think I will scream...'

'Even though I need to run away, to escape...'

When the fear of the fear has faded, more positive set-up statements can be introduced:

'Even though I have this fear of the fear, I know fear can't kill me....'

'Even though I get this fear often, I know it is my body sending me safety messages...'

Physical symptoms

As the physical symptoms of any panic can be extremely vivid you might as well take advantage and tap on the aspects 'in the moment', using sub-modality cues. Submodalities in NLP are fine distinctions or subsets of the modalities (visual, auditory, kinaesthetic, olfactory and gustatory) that helps us encode and give meaning to our experiences.

Far from being arbitrary, submodalities often perfom a critical role, as a means by which emotions, related memories and felt-sense perceptions such as 'importance as presented to the conscious by the subconscious mind, along with thoughts or memories.

By focusing and tapping on the sub-modality descriptions such as colour, size, shape, movement and sound it is possible to regain calmness in a most empowering way even when physical symptoms are being experienced at their height:

'Even though my head is spinning like a top, making me feel faint, I love and accept myself...'

'Even though my heart is thumping like a huge drum, I take note of the messages to slow down ...'

'Even though my whole head is swimming I know that I will be safe again...'

'Even though I can feel sharp tingling in my fingers, I choose to breathe easily...'

It is extremely helpful to tap on physical symptoms that you know you get in panic situations, especially the ones that tend to come first. By gently recreating the negative disruption at a time when you are not threatened, tapping will help to clear the disruption and will be replaced with calmness. The chances of the physical symptoms occurring in the situation that usually causes you to panic will be reduced. This power of future proofing tapping on emotions, thoughts and beliefs for any issue cannot be underestimated.

'Even though I get heat in my chest when I get in a panic...'

Beliefs

Limiting beliefs can be addressed with EFT using the exercise to assess readiness for a new belief (described in Chapter 8). First, measure the VOC rating of the belief statement (1–10).

Roger said, *'When my panic kicks in, I think I am going to die.'* Asked *'How true does that feel for you emotionally?'*, the VOC measure was 10, which indicated that it was totally true. The set-up statement became:

'Even though I truly think that I'm going to die...'

You can continue working on your own thoughts using the exercise instructions in Chapter 8.	Kev had the belief that *'I don't think that I'll ever get rid of the pains in my chest'.* For him the VOC measure was 10. The set-up we started with was:

'Even though I don't think that I'll ever get rid of feeling...'

Gratitude for the fear process

This may sound like a strange suggestion, but appreciation of the process of fear can be deployed in EFT to bring about a significant reduction in all panic symptoms. Recognising and understanding the messages that your body gives you is all important.

At a time of calmness try to make a very precise list of what usually happens to you when you start to panic. A powerful way to heal fear is to appreciate its physical effects, and the thoughts and emotions it evokes through application of EFT on each aspect of your list; for example:

'Even though my body thinks I am in danger and scares me, I appreciate its need to protect me ...''

'I ask and allow for the calming responses in my body to switch on and return me to normal...'

'Even though I get frightened of what happens in my chest and it's hard not to be frightened, I offer peace to my chest right now...'

As always in EFT when addressing intense aspects of any issue, the approach is gentle and gradual. Introduce some of the EFT adaptations outlined in Chapter 5.

Chapter 11
Habits, cravings and addictions

Chapter 11 Habits, cravings and addictions

After a brief introduction to EFT you can use the techniques to achieve short-term immediate relief from the negative effects of habits, cravings and addictions. EFT is regularly the tool of choice for tackling withdrawal symptoms, chronic underlying anxiety, beliefs, obsessions, compulsions and withdrawal symptoms. It can be adapted to address both the emotional and the physical aspects of the most intense issues.

EFT is especially useful for people who find it hard to focus or to keep still. The techniques are employed in addiction and obsessive compulsive groups, and with eating disorders clients. The basic skills are used in self-help groups and then continued by clients in 'out-of-session' time. The methods fit easily with established recovery programmes such as 12-step programmes and CBT-based therapeutic group work.

Habits and addictions

Habits are merely routines of behaviour that are repeated regularly without the need to think about them directly. Our habitual behaviours originate and reside in the subconscious and are simple activities that we practise to keep us feeling safe. Common examples include:

- nail biting
- teeth grinding
- procrastination
- smoking
- alcohol consumption
- substance abuse.

But habits can sometimes overwhelm or take too much control of normal life. What begins as a habit can become an addiction – when you are no longer able to maintain conscious choice over your behaviour. Subtle differences between an addiction and a habit include the following:

- the 'choice' element appears to have been eroded away
- frequency of activity escalates
- long-term outcomes are negative – they outweigh the positives.

EFT is used to treat addictions and habits to address aspects of the issue and addressing root causes, which in turn leads to new behavioural choices. New habits take time to hardwire in the brain via new neural pathways (see the section on the Recticular activating system in in Chapter 7), so continued EFT practice helps to address any new emerging aspects.

The success rate of EFT on more complex addictions is favourable, especially when the client has a positive willingness to participate and change.

Managing cravings with EFT

Cravings are sudden impulses and strong urges that temporarily dominate thoughts and alter moods and actions. They could involve food, nicotine, alcohol or other substances. In this section the focus is on food cravings of all types, but the methods are easily adapted to any type of craving.

Because 'white-knuckling', or battling through craving with willpower, does not work in the long run, heading off cravings with EFT before they happen offers a good alternative. Food cravings are often a result of emotions. Anxiety or stress can cause the body to crave high sugar and high fat foods in an attempt to 'medicate' to a calmer state. During such emotional or stressful states, energy flow within the body may be blocked or sluggish. Using EFT on cravings rebalances disruptions in the energy system without the necessity to rely on 'being strong'.

EFT is used to treat the negative beliefs that underlie food cravings and their associated temporary high, so that the beliefs no longer need to be suppressed. Many people select EFT because it is a gentle and confidential way to work on emotional overeating issues and healthier choices.

EFT for cravings exercise

This 'quick results' EFT exercise can be used both to take the immediate edge off a craving and as a part of a planned programme to reduce persistent cravings.

At first it can be difficult to notice when a craving feeling builds up, and so learning to be mindful of triggers will help. The technique reduces a current craving, so that it operates at the point of the trigger, instead of catching your hand as it is reaching into the biscuit tin, which is already too late. As this exercise can be used in any setting, you do not need to wait until later, until the atmosphere is just right, or until you are alone or in a place where you can relax. You can do it while driving, in a crowd or standing on the corner.

You can try to use this technique on any instant craving. You are encouraged to get right into the smell, texture, taste, the look, or any element that intensifies the craving desire.

EFT for cravings exercise

1 Rate the urge or intensity of the craving on a scale of 0 to 10; for example, *'I need this piece of cake and the intensity is 8.'*

Make sure you fully associate with the food, snack item or beverage. To do so, locate in your body the feeling or sensation associated with this craving. Think about the item you are craving; get a mental picture and imagine it in detail; think about its aroma, its texture, how it would feel in your mouth. Really fire up your taste buds to get a true intensity rating.

---

2 Begin with a set-up on the friendly point, such as:

'Even though I have this ... craving in my ... [area in body where you feel the craving – mouth, stomach, etc.] I deeply and completely accept myself.'

It is usually more effective to verbalise details about the craving sensation and insert those specific details into the tapping statements such as; 'makes my mouth water' or 'the smell of the icing is driving me crazy,' rather than to make a general reference to the craving.

---

3 Follow the usual EFT sequence using a reminder statement as you focus on the feeling in your body. When one round of tapping is complete, inhale and exhale.

4 Rate your craving intensity again by checking the sensation in your body as before. If it is greater than a rating of 2 then follow another round of tapping, adjusting the set-up statement to reflect the current state. Examples include:

'Even though I still have this ..., I deeply and completely accept myself.' With a reminder statement of *'this remaining ...'*

'Even though my taste buds are still working overtime and I want it...'

5 Continue performing successive EFT rounds until the urge or craving subsides to zero or at least to 1 or 2.

If you find yourself struggling with this and the cravings are not going down or are coming back very quickly, then it makes sense to focus on emotional drivers behind the cravings such as lack of sleep or rest, anxiety, depression, being overly stressed, feeling deprived, or a creative block. You are using food as a reward – this is emotional or comfort eating. The underlying issues – root causes or 'drivers' – are the key to overcoming long-term cravings and addictions.

Be very specific about creating accurate set-up statements, taking care to address each of the related aspects and limiting beliefs that can be uncovered. By getting into the habit of really paying attention to what your 'inner voice' is telling you and in particular to any tail-enders, the set-up statements and the efficacy of EFT overall will improve. Examples include:

'Even though I want to ... [eat this chocolate], I deeply and completely accept myself.'

'Even though I still want that sweet taste because it keeps me calm, I love and accept myself anyway.

'Even though it's not that I want to eat them all, it's just that once I start I can't stop, I love and accept myself.'

'Even though I am not sure why I have to do it, I deeply and completely accept myself anyway.'

Make sure that you really emphasise the 'Even though' part of the statement to confirm to yourself that you truly accept you are more than this issue despite how big it feels.

'Even though I hate to limit myself, I deeply and completely ...' or *'Even though I don't want to limit myself...'* or whatever words fit your situation.

Make this process yours and let your personal thoughts guide you. Doing this will help you to unearth core issues and beliefs you may not have realised were there.

Keep tapping until the craving fades and make sure that you congratulate yourself. Watch out for other triggers around you that could be responsible for bringing back craving intensity. These could include: time of day, other people, work and domestic settings. Applying EFT on any likely triggers puts you, and not the craving, back in control.

To test your progress see if you can bring the SUD rating on the craving back up again: pick up the chocolate bar, smell it, close your eyes and imagine it melting in your mouth. Rub it on your teeth, lick it. You are likely to be surprised with the results. That gorgeous chocolate does not smell as good anymore – it's quite sickly. You will probably find yourself selecting a healthier alternative.

Don't make the mistake of stopping tapping once you find that it works. Cravings require persistence at least in the short term while emotional drivers are still in the driving seat. If you are reluctant to keep tapping for cravings you might need to ask yourself why this is. While tapping around the points, ask yourself:

'What's the downside of not indulging in this craving?' Listen for the reasons. Write them down and tap.

Be gentle with yourself. Do not fight; accept. Keep positive. It does not make you a failure; it simply proves you are human. Accept yourself as you are. If you make a commitment to do the EFT exercises you will reach success.

Take back your power. You decide what you will or will not do every day – make your own plan.

Addressing beliefs

With habits and addictions we hold on to behaviours that are unhealthy for us. Usually it is necessary to address limiting beliefs before permanent positive shifts can take effect. While it is true that many substances are in themselves addictive to our minds and bodies, the reason that any addiction is hard to let go of is that it gives us relief from negative thoughts and feelings, and we control these by its use. Addictions of all kinds are used to 'stuff down' or mask negative feelings. When we try to give them up, not only are we left to face those feelings without support but we also face cravings for the thing that we are addicted to.

After working on cravings using EFT negative feelings that have been suppressed are likely to become exposed. The techniques then allow a natural and unthreatening focus on the underlying emotional drivers behind the behaviour, to expose the real villains behind addictive behaviours.

Typical set-up statements that hit home include:

'Even though I ... when I'm bored...'

'Even though I ... when I'm angry/lonely...'

'Even though I overeat to hurt myself...'

'Even though I ... to avoid my feelings...'

'Even though I use ... to soothe myself...'

'Even though I ... because I think I'm worthless...'

'Even though I ... because I don't love myself...'

Case study

Tammy discovered through tapping that she had established a belief early in her childhood about drinking. She had formed beliefs that starting to drink alcohol in the early evening was a way of separating yourself from the *'daily grind'* and that it was sign that you were *'a grown up'*. At the age of 45, and with the start of a drink problem, Tammy decided through a few sessions of EFT that perhaps she did not need to operate with this illusion any more.

Within a couple of months she was well on her way to being calmly satisfied by other more healthy pastimes.

Using EFT on current feelings

Use EFT to target current and concrete behaviours or symptoms in relation to cravings and addictions. There are likely to be many layers underneath a symptom, but easing negative feelings on the surface first is an easy way to get started, using set-up statements such as:

'Even though I'm a ... addict, I deeply and completely accept myself.'

'Even though my ... is calling me...'

'Even though I crave ... at night...'

'Even though I binge at night...'

Tap three times a day on whatever type of set-up suits your inner voice. Do it in the early morning and late evening, for example, and at one other time. If you wait until you have a craving you are less likely to complete the process, although do it during a craving as well.

Attend to triggers and tap on them using set-ups such as:

'Even though I have an urge to .... whenever I ...'

'Even though I have a craving whenever I see the...'

Then move on to the underlying feelings and anxieties that drive the behaviour.

Adapt set-ups to suit your current position and alter them following re-testing and calibration as you proceed.

For many people with cravings and addictions it is also crucial to attend to de-motivating factors such as guilt and self-hatred. EFT helps to reduce these negative feelings and any associated anxiety.

'Even though I hate myself for...'

'Even though I feel guilty when I ...'

'Even though I feel guilty about being ...'

Tapping on the index finger point (the large intestine meridian) is associated with releasing any feelings of guilt. Add this point to a tapping round or simply tap on this point, saying a phrase such as

'I forgive myself for feeling weak.' Forgiving any compulsive behaviour that seems to be out of control reduces self-hatred and will therefore help with long-term success.

The roots of guilt often include a sense of never being enough, of never being a good enough child or similar. A typical thought may be: *'If only I had been smart enough, good enough, clever enough ... Mum would have stopped drinking for me.'* A young child has no understanding of pending addiction at the time they form false beliefs such as this. For so much of our lives we refer to early decisions that may no longer be useful to us (see Chapter 2). Dig deep to get rid of any guilt in order to avoid missing or misdiagnosing underlying anxiety.

Using EFT on past feelings

Using EFT on past feelings and incidents can be explored further. Write down or name three of the worst incidents from your past and tap for them. Ask which is the loudest memory. Which is the most humiliating / upsetting?

Exploring early attitudes, atmospheres and events often brings up new material that may be linked in important ways to the root of negative feelings.

'Even though I'm anxious when I ...'

'Even though I associate ... with fighting/losing/shame...'

'Even though I feel unsafe without ...'

'Even though I ... to feel better...'

Recall and record the sharpest criticisms around your achievements, relationships, image, peer problems, etc. Tap on negative feelings or beliefs such as shame or whatever the strongest feelings are. Upsetting incidents or periods of time might be uncovered and need more work. By going slowly and respectfully the potential to progress can be striking.

Using EFT to test the future

Our subconscious does not distinguish between reality and perceived reality, it simply follows the instructions it is given.

Test to see how you will feel in the future without particular emotions, feelings or behaviours.

Picture yourself not having your particular craving or addiction. Ask yourself how you feel. Listen to your inner voice and feel the reaction in your body. With any negatives – if you feel anxious, angry, lonely or irritable – tap on the response. Take your time and tap on each aspect until the SUDs are reduced to zero. If the responses are all positive, tap and congratulate yourself.

Picture yourself doing whatever your desire is. Ask yourself, *'What happens? How do you feel?'* It is common to have negative feelings about not deserving the thing you desire, or to feel anxious, or to feel unsafe without a shield. Other reactions may include thinking that other people will be envious, or perhaps that others will comment on your appearance. Take your time and tap for whatever fears and feelings arise.

Picture yourself addressing the underlying feelings that trigger the addictive behaviour. How do you feel? Many people often feel anxious or 'resistant' to doing this and admit that they would rather suffer with the problems of the addiction. Tapping might go something like; *'Even though I'm afraid to face my relationship...'* or *'Even though I'm afraid to deal with the rage at my father...'*

Addressing specific sabotaging behaviours using EFT helps to unblock the barriers to progress. Take the VOC measure on the beliefs that emerge. The following are example set-up statements that can be said out loud and to test reaction. Continue to tap using any statements that elicit negative disruption.

'Even though it's not safe for me to...', Even though I don't feel supported by my family members...' or *'Even though I don't deserve to be happy with my body....'*

Tune into any tail-ender thoughts and emotions that emerge from the stated goal. Take each tail ender one-at-a-time and reform into a new tapping set-up. For example if the tail-enders to the stated goal were, *'I have a block...'* and *'I sabotage myself whenever...'* and *'I'll never get over this'* then suitable set-ups are:

'Even though I have a block to ...'

'Even though I sabotage myself whenever I ...'

'Even if I never get over this ...'

Tapping on statements such as these helps to shift unconscious energy blocks to losing weight, or to stopping the out-of-control behaviour. It helps to accept that part of you is not feeling very positive.

Obviously there are many more phrases and issues that you could select. It all depends on your particular patterns. Common themes that get in the way seem to be shame, guilt, self-hatred and anxiety.

You can always use daily affirmations such as *'Thank you God/Universe/purpose for ...'*

Clients will notice that they begin to 'forget' about the constant thoughts that they are usually plagued with and begin to be engaged in other activities. Positive outcomes begin to occur as the underlying issues fade with tapping and the basics of symptomatic behaviour are tapped away.

Substance abuse and addiction

Addictions are cunning, powerful and baffling! They are usually a multi-faceted problem. Using EFT to help treat an addiction to a substance or to a behaviour will be extremely helpful but it can also be tricky. EFT can:

- bring down the immediate craving of food, cigarettes, alcohol, drugs, etc.

- uncover and address any client ambivalence about giving up the problem.

- reduce incredibly strong defence mechanisms that often present as resistance or 'denial'

- collapse the overall addiction by 'tranquilising' the anxiety caused by underlying anger, fear, guilt, trauma or other underlying emotional issue

- remove the need to switch from one form of addiction to another (from alcohol to coffee/cigarettes, for example).

EFT is regularly used to combat some major addictions with considerable success, usually over a period of time and with persistence. When treating rooted addictions it is necessary for continue using the techniques numerous times a day – for serious addiction up to 25 times.

As addictive behaviour is especially complex the person caught in it usually needs support and guidance from an experienced EFT practitioner.

'Almost every client of mine learns to use EFT and continues to gain benefit outside of session time. Two big advantages that they report is that they are actively contributing to their own progress (often in really surprising ways) and that keeping their hands busy helps'

youth addiction counsellor

Working with substance abuse and addiction is a vastly complex area. As a group, people suffering from addiction experience a greater degree of energy system disturbances than most. The set-up within EFT is therefore of particular importance as it is designed to address psychological reversal.

Using EFT it is possible to minimise the time and pain involved in treatment and to get the client to take personal responsibility far sooner than is usually the case with other therapeutic approaches.

The logical levels of experience template is particularly useful in addiction programmes. It assists client and practitioner to identify aspects of the issue and helps clients to understand personal change. Working through stages from addiction to true healing and recovery, using the neurological levels as a guide, helps to ensure that the client's needs are being addressed effectively at every level of human experience (Dilts, 1990).

In guided programmes clients move from problem state through to increasing wholeness and health, and become increasingly self-directed through the process of change at mind, body and spiritual levels.

As the client begins to think about a change, the practitioner can ask questions at different levels:

* environment – where? and when? and who with? – factors that are external opportunities or constraints

* behaviour – what? – specific actions or reactions within the environment

* capabilities and skills – questions about how? – knowledge and skills that guide and give direction to the behaviour

* beliefs and values – why? – provide the reinforcement (motivation or permission) to support or deny our capabilities

* identity – who? – factors to determine our sense of self

* spiritual/greater system/purpose – what or for whom? – goes beyond self-consciousness to relate to the bigger picture about mission.

> An example of using the logical level framework with EFT is in the section on assessing the readiness for a new belief in Chapter 8.

Working alone or with a client, new aspects are uncovered and evolve. Many may even seem to repeat at different stages of healing or recovery as fear re-emerges. A skilled EFT practitioner can move through the complex areas using the logical levels, intuition and inspiration. At each stage an individual will experience specific challenges. The logical levels provide a convenient interface for the complexity of human experience so that we can identify the problem areas for that person, and then use EFT to treat them.

EFT addiction programmes can run alongside established methods in use or they can be used as a treatment model in its own right. It is very effectively used in rehab centres, working with individuals, in groups, or you can use it for working on your own.

Routes in with EFT

When working with our addictions to various substances more perseverance in performing EFT is usually required than for other issues. We seek our addictive substance when we feel anxiety, hoping temporarily to remove that unpleasant feeling. The process of reversing an addiction is an arduous one. We can become even more addicted and feel even worse when the substance leaves our system. This cycle could apply to nicotine, prescribed medication or drugs of any type.

Recovering from addictions can be a long, frustrating and painful process but the extraordinary effectiveness and do-it-yourself basis of EFT brings relief and often works when nothing else does. The typical path to recovery using EFT covers the following areas.

Addressing the context

Addiction can appear to be something that happens to us, on autopilot, seemingly against our normal will. A first step in undoing the power of the addiction is to become highly aware of the context by asking basic questions about the addiction:

- *What exactly are you doing?*
- *Where?*
- *When?*
- *Who with?*
- *What for?*
- *And then what?*

Responses to each of these specific questions provide information on the thoughts, feelings and possibly physical sensations to begin tapping on. For example:

'Even though "it" always happens when ... I deeply and completely love and accept myself.'

'Even though it's somehow connected with that strange feeling in the pit of my stomach...'

'Even though I just have to ... as soon as ...'

Addressing the purpose

Addictions have a purpose. Addictive behaviours appear to be the solution to our problem. When we are overwhelmed or beyond being able to cope, the addictive behaviours are an attempt at a solution to the pain of thoughts such as *'I am not OK/safe/valuable/lovable/confident ...'*

A typical set-up could be:

'Even though I do not feel confident enough to deal with this on my own, I accept myself for now.'

Addictive behaviours occur when the hope for a solution gets disconnected from the negative consequences. The negative consequences are temporarily disregarded. By filling in the blank statements below, useful tapping material is created.

I have to ...[what?] to ...[feel/be/have what?], and then ...[the negative consequence].

For example, a person who binge-drinks might respond like this:

'I have to drink to feel confident socially and then I feel guilt and remorse.'

Or a person who abuses substances:

'I have to inject to stop the pain in my stomach and then I feel guilty.'

With progressive rounds of tapping on the aspects, key *'ah ha'* moments are discovered naturally. EFT provides an excellent set of tools to help with our cravings, anxiety and jitters, and these tools serves a great purpose between sessions for cravings. The short cut version of EFT using a simple set-up brings results:

'Even though I have this craving [anxiety/fear/irritation]... I deeply and completely love and accept myself.'

EFT on the desire

It may be necessary to do at least one round of EFT for any specific desire 15 to 25 times a day. In this way we establish our freedom from it. It is worth the effort!

'Even though I need ..., I deeply and profoundly love myself.'

'Even though until now I have been desperate to have ... I now feel safe, peaceful, happy and free without it....'

'I choose [want, deserve, allow myself, accept] to be free from the urge for...'

EFT on the underlying emotions

A whole range of underlying emotions may need attention with tapping in order to elicit permanent change.

- With guilt or shame of addiction:

  'Even though I feel [guilty/ashamed] because I am addicted to ..., I deeply and profoundly love myself.'

  'Even though until now I have felt [guilty/ashamed] because I was addicted to ..., I now understand and love myself.'

  'Even though until now I have felt [guilty/ashamed] because I was addicted to ..., I now feel safe, peaceful, happy and free without it.'

  'I choose [want/ deserve/ allow myself/ accept] to be free from this [guilt/shame] about my addiction to ...'

Other emotions that are common in addiction include: fear that we may not get our 'dose'; anger towards others; withdrawal symptoms when we cannot get our dose; anxiety when we do not get what we want or when we are without our substance; unhappy because we do not have what we want; or depression because we cannot feel pleasure or happiness without our substance.

Other issues and aspects can grow and occupy an ever-greater portion of our lives. In addition to relieving our anxiety, the substance can also come to represent:

- Freedom to have what we want, thus we would feel suppressed without it:

  'Even though I feel crushed when I do not get my..., I deeply and profoundly love myself.'

  'Even though until now I have felt despair when I did not get my ..., I now feel safe, peaceful, happy and free without it.'

'I choose [want, deserve, allow myself] to be free from this feeling of suppression/lack of freedom.'

'I choose [want, deserve, allow myself,] to be free from this desire for ...'

- A source of pleasure. We would feel unhappy or depressed without it.

- A substitute for affection or other needs or pleasures. We would feel unloved or without happiness without it.

- A substitute for companionship – especially cigarettes, coffee or alcohol, which require a ritual of preparation.

    'Even though I feel deprived of [pleasure/affection/companionship] when I do not get my...'

    'Even though until now I have felt deprived of [pleasure/affection/companionship] when I did not get my ..., I now feel fulfilled, peaceful, happy and free without it.'

    'I choose [want/ deserve/allow myself] to be free from this feeling of being deprived of pleasure [affection/ companionship].'

    'I choose [want/deserve/ allow myself] to be free from this desire for ...'

EFT for the physical symptoms

Physical symptoms that arise can be reduced or removed using EFT:

'Even though I have this [physical phenomenon]... in my [part of the body] *..., when I do not have* [substance] *..., I deeply and profoundly love myself.'* Working on symptoms at other times than 'in the moment' is particularly effective.

'Even though until now, I have had this [physical phenomenon] *... in my* [part of the body]*... I now feel totally peaceful and healthy.'*

'I choose [want, deserve, allow myself] *to be free from this* [physical phenomenon] *... in my* [part of the body] *... when I do not have* [substance]*...'*

'I choose [want, deserve, allow myself, accept] *to be free from this desire for ....'*

EFT for feelings of resistance

Tapping is effective for addressing many forms of resistance which may arise when contemplating freedom from a substance addiction.

'I cannot feel free without this ...', 'I cannot feel happy without this', 'I cannot sleep without this ...', 'I have no other source of pleasure than ...', 'I have no other faithful companion in life than ...', 'This is my frame or reference in life ...', 'This is who I am ...', 'I do not know how I will be without this ...'

While tapping on aspects of any areas mentioned above, connected aspects and new layers may emerge which would then require tapping on individually. Keep a record of what comes up and once or twice a day work in more depth on the various aspects related to this addiction.

Setting aside times of day for tapping - waking up, before or after showering, before and after eating, before work, after work, bathroom visits and before sleeping at night – can help with keeping a routine. Another way to remember is to use a watch that beeps on the hour.

Following tips like these we can try to keep the desire at a very low level. If, however, the level of the desire increases then we should also tap at those times too.

Eating disorders

EFT is used in many professional and self-help settings to help resolve the complex issues connected with eating disorders such as anorexia, denial and resistance, attachment to bulimic behaviours, food addictions, cravings, and compulsion with exercise. EFT is effectively used alongside other therapeutic therapies without conflict. People can keep issues private and still get lasting relief.

'Using EFT in my practice for the last two years has transformed the healing process with my young clients tremendously. They report that the added benefit of EFT is that it gives them the power to break the cycles of despair for themselves. Most of my young clients come up with really creative ways of moving forward. It's quite inspirational'

Linda Walsh, eating disorder therapist

EFT is used in both self-help and guided therapy programmes of eating disorder treatment and recovery to assist in the following areas:

high levels of distress and anxiety	unhelpful thoughts
confronting cravings and managing trigger foods	self-esteem
compulsion to starve	relationship assertion
recovery from laxative abuse	complex long standing issues including trauma, abuse, neglect, abandonment
self-harm	obsessive compulsive rituals
physical symptoms – nausea, feeling bloated, tired, headachy or edgy	getting back to feeling in control

Case study

Paulo, 17, had successfully worked on many aspects of his eating disorder using self-help EFT. He identified a *'hollow feeling'* that *'sits inside my chest like something is missing'*. He had tapped on his feelings around *'filling the void'* but removing the *'hollowness'* feeling was proving difficult. Listed below are some EFT avenues that were explored in further one-to-one EFT sessions and that could be useful in similar circumstances.

Exploring what was *'hollowed-out'* or *'removed'* in the past. These feeling can be about people and situations in the past, and even about 'removing your personality or identity' as it was not safe to be yourself at that past time. Identify incidents from childhood – perhaps in the family or at school – that rise to the surface while using EFT that remind you about where you felt unsafe. These can be addressed directly through tapping.

Emptiness also can be connected to lack of self-worth. Asking the question *' I feel ... [0–10 VOC] worthy.'* Tap for *'Even though I feel only 50 per cent worthy ...* Make a habit of restating the belief *'I feel worthy'* daily and tapping on any tail enders until the VOC about the belief has risen to a consistent level that you are satisfied with.

Ask further relevant questions one at a time while in a tapping round and address the material that emerges by further tapping: *'Is there a void to be filled from a lack of loving and nurturing, or a deprivation?'*; *'If there is one event that shows the opposite, what would it be?'*. Tap for whatever incidents come up.

A void can also represent a lack of self-love. This is not about a big ego, this is about self-acceptance. Ask out loud, *'How much do I love myself'?* If the answer is an VOC measure of 5, then the set-up statement could be *'Even though I love myself only 50 per cent, I deeply ...'* Self-acceptance, or lack of it, is a big issue for many people. Paying attention to this and persistent tapping will improve acceptance until one day you will reach VOC 10 belief. Continued tapping on this area is recommended.

Obsessive compulsive disorder (OCD)

Everyone has minor rituals, behaviours and thoughts. Many people are a bit fussy about something, whether it is cleanliness, double-checking or arranging possessions 'just so'. In small doses these are not a problem.

OCD falls into a different category, however. It covers a wide variety of patterns of obsessive and compulsive behaviour. Sufferers are compelled to carry out their strong obsessional thoughts and ritual behaviour can swallow up great chunks of their day, putting jobs at risk, relationships under strain and generally making life a kind of living hell. The compulsive rituals are carried out to help ease the anxiety caused by the obsessive thoughts. The obsessional thinker will also use 'curing' thoughts such as counting, thinking 'good things', that are relevant to them but probably have little connection with the intrusive thought or thoughts they are used to counter.

People with OCD can also damage themselves physically through the need constantly to carry out the activity with which they have become obsessed, for example continual washing.

Rituals give relief from anxiety, but unfortunately they can easily go on to become a major problem in themselves. Rituals – washing, checking, repeating, etc. – can make such enormous demands on the individual's time that normal life becomes increasingly impossible. In a way, the rituals are like a drug and people can get hooked on them.

Behind the anxiety there may be childhood experiences, or traumas or unpleasant events from later on. In most cases the 'cause' may be difficult to identify for certain, and it is not at all useful to waste time ruminating this. The point is that, as with exaggerated anxiety responses, the mind and body have learned to react in a faulty way. To recover from OCD the person affected needs to 'unlearn' these automatic responses.

'I would like other children and young people that have OCD symptoms to know that there is help. The horrible OCD will fly away. It may seem hard. I used to say it would never go away. You can learn that you are the powerful one'
Anna, EFT teen client (aged 13)

Underlying most cases of OCD is severe anxiety – fear, in fact. Certain 'triggers' – things that may seem perfectly ordinary to other people – bring on the anxious feelings.

The person affected deals with the anxiety by developing a ritual, the purpose of which is to help them face the threatening situation. The stronger the anxiety, the longer and more complex the rituals tend to be.

Typical obsessions include:	Typical compulsions include:
fear of shameful misbehaviour	cleaning
death and disaster	washing
contamination	checking
sexual thoughts	counting
symmetrical arrangements	measuring
intrusive thoughts and images	repeating ritual actions
lucky or unlucky numbers	hoarding things
unsatisfactory body images	confessing imaginary 'sins'

OCD used to be considered quiet a rare disorder as many sufferers disguise their condition and are extremely reluctant to discuss it with anyone. Far from being rare, minor OCD symptoms are relatively common, and 'eccentric' or 'odd' behaviour is quite widespread. Many people tend to keep silent about their condition. Typically, people with OCD live with their problem for several years before they seek outside help.

OCD can emerge as a result of other anxieties such as GAD or depression. Tackling the larger picture is the first priority and medical consultation is always recommended. EFT can be used in tandem to tackle the anxieties, symptoms and thoughts that are debilitating.

EFT as a strategy for recovery

The logical approach to OCD treatment is to:

- ease anxiety around the rituals

- learn to face the anxiety without the need for the rituals.

This is accomplished by a very gentle and gradual exposure to the situations that are feared, so that they can be faced without the urge to ritualise.

Case study

Tony, aged 24, was going through a very difficult period and was on medication for depression. He was having problems with relationships and had stopped working. Using EFT, Tony began to realise that his OCD symptoms were first triggered while visiting his terminally ill mother in hospital.

'Mum had been on a high sterile ward. I was so aware of the need not to pass on any germs, I felt dirty. I used to hold my hands away from my body. On the journey home, I found that I couldn't touch anything - total revulsion.'

Normal life rapidly became impossible. Tony ate with his fingers because he couldn't bear the idea of touching cutlery. He washed his hands so often that the skin peeled and the flesh split to the bone. Eventually Tony was spending many hours a day sitting inside an imaginary *'clean circle'*, only leaving it to go to the bathroom or to bed. In this way Tony ended up, in his words, *'wasting six years of my life.'*

Within a couple of months, with several EFT sessions and good homework, Tony was able to sedate many of the symptoms around his distress. He continues to make good progress and has returned to part-time voluntary work for the first time in five years.

EFT also works well with other similar disorders.

- Body dysmorphic disorder (BDD) is a preoccupation with a non-existent or minimal defect in appearance that generates significant distress or impairment in social, occupational and/or other important areas of life, and involves unrealistic beliefs concerning other people's reactions to this 'ugliness'.

- Trichotillomania is the recurrent pulling out of one's hair, which is regarded as an impulse control problem.

- Ruminations which are morbid preoccupations, usually associated with depression.

Becoming more positive with EFT progress

When feelings change and disruptions settle the way forward with EFT is to introduce new patterns of thinking.

Case study

A 34-year-old client, Dawn, had been using EFT in sessions for several months. Old habits of thinking were fading and her symptoms of body dsymorphia were reducing. New, more positive EFT set-up statements were appropriate:

'Even though I find it difficult to forgive myself for all I've done over the years to myself and my body, I am beginning to truly forgive and release myself.'

'Even though I may never fully accept my body, I choose to be fully delighted by its acceptance of me ... I choose now to be open to loving my body.'

'I choose to have compassion for myself as I learn to take new steps.'

'I choose to release myself from all my harsh judgements.'

'I open myself to the experience of love and forgiveness deep within my body.'

Chapter 12
Stress, trauma and abuse

Chapter 12 Stress, trauma and abuse

Stress is part of our daily existence. It is a response to our mental, emotional or physical demand, whether actual or imagined. We all live with stress but that does not mean we need to suffer so much from it. EFT provides both rapid relief and long-term benefits for all stress-related issues including positive results for issues concerning trauma and abuse. Symptoms and negative emotions are frequently reduced significantly using EFT, and often more rapidly in comparison with other interventions. EFT techniques are adapted for safe and gentle use in order to minimise distress in even the most severe cases. Repeated applications of EFT can eliminate these feelings permanently, In some cases long-term results require continued and more sophisticated uses of EFT to uncover and address deeper emotional causes. Despite the safe nature of the techniques significant trauma cases need to be handled with caution by EFT practitioners with expert training and experience.

EFT, the universal stress-busting gift

Using EFT to provide relief for stress, trauma and abuse can be challenging, but the results are very often favourable. EFT addresses the mind and the body at the same time. Following successful treatment with EFT, the mind-body is able to recall a previously troubling thought (or to be in a previously troubling circumstance) free from the unwanted emotional response. There is precious little long-lasting relief available for those who have been traumatised, who experience violent and disturbing flashbacks, who have suffered severe personal shock or abusive pasts. EFT proves to be a precious gift for many practitioners who are able to facilitate permanent relief, to restore trust, love and optimism in people whose lives have previously been so affected by traumatic incidents. The utmost care is needed in guiding a client to a peaceful new position. Peace can become a realistic option for many sufferers, and if the person so chooses EFT is also a useful vehicle for addressing the desire to forgive and to have understanding.

The benefits of EFT can also be experienced by those with secondary traumatic stress or vicarious victimisation, by the indirect victims of trauma or perhaps by the partner or family member of a person who has suffered trauma who may also experience symptoms.

Stress

'Houston, we've had a problem'
Commander Lovell, Apollo 13 Mission.

Everyone can handle a bit of excitement and adrenaline occasionally. Moderate amounts of stress help people perform tasks more efficiently; they can improve memory function, heart function and make the body more resistant to infection. The biochemical changes of the stress response within the autonomic nervous system (ANS) are excellent adaptive resources suited to periods of change and emergency.

Stress overload

The stress response becomes a problem when the systems involved in maintaining stability do not stop and remain active even when not needed. Stress is a response to our perception of what is happening; so, for example, even though the vast majority of stimuli are not a true threat to our life we still respond as if they are. This can occur dozens of times a day. Prolonged over-activity or chronic stress can eventually lead to physiological problems such as hyperglycaemia (high level of cortisol leads to increased sugar in the blood), high blood pressure, cholesterol increase, weakening immune system, gastritis and other physical problems.

Figure 10 **Areas of the brain involved in the stress response**

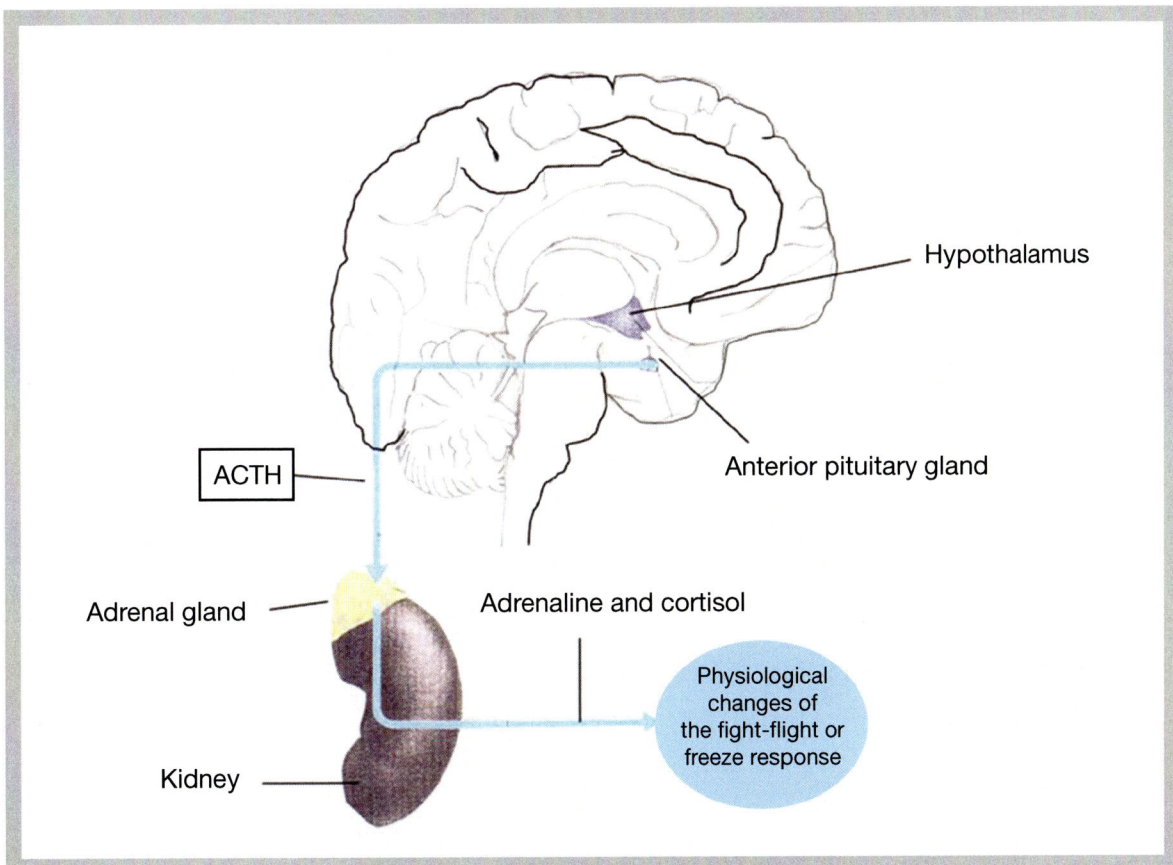

Figure 11 **Physical effects of the stress response**

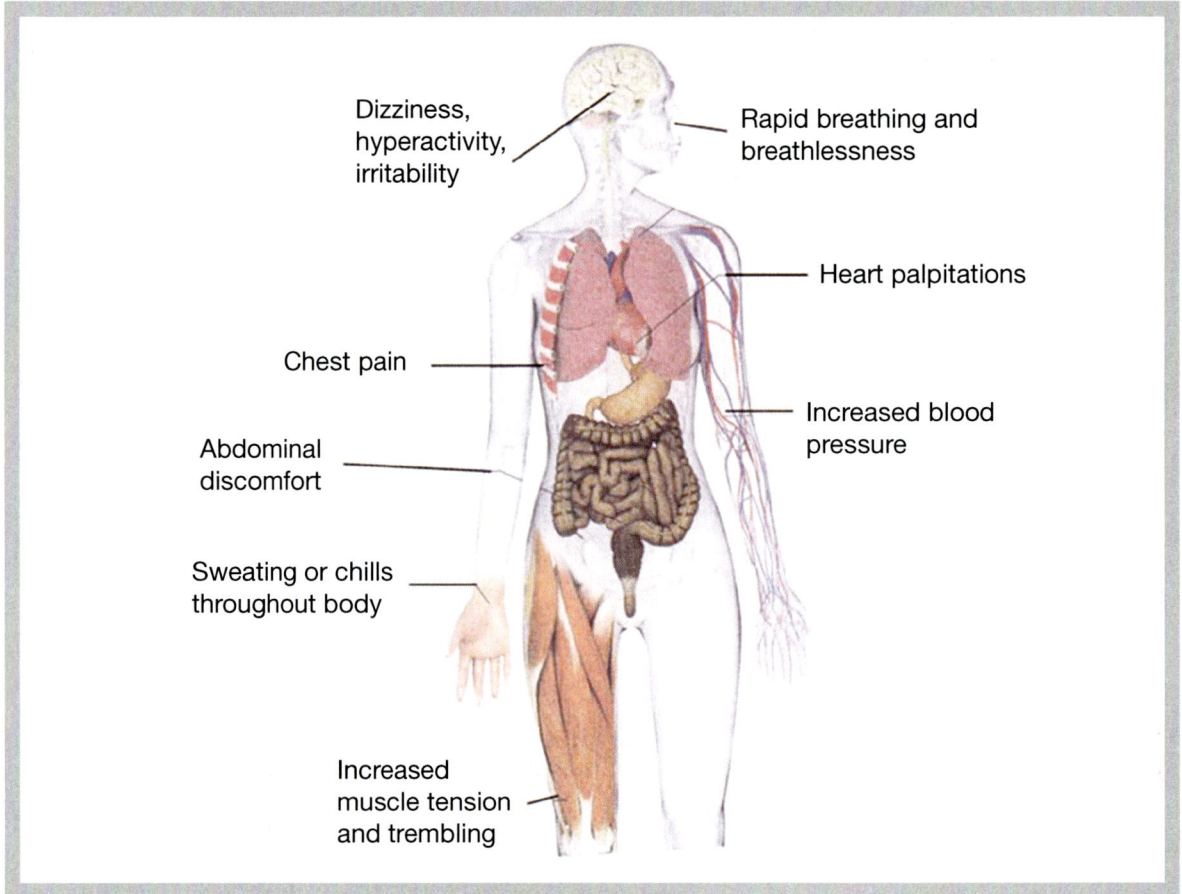

Stress has been linked with a large number of emotional and physical issues such as:

anxiety and depression	colds and flu
ulcers	rheumatoid arthritis
sleeping problems	cancer
heart disease	obesity
stroke	speeding the rate of ageing

We are all aware that if we can reduce stress in our lives we can enjoy healthier lives, better relationships and even recover more quickly from illness and disease. Despite this knowledge, it can be difficult to find effective and practical ways to reduce the stress response when we are 'in the moment' or to erase stress that arises from deeper issues.

EFT for stress relief

The practice of EFT can be equally effective for self-help and when working with someone else.

In the moment

EFT results appear to be unrivalled when used 'in the moment' as a calming technique on stress-producing events or thoughts, on anxious feeling and in emergency situations. Physical and emotional distress can be reduced rapidly and almost instantly in some cases. Once general calm has been regained it becomes possible again to function at your best in the current circumstances. Continued skilled use of EFT can be employed at that point or later to help uncover the underlying roots and ease them for longer term relief.

Most users of EFT report its cumulative effect as the mind-body become accustomed to the positive effects even when just using shortcuts in tapping and after only a few practices. Consequently when a new stressful event occurs users are more likely to choose to tap and the negative effects of the stress response fall away so that calmness is restored more quickly. The empowering effect of EFT is impressive and encouraging to the user.

> *Why allow your body to remain in a constant state of stress?*
> *Sabre-tooth tigers are extinct.*

For chronic stress

Facing continual sources of stress, specific hormones kill hippocampus neurons in certain areas of the brain, resulting in a loss of memory and a decrease in attention and concentration. A marked deterioration in cognitive ability, including in terms of retention of new information and adapting to new situations, are common experiences of people with chronic stress. Until the last decade or so, it was generally believed that the adult brain does not create new brain cells.

> *'Brain cells create ideas. Stress kills brain cells.*
> *Stress is not a good idea'*
> **Frederick Saunders**

Medical science has produced growing evidence that the adult human brain has the ability to create new neurons in a process known as neurogenesis. EFT provides an optimal opportunity for regeneration (see the section on neurogenesis in Chapter 7). When we are able to maintain optimal conditions many of new neurons survive and integrate themselves into the working brain. With continued positive use of tapping, new insights become new ways of thinking. Over a sustained period of time the neural pathways strengthen.

It is to be hoped that this knowledge will provide relief to those who have been led to believe that they can never regain a life free of the effects of chronic stress. We have the ability to heal ourselves and we have the ability to see things differently in life, to shift our priorities. EFT brings us to a place where these insights and decisions come about naturally.

> *'For me, coping with ongoing mental health issues and living in isolation without any support of family is s**t to say the least. Sometimes, it only needed a strange look from someone in the post office and I would find myself getting really stressed out. I used tapping on and off for irritations as they were happening, and the reaction went straight away. I think my body has got used to tapping now and I get rid of the feeling in my chest quickly. If I'm out I just usually hide it a bit and tap across my collarbones but no one takes any notice.*

'I have changed my ideas about quite a few things since I started using EFT about being different, as it used to really bug me. I know I am different but it just doesn't have the same effect anymore. Tapping is like that, at least from what I've seen from other people in the group. It has a kind of well – way of making stuff seem less in your face'

Darren (aged 23), member of an EFT working support group

Trauma

Trauma or critical incident can occur when we are faced with sudden or unexpected events that involve elements of threat, loss or disruption of basic value systems. Traumatic events can range from a single, overwhelming event such as a robbery or accident, to more complicated and enduring situations such as abuse, domestic violence, war or an extreme threat or loss. The effects of trauma are the same, and are equally legitimate, where a person has a strong subjective perception of threat in circumstances that may not be seen as posing a significant threat to other people.

Impact of trauma

The impact of trauma on an individual person is dependent on risk and resilience factors for that person. The negative effect of a traumatic event on the energy system is almost always connected with a person's 'comfort zone' in relation to what is familiar, comfortable and safe. Although the traumatic event may now be over, strong physical and emotional reactions can remain. Following a critical incident, emotional and physical aftershocks are common. Symptoms may appear immediately after a traumatic event or not until weeks, months or even years have passed. All, however, are powerful enough to cause incapacitation, in many cases with overwhelming force (see Table 16 on page 200).

The symptoms of trauma are amplifications of the basic reactions of stress, the very basic responses designed to assist you with coping and surviving. Excessive, more dramatic swings between peaks of arousal and troughs of passivity characterise trauma. Each extremity of the swing has a different effect on the body and mind in emotions and in physiology (see Figure 12).

Figure 12 **Trauma featured by excessive swing between arousal and passive states**

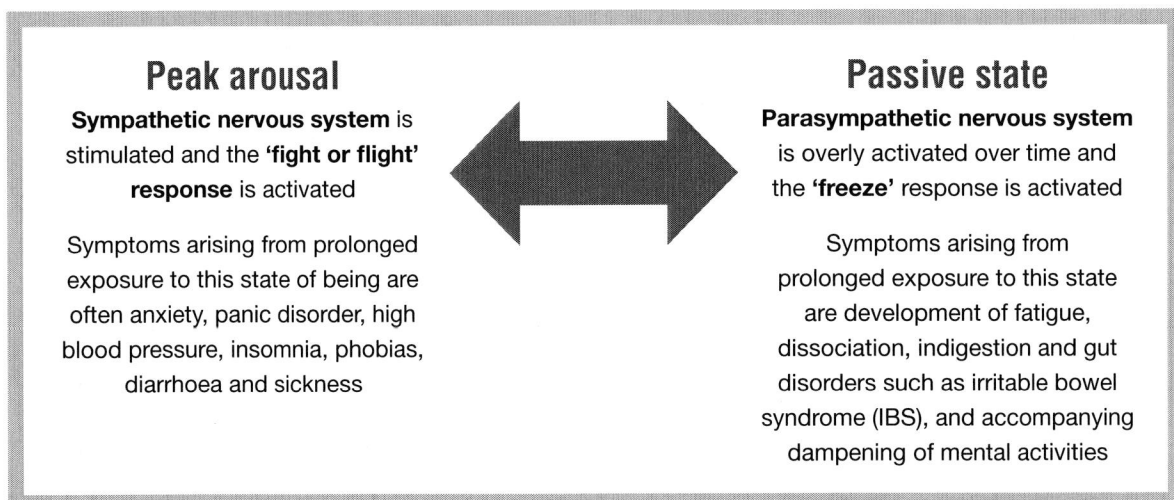

Peak arousal

Sympathetic nervous system is stimulated and the **'fight or flight' response** is activated

Symptoms arising from prolonged exposure to this state of being are often anxiety, panic disorder, high blood pressure, insomnia, phobias, diarrhoea and sickness

Passive state

Parasympathetic nervous system is overly activated over time and the **'freeze'** response is activated

Symptoms arising from prolonged exposure to this state are development of fatigue, dissociation, indigestion and gut disorders such as irritable bowel syndrome (IBS), and accompanying dampening of mental activities

Many people are aware that as mammals we are wired for fight or flight. This automatic reaction propels us into action during times of danger. Few are aware, however, that the freeze response is an equally important and related survival mechanism. In terms of hunter and prey, in the last moments of the chase, when there is literally no possibility of 'fight or flight', the victim will experience the freeze response. When 'fight or flight' is not an option our autonomic nervous system goes into a freeze response. We become immobilised energetically and most often physically at the same time.

There is a growing awareness among neuroscientists that our evolutionary heritage has a greater impact on the nervous system than was previously thought. Unlike most mammals which are able to shake off the freeze response and go into fight or flight, in some situations humans are unable to shake the freeze response mechanism and suffer the negative consequences. Many who seek counselling for relief from the symptoms of trauma are puzzled when they recall how they froze in the face of inescapable danger. Indeed, they are frequently filled with shame about their lack of ability to react more actively to the original event.

To explain the freeze response it is useful to understand the function of regulation in the nervous system. Regulation in human beings is reflected in the way the nervous system handles stress, the way it handles emotions and more generally, the way it manages energy. During a traumatic event an enormous amount of energy is released by our neuroendocrine system. If there is sufficient resiliency in the nervous system then this energy can be discharged without trauma. For some people, however, a life-threatening experience sets the stage for dysregulation, which means that the energy cannot be discharged in a timely manner. The nervous system non-consciously and physically holds onto the stress in the muscle and fascia tissue throughout the body. The energy mobilised by the perceived threat gets 'locked' into the nervous system when we go into freeze. The individual can feel wired yet exhausted at the same time.

Our survival instinct is extremely strong. It is not easily overridden by the neocortex (that is, our intentional self). You cannot tell yourself not to freeze – the body chooses. It's the optimal response at the time. Freezing does not refer simply to being motionless; it also relates to how the nervous system manages arousal during moments of traumatic stress. It is this type of response that causes some of us to develop trauma symptoms long after the danger has passed. In other words we may go into freeze yet not be aware of it.

In these situations you may not realise that you went into freeze yet several months later still be reeling from the effects of an accident. One theory is that the nervous system has not yet discharged the energy that was mobilised for fight or flight. This freeze response sometimes reveals itself when you breathe. Holding your breath and shallow breathing are both forms of freeze. The occasional deep sigh is the nervous system catching up on its oxygen intake.

This has theoretical possibility for preventing post-traumatic symptoms (Scaer, 2001). It appears that the more the nervous system is dysregulated, the greater is the tendency to move into freeze. All of this has exciting implications for techniques like EFT. Clinical practices show that integrating disrupted energy patterns during EFT tends to restore resiliency to the nervous system, a key factor in its efficient regulation.

EFT for trauma relief

The relief of trauma is one area in which EFT has a huge amount to offer. EFT can effectively be applied at any stage of trauma.

The techniques are an excellent addition to the toolbox of professionals who work alongside victims of abuse and trauma. With experience and training, they are able to offer interventions ranging from full therapy sessions to quick-fix techniques to restore calm. Table 16 outlines example applications of EFT for the various phases of trauma.

Table 16 **Applying EFT 'in the moment' or when recalling trauma**

Phase of trauma	Symptoms	Example set-ups
Shock	Senses are overwhelmed Brain is unable to process it all and begins to go emotionally numb Time, auditory and visual distortions can occur You may be aware of physical symptoms, including agitation, hyper-alertness or over-activity	**Tapping 'in the moment'** *'Even though I feel completely stuck and I don't want to move, I accept myself.'* **Tapping when recalling** *'Even though I wanted to stand up for myself I was unable to speak, I love and forgive myself.'*
Impact	Frequently brings confusion as you come to realise and assess the extent of the damage, death or injury You may become highly emotional	*'Even though I feel a stabbing in my chest about that night...'*
Recoil	Return to a near-normal state and some stable days Start of a decrease in the symptoms present during the impact phase. A gradual return of awareness, reasoning ability, recall and emotional expression	*'Even though, I am so angry that he thought he could get away with doing that...'* *'Even though some days are still painful, I choose to recognise the moments that are pleasant ...'*
Post-trauma resolution	A routine pattern; the trauma's impact shows in changes in behaviour, thinking and perception Acceptance of the event and your actions, along with a positive re-evaluation of your goals and values is possible Can be a lengthy process; without trauma resolution a strong likelihood of a chronic struggle with distress	*'Even though it was awful, I choose to be grateful that I survived...'* *'Even though I lost the man I loved, I am open to the possibility that I will feel peace again...'*

The techniques are also powerful self help and even with the most basic training EFT can be used anywhere. In the moment of a trauma situation tapping shortcuts are precious ways to calm the physiology and the emotions.

Applying EFT in an emergency for yourself or for someone else can reduce immediate symptoms and can also reduce the likelihood of the effects causing longer term problems. Simple and calm tapping on the friendly point or the collarbone are both excellent for reducing anxious feelings, panic and negative thoughts 'in the moment'. The words to tap on are less relevant as the negative disruption is already present. You are fully in touch with the feeling; just calmly tap a few points or do a couple of rounds until the stress response fades.

EFT is also extremely helpful with traumas that have been held in the body for any length of time. Energy disruptions can remain at cellular level for decades. Using EFT diminishes the various effects on the physical and mental systems, and allows a return to homeostasis. When disease and illness is already present, or symptoms of past traumas are evident, the use of EFT can still greatly enhance the body's resilience capacity.

While conventional approaches encourage a traumatised person to talk about, understand and come to terms with their experience, the issues do not always fade sufficiently. Gaining freedom in the logical or cognitive frame is not usually enough to provide emotional freedom, and the effect is that the body's energy system remains disrupted. Gentle EFT approaches (see Chapter 5) can enable intense negative emotions to be released effectively without the necessity for a very extended series of talk sessions. The results of using EFT in cases of trauma are overwhelmingly positive, especially when applied to specific events.

Table 17 **Example EFT applications for trauma**

Physical	*'I can't breathe.'*
Cognitive	*'I nearly died.'*
Emotional	*'I'm so furious with her.'*
Behaviour	*'I can't be in the house on my own anymore.'*

So an example set-up may be, *'Even though I am so furious with him...'*

Features and benefits of using EFT for trauma

- Adaptable in many applications, ranging from first-aid quick fixes to therapy sessions.
- Excellent as a self-help tool to be used anywhere, anytime, for all age groups.
- Equally suited for addressing present-day effects and underlying issues and roots.
- Immediate relief from panic and anxiety is achievable.
- Less need to talk about intense/overwhelming details.
- Addresses emotional, cognitive, behavioural and physical elements in unison.
- High success rate compared with other interventions.
- Very cost-effective therapy solution.
- Results are typically permanent.

Case study

David felt trapped with traumatic memories of his car collision, in which a motorbike passenger had been killed. His home life and his health were suffering and he was on the verge of resigning at work because he was not coping. Unable to concentrate, and finding it difficult to make simple decisions, David was also haunted with vivid flashbacks every day.

In session, the effects of trauma were gradually eased using EFT. We started to use the tearless trauma technique (described in Chapter 5). I asked David to give a general or vague title to the traumatic memory. He called it *'The collision'*. We started to use the basic routine, tapping *'Even though the collision happened, …'* We kept tapping for four rounds until David agreed that he was comfortable to move on.

Taking a couple of steps back and starting with a less intense part of the event, I asked David to describe events leading up to the actual incident while starting to tap again, using the softly, softly technique.

'Even though the light was fading and I didn't have my headlights on…'

As we progressed, the set-ups were altered.

'Even though I don't think I was paying full attention…'

'Even though he seemed to come from nowhere…'

At each new frame David and I used EFT tapping until the emotional or physical intensity reduced to a comfortable SUD level. This was further tested by inviting David to repeat the details of that portion of the event and seeing that he was able to do so without registering intensity. Several times David was tempted to add several intense aspects at once as they flooded in, but instead we gradually added each new piece to the scene only after the previous intense aspect had been sufficiently addressed and tested. Using EFT in this manner allows gradual healing and reduces the chance that any energy disrupting aspects remain.

Within a handful of sessions the flashbacks were no longer a problem for David and he continued EFT practice at home on other aspects. The following year he attended an EFT training course and happily reported that within three months of his initial EFT sessions and practice, he had cleared his relationship problems and was *'feeling normal again'*.

When working with any trauma I tend to use the full basic EFT routine with the nine gamut routine more often than the shortcut EFT recipe. The nine gamut procedure is particularly effective for facilitating the brain in reprocessing memories, and this has obvious significance when the memories are traumatic (see Chapter 3).

Removing trauma quickly using EFT

An article on trauma energetics by James Oschman (2006) explores energy psychology in terms of a high-speed electronic information processing system in the body. What is described is a connective tissue matrix that reaches into every cell in the body – a whole-person physical system that senses and absorbs the physical and emotional impact of any traumatic experience. It is suggested that the living matrix stores traumatic memories and can be resolved.

EFT is a powerful therapy which applies the principles of electromagnetic fields to medicine. It gives us access to the realm of quantum healing, and the time required to heal psychological traumas can dramatically shorten. To professionals accustomed to lengthy courses of psychotherapy, or to drug therapies, EFT can indeed seem like a miracle. All the techniques work with the body's electromagnetic signalling system to produce healing in the emotions and cells directly and quickly, without the need for extended courses of therapy, and sometimes without even needing to identify the experiences that have caused the disturbance. It is suggested by Oschman (2006, p32) that what is at work in these cases is that the techniques allow for:

> organized or non-chaotic energy to spread suddenly throughout to create new structures, functions, and order. This concept is important as a frequent observation of practitioners of energy psychology is a sudden and beneficial 'sea change' spreading throughout as trauma or other disorder is resolved, and the whole body reintegrates accordingly.

> ... stored trauma can be resolved as quickly as it was set in place. The body is continuously poised to resolve these afflictions and all of the physiological and emotional imbalances they create. This process goes to the deep energetic level that organizes or incarnates or underlies conscious experience itself. When this happens, the patient may suddenly know that the issue or discomfort will not bother them again.

Trauma in young people

Children and teens can have extreme reactions to trauma, but their symptoms may not be the same as adults. In very young children these symptoms can include:

- bedwetting, when they had learned how to use the toilet before
- forgetting how or being unable to talk
- acting out the scary event during playtime
- being unusually clingy with a parent or other adult.

Older children and teens usually show symptoms more like those seen in adults. They may also develop disruptive, disrespectful or destructive behaviours. Feelings of guilt for not preventing the traumatic events may also arise. Thoughts of revenge are also fairly common.

Post-traumatic stress disorder (PTSD)

This is a severe anxiety disorder that is the result of an individual being subjected to threatening stressful events. Violent assault, a single abusive event, extreme mental and physical duress such as torture or anything perceived as torture by the individual, natural disasters such as floods, earthquakes or tornadoes, war or terrorist bombings, automobile or plane crashes, road accidents, or any event accompanied by extreme fear and a sense of helplessness can give rise to PTSD.

It is natural to have emotional and physical symptoms after a dangerous event. Sometimes people have very serious symptoms that go away after a few weeks. This is called acute stress disorder, or ASD. The majority will recover. Not everyone who lives through a dangerous event develops PTSD, and in fact most will not. A minority, however, develop the chronic mental health problems that characterise PTSD.

Frequently, people respond to PTSD symptoms by minimising, dismissing or medicating them with alcohol, substance, over-medication of prescription drugs, self-harm or feel-good foods. Relationships are often badly affected, and divorce, unemployment, homelessness and violence are not uncommon features. If the symptoms are not recognised and treated individuals may be left feeling like they *'can't stand it', 'can't cope', 'feel like I'm losing it', or 'have no idea what's going on'.*

PTSD symptoms

Symptoms can be grouped into three categories, as described below

Re-experiencing symptoms:

- flashbacks – reliving the trauma over and over, including physical symptoms like a racing heart or sweating
- bad dreams
- frightening thoughts.

Re-experiencing symptoms can regularly cause problems in everyday routine. They can stem from the person's own thoughts and feelings or they can be triggered by words, objects or situations that are reminders of the event.

Avoidance symptoms:

- staying away from places, events or objects that are reminders of the experience
- feeling emotionally numb
- feeling strong guilt, depression or worry
- losing interest in activities that were enjoyable in the past
- having trouble remembering the dangerous event.

Things that remind a person of the traumatic event can trigger avoidance symptoms. These symptoms may cause a person to change their personal routine; for example, after a bad car accident a person who usually drives may avoid driving or riding in a car.

Hyper-arousal symptoms:

- being easily startled
- feeling tense or 'on edge'
- having difficulty sleeping and/or having angry outbursts.

Hyper-arousal symptoms are more likely to be present constantly and are independent of triggers. The effects of hyper-arousal can make the person feel stressed and angry. They may make it hard to perform daily tasks such as sleeping, eating or concentrating. Personal relationships commonly suffer too.

Factors influencing the onset of PTSD

Many factors play a part in whether or not a person will get PTSD. Risk and resilience factors are present before the trauma and others become more relevant during and after a traumatic event. The balance between the factors determines the likelihood of developing full PTSD.

Table 18 **Risk and resilience factors in PTSD**

Risk factors	Resilience factors
Living through dangerous events and traumas	Having coping strategies, or a way of getting through a trauma event and learning from it
Having a history of mental illness	Finding a support group after a traumatic event
Getting hurt	Seeking out support from other people, such as friends and family
Seeing people hurt or killed	Feeling good about one's own actions in the face of danger
Feeling horror, helplessness or extreme fear	Being able to act and respond effectively despite feeling fear
Having little or no social support after the event	
Dealing with extra stress after the event, such as loss of a loved one, pain and injury, or loss of a job or home	

Originating traumas may lie hidden for years only to surface much later when stressors trigger these unresolved memories. Sufferers can be plagued by a huge range of intense and frequent symptoms which can appear out of the blue, with no apparent cause. Trauma from childhood events can range from loss of a parent to hospitalisation, from an incident of near-drowning to anaesthesia. Events that activate unresolved childhood trauma may seem simple on the surface such as a minor car accident, minor surgery, whiplash, a move to another town, and seeing violence on TV or in real life.

Easing PTSD with EFT

It takes courage to seek help as many PTSD sufferers are embarrassed by their emotions and behaviour, and often they are simply not the same person as they used to be. PTSD is a chronic mental disorder and as it is very difficult to determine the exact cause or a good treatment using the existing standard medical paradigm.

Those who use EFT for PTSD find that results are regularly effective. Approaching an EFT practitioner qualified in handling PTSD can help ease the issues and can feel less threatening than other face-to-face interventions. A broad level of experience with EFT is required for successful elimination of the negative energy of fear and helplessness associated with PTSD. This is not the place for a novice to begin as the fear and feelings are intense and require very careful handling.

EFT has been used with war veterans suffering from chronic insomnia, nightmares and other symptoms of PTSD. Many have responded surprisingly well to EFT, despite considerable previous medical interventions. Notably successful EFT work has been done with Vietnam veterans who were still suffering decades later from extreme symptoms despite therapy and extensive medication; this work is detailed in the book *EFT for PTSD* by Gary Craig (2009). Reduction in symptoms in recent trials of EFT for war veterans suffering from PTSD after six months measured 86-90 percent (Feinstein, 2010).

With skilful EFT intense feelings from flashbacks and intrusive memories either fade or are materially reduced within a small number of sessions. Repeated use of EFT often permanently eliminates residual layers and disruptions. Energy techniques including EFT have been used in disaster operations with victims following 9/11, the London bombings in 2005 and hurricane Katrina, as well as with war trauma victims in Kosova and Rwanda.

Even more than with other stress and fear-related challenges, it is essential first to find a safe starting point for the treatment when applied to PTSD clients. The initial set-up statements need only to be vaguely suggestive of the suspected traumatic event. Used well, the gentler methods of EFT (see Chapter 5) provide a pathway for a client to revisit aspects and events while keeping the trauma and pain at a reasonable distance. With skilled guidance the SUD intensities are reduced one at a time, working through the various layers toward the core issue and being mindful of what is comfortable and safe for the client by constant and thorough testing.

The approach of EFT differs from other therapeutic interventions where substantial talking is required. The problem is that, especially with PTSD, despite reliving and rationalising events, the pain and trauma live on in your system. It does not have to be this way. Reliving pain is not necessary when using EFT and indeed it is avoided. Nor is it necessary to devise coping strategies to deal with PTSD. Using EFT, burdens are lifted in a way that is evident immediately, which adds substantially to the healing process.

Using EFT close attention is paid to the emotional reactivity of the fears, sensations and feelings that arise in relation to the suspected traumatic event. A fear is never approached further or deeper than a level dictated by complete comfort. Set-up statements are based on the truth of the emotional response of the moment, and need to be general and broad in the early PTSD treatment:

'Even though I have had this problem for so long and I don't really want to deal with it head on yet...'

This type of fear and belief is common for many who begin an EFT session for PTSD.

Case study

Liz experienced a major traumatic event in her late teens which was still having a significant negative impact on her life some 30 years later. Now aged 50, she had tried many types of talk therapy and medical intervention but was still suffering regular severe panic attacks, dizziness, a lack of self-worth and bouts of depression.

By the second EFT session Liz was making very good progress on elements of panic. She continued to tap between sessions using the suggested set-ups that we formulated together. By about the third session, and despite using some of the gentle techniques, Liz repeated her concern that she would need to tune into the real emotions of that specific event in order for it to ease. So we tapped:

'Even though, I feel the need to get my real feelings out about what happened...' This is not an unusual need. Commonly the brain goes into self-protect mode when we experience trauma. We tapped further creating new set-ups as Liz's descriptions became more detailed, *'Even though I feel that there is a mesh net all around me...'*

Liz brought her memory box to the next session. She collated the contents of the box when she worked abroad as a teenager. At the start of the session Liz left the box outside in her car: just getting it down from the shelf in her cupboard had been upsetting. We spent the next hour tapping on all the emotions that arose concerning the box and its contents, the memories, the places and people. They were all indirectly connected with the traumatic event of one evening. Finally when Liz wanted, and when testing confirmed her readiness, she retrieved a letter from the box. We continued tapping many rounds for all the aspects that arose (see the sections 'In touch with the issue literally' and 'Protection using codes' in Chapter 5):

'Even though I feel sick holding this horrible excuse letter ...'

'Even though it's 29 years since I read this horrible letter ...'

'Even though I can smell that disgusting pig now ...'

Liz had gradually managed gently to retrieve the emotions that she had felt sure would never be expressed. We also tapped extensively for the physical aspects that came up for Liz. Eventually we revisited the movie that Liz had named in a previous session. This time, Liz reported that even though the details were now more vivid, real and more connected, they strangely did not cause her any discomfort. She was able to re-tell the story without distress and she reported that it was OK to let the past fade.

Following the next few sessions and by using the personal peace process at home Liz was able finally to free herself of recurrent nightmares and of the specific events and memories that had been associated with dizziness and panic attacks.

Going back to the root

It is easy to imagine that the root of PTSD is easy to identify but this is not always the case as the origin of the challenge may be deep, below the obvious. Care is required to attend to what is being said at all times and the body's cues give vital information on progress (see Table 8 in Chapter 4).

Case study

Peter was unable to function well. PTSD had originated four years earlier while he was working as a news reporter in a war zone. Peter had been clear from the outset that he needed to accept *'my part in what happened'*, and *'to be able to talk'* in order to move on. Despite being unaware of what this meant exactly, I recognised that these aspects would require careful attention when the time was right.

In initial sessions Peter was able to relieve many of the physical and behavioural symptoms that had being plaguing him by using standard tapping techniques. We began the gradual process to clear the more intense levels of distress by using a variety of the gentle techniques outlined in Chapter 5.

Several sessions passed before it became more apparent that *'my part'* involved the death of Peter's work colleague. We continued with gentle EFT using set-ups such as *'Even though my legs are shaking at the thought of talking about that day...'*

Peter uncovered a belief in the fourth session that proved crucial to his recovery. Clues had been noted in earlier sessions when he had made references such as *'I shouldn't have let it happen'*. In this latest session, while tapping around the points, I asked him if he was able to clarify. He said slowly, *'Mum always said that mates should be there for each other'*. It emerged that Peter had been away from his team trying to negotiate new accommodation on the morning that his work partner got shot.

Even though we had already tapped on feelings and beliefs around loyalty and guilt in general using EFT, reviewing the specific writing on Peter's wall was crucial (see the section on graffiti in Chapter 6). His belief around *'mates should be there for each other'* was strong enough to provide continued resistance and prevent him from moving on. Until that point Peter had never made a conscious connection between the strong source of this underlying belief and his current guilt. Logically he knew that the connection did not make sense, but there was no doubt that his energetic body registered differently.

'Even though I was trying to get better beds for my mates, I wasn't there...' and we continued.

Using EFT to help PTSD usually involves many layers, and in this case resistance was one of these. Understandably sufferers avoid intrusion on the fearful and painful memories or on deeper earlier events that have caused the PTSD reaction. This is exactly what they feel they cannot tolerate as it would be just too intense. In time, using gentle EFT variations such as the tearless trauma technique it is possible gradually to ease the intensities using personalised set-up statements to fit an individual person and situation.

>>

Case study continued

'Even though I ... [insert problem]..., I am willing to accept my feelings without judgement...'

'Even though I ..., I am open to the possibility that...'

'Even though I ... I am ready to bring healing to...'

For someone who finds the acceptance part of the phrase difficult or unacceptable:

'Even though I don't accept myself, I am ready to begin to bring healing to ..., and I accept who I am right now ...'

Within a few hour-long sessions Peter reached natural re-frames that were not just logically true but, much more importantly, emotionally true for him. He gradually altered his own perspective until he was finally able to vocalise calmly for the first time the phrase, 'He died at my feet.' Peter showed visible relief that he was now able to begin talking about losing one of his team for the first time. Across the following months, he continued to reduce physical and emotional symptoms in further sessions.

EFT treatment has provided relief for the chronic and previously unresponsive stressful emotions of PTSD and new research programmes are in progress. In the UK, evidence-based research in EFT treatment for PSTD (alongside a host of anxiety-based issues) is being coordinated by the National EFT Research Programme. In the USA, the Iraq Vets Stress Project[1] is a recent initiative of Soul Medicine Institute. It was set up in a non-profit research and teaching institution to assist troops returning from combat to release PSTD and other emotional distress.

Abuse

Abuse is an ugly feature in every society and has many guises, including domestic abuse, violence, recurrent physical abuse, emotional abuse, sexual abuse, emotional and physical neglect.

Some of the psychological and physical symptoms associated with abuse include:

worry	guilt	fear	anger	health issues
anxiety	conflicting feelings	self-harm and injury	mental illness	alcohol and substance abuse
embarrassment and shame	depression	phobias	panic attacks	suicide
relationship difficulties	pain without physiological cause	low self-worth	stress	denial and repression

Abuse is often referred to as the 'silent problem' because people are either afraid to tell, having been threatened, or are too young or too ashamed to put what has happened into words. Conflicting feelings around the abuse can result in shame, resentment, guilt, self-blame and a sense of betrayal. Very often victims will have a fearful view of the world if they have been abused as children. Generally decision-making skills are reduced at least temporarily and because normal trust has typically been damaged feelings are commonly repressed. If victims close themselves off, they may begin to feel helpless which can have long-lasting effects on future relationships and emotional health.

EFT has been used extensively to clear the intensity attached to emotional and physical aspects of abuse for adults and children. In most cases, with expert help, the feelings of anger, fear or guilt fade away and with repeated applications are eliminated permanently. Gentle techniques of EFT are employed which means that the person does not have to relive the trauma details when this would be too intense. At each step using EFT energy disruptions are addressed, allowing the effects of anxiety and the other attached negative emotions to dissolve.

Emotional abuse

Emotional abuse is a serious form of violence but the damaging effects may be underplayed in cases where physical violence is absent. It can include elements of rejection, degrading of self-worth, and can include humiliation, exploitation and insulting behaviour. All forms of emotional abuse, whether they involve terrorising or isolating a person, are a cruel way of controlling people through fear.

A client who had suffered terrible abuse wrote:

> *'EFT has given me my life back in a way that I had not dared to believe possible. Those vivid, sordid memories that used to flash before me virtually every hour are now in some a dusty vault that I have no interest in. I am creating new movies for my future.'*

Many EFT practitioners are able to offer specialised help in this area and in recent years increasing numbers of practitioners from professional support agencies have become qualified in EFT. Tapping offers the opportunity for emotional resolution in a safe and gentle way by addressing and healing the successive negative aspects connected the abuse of an individual.

Sexual abuse

> *'I suffered repeated sexual abuse as a child for about six years. As a young adult I drank too much and got hooked on drugs. I entered a rehab unit at 30 and I have been in many forms of therapy and programmes since.*
>
> *My saving grace was being introduced to a great EFT therapist three years ago. We covered ground where no one had been, not even me. I do not know myself now. I no longer have the nightmares, my depression is … well, it isn't!*
>
> *I have looked at the sky for the first time - literally.*
>
> *I am alive and beginning to live'*
> **EFT client**

Gentle EFT techniques were employed to help this client. He was comfortable with the movie technique and code words which helped him approach and clear the negative emotions around each memory and event safely and without any significant abreaction.

In between sessions when some positive movement has been made many clients choose set-up statements to continue the healing process. Creating set-up statements that focus on where they would like to be in the future provides a personal and safe focus on the goals of wellbeing and greater empowerment even though this may not yet feel entirely achievable. Fortunately, under the right conditions our subconscious can attend to goals like these for us (see the section 'The Reticular activating system' in Chapter 7). This begins to bridge the gap between the not-so-pleasant here and now to a place of relief and comfort, for the first time in a long time. Set-up statements can be adapted to suit, such as:

'Even though I am utterly overwhelmed by my past, I allow myself to feel safe right now...'

'Even though my past is haunting me, I am learning how to release it...'

'Even though he controlled me, I am choosing to claim my life back now...'

Like other EFT practitioners I am introduced to countless clients who have been in therapy for years but still remain very troubled. Often they have learned to cope in the cognitive sense but they have not resolved their deeply painful issues on an emotional or energetic level, and so day-to-day existence continues in anguish. Thankfully, using EFT regularly provides the way to resolve the layers of pain gently by recreating energy disruptions piece by piece and rebalancing the body's energy each time.

Case study

Last year, I met Michael, aged 21. He was not impressed that he had spent so much time talking (and not talking) in other therapies. He had gained insights about himself and his situation across the years but his body still held on to significant disruptions and therefore the negative effects remained.

In desperation he had come across EFT during his own research and wanted to *'give it a go as nothing else has helped me'*. As we started our first session Michael said, *'I always feel the same'* and when I asked him to clarify, he reduced his emotional state down to one word *'S**t'*.

He then added, tongue-in-cheek, *'The only difference is that I know that I have chronic stress due to the physical and emotional abuse by my drug-taking mum – but it still feels like s**t to me!'*

I love working with young people. Other clients are not always so direct but being direct is key in EFT as the words go directly back into the set-up statements.

We started *'Even though I feel like "here I go again", she wants to hear why I feel s**t ....'* Michael had to laugh with the statement but he engaged immediately and continued to make superb progress in many areas.

>>

Case study continued

EFT is so different in that the client is empowered from the start to create their own set-up statements and clear their energy system. By facilitating the EFT process using skills and experience the practitioner and client are engaged on a journey chosen by the client.

The last time I checked, Michael was currently feeling *'sweegy'* – which is apparently good!

Chapter 13
Health and healing

Chapter 13 Health and healing

It is difficult not to be really enthusiastic about the potential of EFT in the healing arena. The techniques gently heal the mind and body, and in the hands of trained practitioners and health care staff they produce remarkable clinical results that are astonishing even to the most casual observer. In the hands of patients, carers and families and the young, basic techniques have delivered equally dramatic shifts in symptoms and pain.

The principles of tapping can be learned easily, making EFT the empowering self-care toolkit of the 21st century.

EFT is non-invasive, and it makes sense to consider the techniques as the first option to consider seriously before medication or surgery in a huge range of cases. Increasing numbers of health care workers, NHS staff, speech and language professionals, and GP counsellors choose to employ EFT daily. The techniques offer extremely cost-effective, quick and efficient solutions when compared with other interventions and therapies. The issues and case examples offered in this chapter are just a small collection from my personal records but the applications within health care appear to be almost limitless.

Despite the safe nature of EFT, it is wise to consult appropriate medical opinion to manage any persistent health issues.

EFT health and healing pathways

Health issues can be approached from two angles.

- General: using EFT as a daily lifestyle technique encourages good energy flow in the body. While not focusing directly on any health issue, this can create within your body an energetic environment that supports your overall health, vitality and healing. The cumulative effect of gratitude tapping is attractive (see the section on attitude to gratitude in Chapter 8).

- Focused: by bringing to mind a health concern and working on the physical and emotional aspects and underlying beliefs, the targeted effects of EFT work very efficiently. As the aspects of the health concern are addressed one by one, the mind and body increase in strength and the health condition improves.

Healthy option scanning

Most people find that they have a recurrent health issue that keeps coming back. Perhaps it is a dodgy knee, a stomach upset or frequent headaches. Messaging signals call our attention – *'Hello, could you please attend to me?'*, but in our busy lives most people are disconnected from the constant feedback that is offered and we are usually too distracted to notice the subtle messages. So, we do not notice the shoulder tension caused by work stress, for instance, until a more painful spasm occurs. Left too long, subtle messages turn into health problems and the worst-case outcome is longer term damage and disease.

A healthy method to take note of these timely messages is to adopt a simple scanning technique as a regular mini health check. The healthy option scanning exercise below helps to flag up early signs that you can act on using EFT. This does not mean that you are going to be focusing obsessively on what is going wrong; it is just a simple way to be mindful. Investing a little time to do some checks and you could save years of treatment or medication in the longer run.

Case study

Angie suffered with severe panic attacks for years and was virtually housebound. Despite the many facets of her problems, the progress with EFT was impressive. Angie's days were becoming a lot calmer and she was able to cope more easily, but she was still getting migraines and had problems with her wisdom teeth. Doing a two-minute body scanning exercise, Angie had the answer for herself.

She discovered that she was unconsciously clenching her jaw at the first sign of stress, on and off throughout the day and night. We used EFT on a variety of her stresses and limiting beliefs. The symptoms of the physical issues faded even though we did not tap on them directly.

Angie created a healthy option tapping exercise for stress using worksheets and puts this to use whenever she feels the need.

Healthy option Exercise 1: scan

Tune into your body and mind to discover your healing pathway.

1 Sit somewhere comfortable and place your feet flat on the floor. Unfold your arms and rest your hands in your lap. Close your eyes and take a few nice easy deep breaths. Alternatively lie flat and relax.

2 Once you are resting comfortably let your mind run a healthy option scan slowly through your body from head to toe, paying attention to any aches, pains, stiffness or congestion in your energy. Take your time as you do this. You will notice parts of your body that require attention.

3 Make a mental note of how you would assess each sensation. Perhaps you will use some sub-modality descriptions (what size, shape, colour, texture or sound?), an SUD measurement, or ask yourself a question such as, *'What is that ache or pain saying?'*

4 Continue this process as you move through your body. Identify any limb, organ or structure that is asking for attention. If you have lots going on then you may need someone to take notes. Pay attention also to the outer boundaries of your body.

5 When you have completed the scan, review what you have found and choose one to start using with EFT. Adopt any of the tapping methods you have learned that suits what you have found: these might include: managing pain, emotional aspect, beliefs, internal tapping, conflicts, parts, gratitude that your body is sending you a message, choices .... Tapping can use positive set-up statements with gratitude on the areas of your body that are functioning well, and you can even tap on some functions that you may never have noticed or paid attention to before.

The details revealed in this exercise can be quite profound for some people. It may be the first time that you have really attended to your body's needs. Present health and emotional issues can arise to the surface as well as past unresolved issues. By using the scan exercise regularly you can track your progress and become more mindful of those early messages.

Reproduced from: Tapping for Healthy Options 2008 ©

Metaphors in health and healing

Words are so powerful and metaphors that are woven through our language reveal a rich source of information about our emotions and beliefs as they are usually uttered unconsciously. By actively listening to your own metaphors and those of others, interesting patterns can be noted. *'My shoulder is giving me grief'* begs the question; *'Who is it that is giving you grief?'* Listen to your metaphors about life. If *'life's a struggle'* is one of yours then guess what – it will be!

Case study

A local GP recommended that Nick attend a programme of EFT sessions. He had hypertension, irritable bowel and anger issues at work. With initial contact on the phone, Nick described his workplace as being like a war zone – *'the battlefield, the conflict, defeat, ammunition and the enemy'* – all within a couple of minutes. It sounded exhausting for Nick.

When we met, he talked about his *'wounded pride'* and *'a time bomb in his chest'*. His job? He was a primary school teacher. Within a few EFT sessions, Nick addressed some past issues around *'letting go'* as well as some limiting beliefs that he figured needed revaluation. Physical symptoms began to fade within the first few weeks and he also began to notice changes in his outlook.

Across the course of a couple of months Nick began to find it easier to notice and alter his language patterns. Luckily EFT techniques helped him discover the patterns and source of his 'battles' in a natural, unthreatening way. We used another healthy options exercise to help.

>>

Case study continued

Now Nick describes his career in terms of a journey (a description that he naturally found during a session). Working with EFT, we revisited many of his original 'battles'. Several months later when I was running a workshop within his school he contributed with his colleagues:

'... one of the main things that I learned about myself using these techniques is that everything used to be about victory or defeat; now I choose to take a walk and everybody survives.'

Further metaphor links showed up during Nick's sessions. He found that the friendly point (FP) and little finger (LF) were powerful release points for him. Interestingly, these points are on the heart and small intestine meridians which were both areas that had been giving him physical problems. In Chinese medicine terms, 'letting go of the old' is how these meridians are described when energy is flowing freely through both meridians. It was so fascinating to hear Nick use this very phrase during our first session even though he had no prior knowledge of the emotional acupuncture system. For those interested, a simple summary of the emotions associated with meridians and organs is supplied in Appendix 2.

Case study

Jan had had a hernia for the last 12 years. She was on medication and was waiting for a surgery date. She had booked EFT sessions to try to give up smoking, to deal with general worry and to get better sleep. Many layers and aspects came up during the first couple of sessions and interesting metaphors gave some clues to underlying patterns and beliefs. All of the outcomes surprised Jan.

When reviewing her intake form at the beginning of the first session, I asked Jan about her hernia and her proposed surgery. She told me that none of this bothered her and that everything was in hand.

We covered the basics of tapping by doing some tapping on the global topic of worry. Some of her statements included: 'I worry for England, but only at night', 'I can't sort the problems out', 'things just go round and round', and 'I feel powerless to sort any thing out'. As we progressed Jan scanned her body to try to locate her worry. It was in her gut – the place of her hernia – but Jan was quite clear that she was not bothered by the hernia. I invited her to tune into the worry feeling.

>>

Case study continued

'It's a coil ... hot ... and tight ..., about the size of a clock.' We continued tapping on the many aspects connected with worry and frustration at home and at work. *'I worry and I get upset but I just can't sort things out ...'* This phrase sounded interesting and had popped up in various forms several times, but I mentally shelved it for a moment until we had finished tapping and measuring on the current aspects.

We continued, *' Even though, I have this hot red coil of a clock that gets wound up every day ...',* The SUD measurements on the coil were now down to a 4, but I sensed that there was still more to this.

While we continued to tap, I asked, *'When was the first time you remember this coiled feeling?'* Jan was very clear about this. Initially as she spoke and tapped she was unaffected emotionally. There was no discernable SUD reading so we continued.

Jan tapped and told me that from the age of 4 she was *'a good girl'* she *'went to bed and didn't get up'.* But night after night for 12 years there were fierce rows between her parents as soon as her bedroom door was closed. Key statements picked out to go into set-ups included: *'I couldn't sort it out', 'I wanted to be brave', 'my feelings went round and round', 'the lessons I learned at night', 'I couldn't say anything', 'I was powerless', 'the feelings went round and round', 'look where it got me!'* Jan tapped and realised that the coil of worry in her gut that had wound up from the age of 4 was the worry she was still holding. The connected message was that she could never do anything to sort it out. As a child, she lay in bed every night with the worry going *'round and round'.*

During two sessions we covered a lot of feelings, beliefs and metaphors.

Because of various circumstances we did not get together for the next three months until Jan sent me an email to book on to a workshop.

'Hi Christine ... As you know, I continued tapping, a bit here and there ... I've been promoted at work. I go to sleep peacefully every night and I do not use any hernia medication and the surgery is cancelled. I forgot to mention to you before that I don't smoke any more – I just didn't fancy them any more (22 years – but not a heavy smoker anyway). I also laughed the other night when I shut my bedroom door and realised that I do it now without feeling anxious at all. I have never liked my door shut at night but never knew why. It was always difficult for me to stay in hotels because I disliked the door being shut at night. Now it doesn't bother me at all.'

Pain

'EFT offers great healing benefits'
Deepak Chopra

Properly applied, a high proportion of people reduce the emotional contribution to pain within a few minutes and, depending on the underlying cause, the results can be long-lasting. Pain relief techniques without medication or surgery are surely worth a try and can work equally well as a self-help method or practised with an EFT practitioner.

EFT is employed to address the causes of pain in a way that is largely outside the western medical approach. This is why EFT often works in pain relief for so many people where none of the usual methods have worked. The techniques address the energy disruptions in the body which are the cause of negative emotions.

- **Disrupted subtle energies**
  The free flow of subtle energy in our body is vital to our health. Repairing any disruptions in these subtle energies with EFT can lead to symptom reduction and pain relief.

- **Negative emotions**
  It is a well-established medical fact that our emotions trigger chemicals in our bodies. Joyous emotions can produce healing chemicals while negative emotions of all descriptions (anger, trauma, fear, confusion) can trigger disease-causing chemistry in our systems; for instance, stress might contribute to ulcers or high blood pressure. Negative emotions can therefore be a major source of pain. When EFT is used to address negative emotions pain subsides.

The EFT process addresses both of these elements simultaneously and regularly provides us with the catalyst to alleviating the underlying causes of poor health. EFT well deserves its description by Gary Craig:

'the universal healing aid, as the benefit extends well beyond pain management.'

Managing pain with EFT

Sometimes pain just shifts while using EFT on another issue like past trauma, anger, grief, sadness. At other times, you may want to do EFT while focusing specifically on pain in the body.

Here are three ways to work with pain in the body.

1 Focus on the actual pain

'Even though I have this tight wrench feeling at the base of my spine...'

'Even though I have this red pulsating knot headache in the front of my head...'

'Even though I have this spongy numbness in my lower legs..."

Sometimes this alone is enough to reduce the SUD to zero. Amazing results can be achieved in pain reduction even in severe migraine cases and with kidney stone spasms.

Careful checking and testing along the way is essential, as expected. Other aspects that are present will mask and interfere with overall progress. If progress does seems slow, then it is likely that by turning attention to tapping on the emotional content of pain better progress will be achieved.

2 Focus on how you feel about the pain

'Even though I'm afraid that this tightness in my fingers will mean I can't type anymore...'

'Even though I'm worried that she'll get fed up looking after me...'

'Even though I'm frightened that I'll never get rid of this...'

'Even though I'm annoyed that I can't train in the gym...'

3 Find an emotion or quality in the pain or in the part of the body affected

'Even though I have this resentment in my fingers....'

'Even though I have this worry in my lower back – I worry who will support me if she gets fed up?...'

'Even though I have this shame/grief/sadness [whatever it is] in my...'

Residual pain

A sudden event, shock or accident can leave us in pain for a considerable time after any physical injury has healed. Using EFT to address the underlying emotional content of any accident or illness can vastly improve the healing rate of residual pain.

Case study

Gerry still had residual neck pain from an old car accident. He used EFT on the physical aspects but, unexpectedly for him, blame and anger showed up.

'Even though I'm sure he wasn't looking in my direction when he came at me head on...'

'Even though I have spiky purple spasms of anger on the right side of my neck...'

Steadily working through the layers using EFT, Gerry released his unresolved feelings of anger at the other driver. The neck pain faded that day and he has not been troubled by it since. This is by no means an uncommon occurrence when using EFT.

If you are under treatment by your doctor for chronic or recurring pain and are looking for additional relief from this stress, you may find EFT effective, easy to learn and quick acting. EFT offers a drug-free approach to managing your pain better.

Caution, however: be mindful of the fact that pain is the body's warning that something is wrong. You are advised to seek medical advice for any significant symptoms before treating them with EFT.

Communication and speech difficulties

EFT works extremely well on a huge range of emotional and physical aspects of many speech disorders such as forms of mutism, stuttering, developmental delays and exceptional needs.

Mutism

Case study

Sean's voice did not return following a throat infection. He did not speak at all. He had several visits to his GP, hospital specialists and to a speech team, yet no physical reason could be determined. Following many assessments, he was diagnosed with a form of traumatic mutism.

Six months on, despite speech therapy and regular interventions, Sean, now aged 12, had made no improvement. He did not display signs of social anxiety but did not vocalise in any setting despite great determination on his part.

After just two EFT sessions Sean was making tiny – and I mean tiny – croaks of a whisper. He tapped every day at home using the tapping song (a song written and recorded by teenage tappers which provides an easy to use general energy system workout for daily use for all ages) and using a tapping routine at bedtime. We had two more sessions, which were a mix of webcam and skype messaging, before returning for his check up with the speech therapist. His voice came back gradually and he was absolutely delighted with himself.

Sean was able to settle back into school life, which had been severely disrupted. He has had no further problems. Two key areas had been very important and were resolved using EFT:

- the need to calm feeling around several specific emotional events of family hostility and his interpretation of them

- anger and frustration about *'What the expert said'* to him early on in his illness, which centred around, *'Don't speak at all for as long as possible, as it might cause damage to your throat'*.

During this time tapping had become a family affair. Connected both energetically and emotionally, several members of the family joined in family EFT sessions. Mum had tapped on:

- her worry about whether Sean would get his voice back

- guilt, anger and feelings of inadequacy connected with underlying tensions at home that had contributed to stress over the last couple of years

- annoyance at how stupid the expert advice had been, especially as she had continued to back up this advice at home with *'Don't talk, Sean; remember the doctor told you that you will damage your throat if you talk.'*

>>

Case study continued

Sean's speech team took an interest in EFT:

'There is a need for tools like EFT in the recovery for clients with stress-related symptoms. EFT fills a huge gaping hole in addressing the patient's emotional needs. It provides superb results quickly and efficiently and often on the spot. We are now in training to use EFT techniques within our team', J. Taylor, speech and language therapist

Stroke recovery

Physical and emotional relief using EFT in stroke recovery can be gained quickly, although persistence may be needed in some cases. Friends and family can help too if invited! Any restriction in accessing all tapping points need not be a problem. Remember that physically reaching a few tapping points, comfortably, is more important than trying to stretch to them all.

Table 19 **EFT application in stroke recovery**

Trauma	Circumstances of stroke, shock, acceptance, denial
Frustration	Having to do exercises, slow communication, lack of understanding, not being able to find the right words, not being mobile, inability to write, unable to cope, lack of control, people over-compensating by filling in the gaps and not allowing the person to try to speak, move, help themselves
Embarrassment	In public, with friends, family, hygiene, pride, privacy, speech and communication, looking different, being different
Guilt	Dependent on family members, beliefs around cause of stroke
Loneliness	Silent world, inability to get out and about, change in identity
Worry	Money issues, relationships, responsibility, coping, ability to recover
Anger	Why me? Why is it taking so long to recover? Treatment and quality of care
Lack of hope	Beliefs around getting better, giving up, pace of recovery
Jealousy	Envy of able bodied, loss of function
Sadness and grief	Loss of former self, loss of identity
Physical	Loss of movement and speech, speech dysphagia (swallowing difficulties, muscle restriction), pain

Internal tapping

A useful addition for managing wellbeing is internal tapping. For stroke patients or anyone who is unable to tap for themselves the complete tapping routine can be performed in the mind. With a little focus, the effect can be just as powerful.

Instead of using your fingers to tap, you put your intentional mind to use. Even if you are not tapping or saying the phrase out loud, your intention on the tapping points will clear disrupted energy in the body, encouraging calm, peace and positive emotions. Even though it sounds odd, internal tapping works very effectively.

Select an issue, emotional or physical, or if you are 'in the moment' then that is the issue.

Using SUD, rate the issue. Relax and sense your body as best you can.

Create a short set-up phrase like *'Angry with him, accept'*.

Focus your mind or energy on your friendly point (FP) and focus on the phrase; for example, *' Anger with him, accept'*. Say or whisper it. Continue internal tapping for a round, and test and assess as normal.

Other tapping methods

You can also adapt the internal tapping technique described above for tapping in bed to help you go to sleep or for going back to sleep if wakefulness is an issue.

'I find internal tapping very useful when I'm having difficulty getting to sleep. If I'm comfortable in bed, it saves me waving my hands around, making me cold or distracting me from relaxation. It also means that you can get the benefits of tapping without disturbing a partner's sleep too. After years of insomnia, I have never slept so well or so much!

I also use internal tapping when I'm in a conspicuous place and feel awkward about drawing attention to myself. I imagine tapping my upper chest point (which works as a good release point for me) and give myself permission to relax'

Rosie

While I tend to encourage people to tap on their own energy system (mainly to experience personal empowerment), particularly in the case of stroke patients, great results can be achieved by tapping on the person. In this way family members can gently help those patients who are unable to tap for themselves to address the physical and emotional aspects present. The effect is often powerful and helpful to both. Surrogate tapping is also a fascinating variation which brings significant results in many cases (see the section in Chapter 14).

Chronic illnesses and serious diseases

EFT has revealed significant relief for patients of chronic illnesses and serious diseases. Most practitioners aided relief in a range of issues including cystic fibrosis, chronic fatigue syndrome, fibromyalgia, Parkinson's disease, multiple chemical sensitivity, arthritis, asthma, sciatica, diabetes and hypertension.

'I have Lupus, an auto-immune disease. My immune system creates antibodies which, instead of protecting my body from bacteria and viruses, attacks and destroys my tissues. In the past, on some days the pain was too much to bear and I had very limited movement. I have had steroid treatment and physical therapy.

Three years ago when I just couldn't bear the pain any more, I was told about EFT. Frankly I didn't hold out much hope, but I was also desperate. After being guided through a tapping sequence for about 10 minutes, the excruciating pain in my wrist had gone completely. That was too weird to describe. I couldn't believe it! I kept mentally searching throughout my body for the pain. It just wasn't there!

I still get pain a lot of the time and life gets on top of me some days, but tapping definitely helps or I wouldn't bother with it.'

Strategies for restoring health

Some strategies will be appropriate in one case and not another and the list below is presented in no particular order. Additional details of the techniques are outlined in earlier chapters.

- **Daily tapping** – many rounds of EFT tapping are recommended daily to keep the body's subtle energies flowing freely. An easy way for the client to remember to tap is to associate it with a regular and convenient time of the day.

- **Tap for symptoms and then emotions** – starting EFT with *'Even though I have this numbness in my left hand...'* will often give symptomatic relief. If the symptoms do not fully relieve, then emotional drivers may be present. Ask, *'If there were an emotional reason for this symptom, what could it be?'* and proceed to a suitable set-up statement based on the response.

- **Metaphors** – listen out for metaphors and meanings. Ask questions to elicit meanings, such as *'What does the hot itching look like inside your body?'* or *'What does your doctor tell you is going on?'* which produce rich and informative responses. Create fresh set-ups and apply EFT such as, *'Even though it feels like I have someone really irritating in my joints ...'* or *'Even though he said that it would probably always be a nuisance to me...'* If working with someone else, take care to avoid over-interpreting what is being said by the other person. Remember, the key is that you are facilitating the process. Take care not to get attached to the outcome or know the answers. You remain on the side-lines at all times checking your understanding of what is going on and never leading the other person where you feel it is best for them to go.

- **Employing gentler techniques** – softly, softly technique, tearless trauma technique, movie technique and tell the story technique are all designed to suit applications when reducing the initial intensity of potentially upsetting memories is advisable (refer to Chapter 5).

- **Being specific** – when the requirement to be gentle is less of an issue then the most efficient strategy is to attend to the specifics of an issue. Getting to the identifiable basics of *'I have hypertension'* permits substantial improvement of the underlying problem; so, for instance it is better to use a more specific set-up such as *'Even though my blood pressure is 170/95...'* or, *'Even though I can feel my chest thumping and it frightens me...'*

- **Emphasis** – getting connected with the issue is always important before the negative energy patterns fade. For some people, tuning into emotion is challenging but necessary before the patterns will shift and healing can occur. If this is proving difficult then strongly emphasising the EFT set-up statements and reminder phrases is a very effective way to increase the connectivity. This may mean raising your voice level, imitating a voice or any gestures or body movements in order to increase the emphasis and re-create negative energy patterns. This can turn a 'go-nowhere' session into a productive one.

- **Get to the core issue** – By using variations on the questions here while performing continuous tapping on the friendly point or around the tapping points, material usually emerges which if fed into further set-up statements leads the way to clearing core issues.

  If an emotional contributor to that symptom existed, what could it be?

  If you had life to live over again, what person or event would you prefer to skip?

  What would it be like to have none of your symptoms?

  What benefits are you getting from this illness?

  What would you have to give up if your illness went away?

  Who or what are you most angry at?

  Why might you deserve this illness?

- **Chasing the pain** – one principle of EFT, as mentioned above, is that when appropriate it is more effective when we are able to focus on the specific. This is just as relevant when addressing pain and healing using EFT as the location of pain typically moves and/or changes in intensity or quality, and needs to be tracked. For example, before tapping a round, when assessing discomfort a toothache might be described as *'a throbbing ache in my upper right jaw'* with an SUD intensity of 8. After some rounds of tapping, typically the location, sub-modality description and intensity will all have shifted when they are assessed. The toothache may now be described as *'a dull hazy throbbing in my gum'*, with an SUD intensity of 4. By 'chasing the pain' using EFT and closely attending to the specifics of what is happening, the negative effects will usually go to zero or some low number. In the process, the emotional issues behind the discomfort can also collapse.
  This provides a very powerful and effective way to help erase an intense emotional issue where physical symptoms are also present, which they usually are. By tackling the physical symptoms first and chasing the pain as these symptoms shift, you will often collapse the related emotional issue without ever having to deal with it directly.

- **Allergies** – the fact that many allergies or substance sensitivities have been treated successfully with EFT again shows that there is often a mental/emotional component as well as a physical component to these kinds of issue. Frequently the emotional trouble manifests itself as a symptom in the body and this perhaps is the body's way of drawing our attention to the problem. Some EFT practitioners specialise in treating allergies.

- **Testing** – thorough and consistent testing is a very important step as, without it, you can wrongly think that aspects and an issue have been sufficiently healed. To test the erosion of an aspect try if possible to re-enact a bothersome memory; or vividly imagine it to see if you can get upset; or bend, move or do whatever is necessary to bring back the symptom (taking care, of course). If careful testing is not carried out then you risk other aspects or related issues showing up in the future, keeping the overall issue supported.

- **Personal peace procedure** – this procedure which was outlined in Chapter 5 is an especially beneficial course of action to follow at home using EFT on a daily basis to collapse each item on the list, health-related or otherwise. The more negative disruptions that can be removed, the greater the chances of regaining long-term health and peace.

- **Humour** – laughter can be used sensitively to help clients create new associations regarding the severity of any emotional issues they may have. It is a very good intuitive a form of testing progress but excellent rapport skills and trust are essential if working with someone else.

- **Imagine perfect health and observe tail-enders** – by vividly imagining perfect health (that is, completely without symptoms) we can tune into any resistance that shows up as self-talk or secondary benefits (see Figure 6). These are the subtle emotional aspects that can be powerful enough to hijack us into subconsciously holding on to ailments. By identifying the clues to the real impediments to healing we can use EFT as an antidote.

- **Introducing choices and gratitude** – when some significant negative disruptions have been shifted it becomes appropriate to inject positive direction into healing by using set-up phrases of the form, *'Even though my body is holding on to so much ache, I choose trust my body to let go of some...'* (see Chapter 6).

Introducing healthy options tapping

As an extension of positive choices in EFT, here is another exercise from the healthy options tapping handbook. It is a quick and easy workout for the energy system for anyone who has difficulty with blood sugar level.

Perform this healthy option routine for a few minutes daily.

Healthy option Exercise 2: energy balancing for blood sugar levels

The points used in this exercise correspond with your spleen, pancreas, kidney, liver and triple warmer meridians whose functioning are all important for balancing blood sugar levels.

Table 20 **Tapping points for balance of blood sugar levels**

Tapping point	Location	Meridian
Both collarbone (CB) points	Shallow depressions below each collarbone	Kidney
Both under arm (UA) points	Approx 10cm below armpit	Spleen/pancreas
Both nine gamut (NG) points	In the crease on back of hand between little finger and ring finger	Triple warmer
Both liver points	For men, approx 2.5cm below the nipple. For females, beneath the breast, one rib down.	Liver point

Healthy option Exercise 2: energy balancing for blood sugar levels

1 Choose a positive image that helps you feel relaxed and positive about your health. Perhaps you can call to mind a specific image of a happy holiday, a smile from a loved one on a special day, taking in a sea view when the sunset was stunning. Relax, breathe slowly in and out, and as you do test this image. If it feels good, make it bigger, brighter, bolder, recreate the sounds. Use all your senses. Relax. If you detect any negative triggers associated with the image, so that it does not feel good, switch the image and try again. For this exercise, avoid scenes that are going to conjure up any negatives.

2 Select a short, positive healthy option phrase. It can be anything that makes you feel good and positive. Relax, breathe in and out slowly, and say it out loud slowly three times. Examples can be, *'sunny relaxation'*, *'no worries'*, *'feeling in balance'*, *'I thank my body for healing'*.

Alternatives to Steps 1 and 2:

If you have knowledge of the reasons for your blood sugar problem and you would like to be specific on this, then example set-ups could be: *'I choose to let my immune system relax'* (suitable for Type 1 diabetes), *'I choose to let my insulin receptors do their job easily'* (suitable for Type 2 diabetes). Create a visual image that represents what you are saying.

3 Start tapping on your collarbone points (CB) as you gently breathe in and out, repeating your phrase slowly and imagining your happy or healthy scene. You can tap on both collarbones at the same time and cross over your hands if you wish. If you are able to focus easily then you can continue by visualising the image and repeating the phrase silently five times.

4 Switch to tapping on your under arm (UA) points, visualising and feeling the image and saying your phrase. Here you can tap 'monkey style' (the name given by young people tapping under both arms at the same time like a monkey) or cross arms over.

5 Continue on the nine gamut (NG) points on either hand and then on the liver points.

Relax and thank your body for doing a marvellous job. This exercise is also great to boost vitality and the immune system.

Notes:
1 If you have reasons to believe that you have resistance to balancing out your blood sugar or feeling negative then you can always start a regular tapping round on your friendly point.
2 It is not essential to tap on both sides of your body at the same time. Tap where you can and as you like.

(Reproduced from: Tapping for Healthy Options 2008©)

Negative feelings and hopelessness

It is difficult to feel positive in the face of particular health issues but holding negative beliefs about the potential to heal creates even more negative emotions. Fear, frustration, depression and anxiety all stand in the way of healing. Test out your beliefs about your own ability to heal and ask *'How true is that for you?'* to provide specific material that may be tapped on (see section in Chapter 6). For instance if your true current belief is 'I don't know why this had to happen to me now' the VOC measure may initially be a 7. A suitable set-up statement could be, *'Even though I don't know why this had to happen to me now, I deeply and completely love and accept myself.'*

By stating a desired outcome, *'I have pain-free days'* or *'I enjoy my worry-free life'*, the feedback or the tail-enders that pop up could be, *'Me, never'*, *'It's all I can remember'*, *'I just can't imagine it'* or *'I wouldn't know who I was without worry'*.

Set-up statements can then be created which address the negative view of your ability to heal:

'Even though I wouldn't be me without worry, I accept that I'm doing the best that I can ...'

'Even though I am frightened that I won't get better, I love myself and all my parts ...'

'Even though my stomach has always given me trouble, I'm willing to notice the parts that are working well...'

'Even though I feel hopeless, I'm not beyond God's help [or any variation]...'

'Even though I have no idea how I can heal, I accept that I can heal anyway.'

Create set-up statements that have meaning for you and tap on them. Relief from negative feelings and helplessness by clearing the tail-enders improves your overall success with healing.

Depression

It is no surprise that the negative emotions associated with depression tend to generate many more physical ailments. In addition, side-effects of medication can contribute to a number of physical problems.

Depression responds well to EFT in comparison with other interventions. Specific events and beliefs can be addressed using gentle EFT methods. In a great number of cases when EFT is used skilfully the depressed feelings vanish or are materially reduced. As the depression symptoms abate, so do numerous physical ailments.

Introducing more positive choices as progress starts to be made often helps for 'the light at the end of the tunnel' to become a reality (choice statements are in Chapter 6). Repeated applications of EFT often eliminate these feelings permanently so that they no longer reappear.

Chronic fatigue syndrome

EFT is an ideal set of techniques in the support and recovery of chronic fatigue syndrome to address aspects such as, energy levels, general health, tension, stress, depression, outlook and unresolved underlying issues and beliefs.

As low energy is a key issue in many chronic conditions including chronic fatigue, following this exercise from the Healthy Options Tapping handbook may help. Perform this daily healthy option routine for a few minutes.

Healthy option Exercise 3: gaining energy

Table 21 **healthy option**

Tapping point	Location
Top of head (TH)	On midline, slightly forward of centre
Wrists	Both inside and outside – approximately 2–3cm from the hand crease
Ankles	Inside and outside – approximately 2–3cm above ankle bone

Healthy option Exercise 3: gaining energy

1 Choose a positive image that reminds you of healthy energy. It could be a real memory like a walk by the sea or just something that helps you feel energetic like a windmill or a jet-ski ride. Relax and breathe. Close your eyes, test your image, breathe slowly in and out. If it feels good, make it bigger, brighter, bolder, add sounds. Use all your senses. Relax.

If the image creates any negative feedback, then switch to another and test again. Avoid scenes that are going to conjure up any negatives for this exercise.

2 Select a short, positive healthy option phrase that you can focus on. It can be anything that makes you feel good and positive. Relax, breathe in and out slowly, and say it out loud slowly three times. It can be anything that reminds you of positive energy. Examples can be, *'I invite vital energy into my body as I breathe', 'I am grateful for the energy I am receiving'.*

Alternatively if you have knowledge of the reasons for your lack of energy and you would like to be specific on this then choose a phrase to suit. Examples could be 'I invite energy to boost my immune system', 'Easy flowing energy for my immune system'. Create a positive image to match.

3 Start tapping on your top of head point (TH) as you gently breathe in and out, repeating your phrase slowly and imagining your healthy option scene of energy. If you are able to focus easily then you can just repeat the phrase in silence while imagining the image.

4 Switch to tapping on your wrist points, thinking of the positive image and saying your phrase.

5 Continue with tapping, visualising and repeating your healthy option phrase on the ankle points.

6 You can follow with a round of positive tapping using, 'I love and accept myself unconditionally as I access my energy easily', and a reminder phrase of 'easily accessing my energy.'

Relax and thank your body for doing a marvellous job.

(Reproduced from: Tapping for Healthy Options 2008©)

Your journey through health care

Patients in diagnosis, treatment and recovery can gain much benefit from using EFT on many levels. Many professional health care staff introduce patients to EFT for on-the-spot relief while others use it with a more structured treatment plan. The potential applications are numerous: minor upsets, delays in treatment, pain management, fears, phobias, and so on. Many patients continue to use EFT for long-term health management and many follow a personal peace procedure.

Case study

Many patients in chemotherapy wards respond well when using EFT for pain relief and to cope with any side-effects. Shirley was able to relieve the nasty taste in her mouth so that it did not bother her anymore.

'Even though my throat tastes of plastic...'

'Even though this plastic taste makes me want to vomit...'

'Even though my throat is jammed with plastic...'

Other EFT applications in this area include the following:

- identify and release the negative emotions and rebalance your body's energy system
- get over the shock of the diagnosis
- reduce the fear about the uncertainties of the treatment
- gain a more positive outlook on your situation
- integrate body, mind and spirit, supporting your desire of regaining your health
- make the transition to a more healthy and fulfilled life
- for your support team to relieve stress.

Basic tapping methods have resulted in improvement in headaches, back pain, stiff neck and shoulders, joint pains, chronic fatigue syndrome, lupus, ulcerative colitis, psoriasis, asthma, allergies, itching eyes, body sores, rashes, insomnia, constipation, irritable bowel syndrome (IBS), eyesight, muscle tightness, bee stings, urination problems, morning sickness, PMS, sexual dysfunction, sweating, poor coordination, carpal tunnel syndrome, arthritis, numbness in the fingers, stomach aches, toothaches, trembling, and multiple sclerosis, among many other physical conditions. This is not to suggest that the basic recipe of EFT replaces medical care, but it is interesting that an approach designed to address emotional problems is so frequently reported as helping with physical problems as well.

Putting together the scientific studies of EFT, the thousands of case histories reported, and our growing understanding from connected perspectives (as offered in Chapter 7), it is apparent that hugely beneficial techniques are in use that are safe, swift and effective. We are no longer limited to a repertoire of medications and surgery for our wellbeing. The new medicine also offers each of us a degree of control over our wellness, down to the very level of our cells – one that science never even dreamed of a generation ago.

Chapter 14
The gift of sharing EFT with our next generation

Chapter 14 The gift of sharing EFT with our next generation

There is no doubt that every child and young person can benefit from a daily energy clearing of any negative emotions and events. This has benefits in the short term and helps to prevent the development of a negative cumulative effect into adulthood. EFT is an extremely effective, flexible and safe gift to share with our next generation. It provides a natural 'missing link' in the practitioner's toolkit for work with families, in education and in support agencies concerned with young people's emotional, behavioural and social resilience. Children are infinitely better than adults at accessing and trusting their unconscious and creative qualities.

With careful tweaking of the basic techniques, EFT is also an attractive option in the hands of young people themselves, as they are empowered to facilitate change in their thinking and feeling in astounding ways.

Young people use EFT by themselves or with their friends, family, staff at school or within more structured sessions with a counsellor or therapist.

One-stop emotional health

EFT techniques are suited to a huge range of emotional and physical issues across all age ranges and settings of young people, including:

phobia and fear	performance	self-worth and esteem
anger	pain and ailments	behavioural challenges
learning challenges	trauma and abuse	sleep issues
depression	learning difficulties	confidence
family issues	habits, addictions and obsessions	friends and relationships issues
attachment issues	fears and phobias	anxiety and stress

Why tapping suits young people

- It can be used anytime for simple self-help issues.
- The process is active and engaging.
- Given the right encouragement participation is high.
- They share the techniques and benefits with friends.

- Tapping can be used anywhere and at any time – it is portable and free.
- It is perfect for young people's intuitive and creative skills.
- They become empowered to support their own needs.
- They quickly learn to relieve physical and emotional negatives as these happen.
- They learn that they not need remain stuck.
- It works.

What young people say

The words that are used in set-up statements in EFT come directly from the individual. An EFT practitioner resists the urge to reframe or add meaning or vocabulary. This absence of jargon in EFT is refreshing and attractive to young people – it is their own language!

'Even though I get so angry that I could smash the windows, I am a good mate.'

With guidance a young person identifies where they feel *'angry'* in their body. They may be asked, *'What does it remind you of?', 'When did you first have this feeling/memory?', 'Where were you?', 'What colour is it?', 'Is it moving?', 'If it was saying something to you, what would it be saying?'.* These questions typically elicit a rich supply of words and phrases for fresh set-up statements which can elicit energy shifts and reframes in thinking and behaviour patterns.

'Even though it feels like an explosion of nails in my head when I get angry ...'

What young people say about tapping

Case notes

Joe, 14, said: *'We tapped on exactly how I felt – the heavy sadness in my chest."*
Newcomers to EFT sometimes query the sense of stating negative phrases so readily. Following standard EFT we outwardly state a problem in the first part of the set-up statement and follow it with the accepting phrase at the end, such as, *'I'm OK', 'I'm a good friend'* or *'I'm a great footballer'.* The acceptance phrase allows our subconscious to recognise that we are acknowledging a negative feeling and accepting ourselves anyway. In effect we are saying to ourselves, *'it's only part of me and even though I have this problem, I accept myself.'* Naming and claiming each aspect of an issue allows us to 'hug the monster' in a safe and manageable way so that the cumulative effect is that the emotional intensity (SUD) ratings fall.

'I liked it, as I didn't say too much. We tapped on the feeling', **James, 11**
EFT can be content-free. During an EFT session, the talking part helps gently to recreate the feeling of disruption in the body's energy system. If a young person is 'in the moment', then it is not necessary to verbalise, yet EFT still works. Client and practitioner can tap quietly (with the guidance of the practitioner) without the need for many words. Code words, objects and other variations on talking are often used in the process.

>>

Case notes continued

'I can tap anywhere', Elisa, 9

EFT is an active process and young people like the physical elements for a variety of reasons. Often, I will work with young people while they are standing up or engaged in the activity that is connected with elements of the issue concerned. For instance, in working with children who have attention and concentration problems EFT is a real bonus as they can help themselves to focus, slow down and feel motivated while still being active. Young people tap off-stage during a performance, outside the exam hall or in the playground. Many pupils tap on their friendly point (FP) under the desk at school which happens to be a very effective shortcut and is often sufficient to cut anxious feelings, anger or lack of confidence before the effects become overwhelming.

'I use tapping for worry, my confidence and headaches', Sarah, 13

The same techniques will improve any issue that has some emotional content and that includes a fair proportion of physical issues such as headaches, stomach aches, pain and illness. Having become confident with basic EFT techniques, young people use them as a daily energy clearer and as a quick fix for any physical or emotional symptoms.

'It's me, helping myself', Joe, 16

'Even though you helped me with the real big stuff, I still use tapping now for myself for things that happen at home and at school', Jessie, 12

Whether the young person is using EFT alone or with the guidance of a qualified practitioner, they gain a real sense of empowerment for altering how they think and feel about something. Using their own words and feelings (no adult or psychological reframing allowed!), a child becomes responsible for the shifts made. Even from a very young age, a keen tapper soon starts to make connections about how, when and where else they can use tapping to help themselves – before going in front of class, to calm down, to go to sleep after a bad dream.

'My little sister is 3. She used it when she was angry with her friend', Ryan, 8

Slightly altered EFT techniques can be used by any age and for many emotional issues big or small, whether from the past or in the present. EFT is also very effectively used by young people for fears and anxiety about the future.

The writing on young people's walls

The 'writing on our walls' (outlined in Chapter 6) refers to the beliefs, values and attitudes that have their roots in early childhood and are mainly the result of influences from parents, teachers and other primary adults. Most beliefs about our worth, our gifts and our abilities are set by the end of childhood. Ideally, these messages are positive and affirming: *'Believe in your self'* or *'You can achieve anything you put your mind to'.*

Unfortunately, too frequently, they are not positive or affirming: *'You're so disorganised, you're a nightmare', 'You must get things right'* or *'Something is not worth having if you haven't worked hard for it.'*

Working with adults consistently reaffirms my passion for passing on the gift of EFT to our next generation as I see how limiting beliefs that are set in early years keep people trapped. If we are not careful it is all too easy to spend the rest of our days referring to angry, impatient and misguided messages from our history (see Chapter 2). Risk and resiliency factors dictate whether or not disparaging comments from parents, carers and teachers become reference points for us even when the comments are illogical.

Introducing EFT, children become empowered to rid themselves of fears, doubt and unhelpful negative emotions allowing them to be calm, make good decisions, think and feel as best they can despite any adverse circumstances.

Case study

James, aged 17, had become an 'expert' (his words) at thinking that he was a *'failure at everything'*. He said that *'everything had got too tough to deal with'*. Using EFT, he addressed some specific events based around exams, pressure and expectations from others, and some underlying beliefs about his worth.

James continued to use tapping and a couple of additional exercises at home. Over the next few months he gathered positive comments from friends and family about his new confident outlook. James also picked up a few key furtive tapping points to help his focus in sports. He very happily reported his improved exam scores and success on the athletics field a few months further down the line.

Young people and families

The applications of self tapping for the family are endless – for issues around self-worth, behaviour, self-esteem, confidence, phobias, relationships, homework, peers, boundaries, trauma and emotional roots of physical issues. All family members can benefit for free and there are no side-effects.

For more complex issues you may wish to engage an EFT practitioner who specialises in working with the issues of young people. Whether it is a simple issue that takes only a few sessions or more complicated work, other family members can be actively involved in the healing process. This may mean attending family EFT sessions, helping to encourage tapping out of sessions, or attending individual sessions. In the case of more serious issues such as trauma or abuse, professional intervention from an EFT practitioner with relevant skills and experience is recommended.

Parents, you first

Using EFT with your own children can be a most rewarding experience. It can also be extremely frustrating if you are experiencing negative emotion – anger, worry, guilt – or if the child is unwilling to tap. If your child is expressing a negative emotion or displaying an undesirable behaviour you are likely to want them to change and you are also likely simultaneously to be experiencing negative emotion yourself. In these circumstances it will be a challenge for you to be able to draw on your most productive parenting skills.

In addition, the chances that you will be able to entice your child to tap are low. My advice would be to withdraw from the conflict and tap to help remove your own disrupted energy so that you will be better able to see how to proceed. Young children especially tend to be tied intimately to your emotional state as a means of determining how they themselves feel. The emotional transfer between family members should never be under-estimated. Our children are adept at tuning to our emotional states. The advice is always the same:

> *'You need to tap on yourself first.'*

Tiredness and frustration can create a parenting mode that is not particularly useful. By using the EFT on yourself first you reach a more resourceful position to help your child. This not only helps you to be more present fully but you are also likely to find your child more receptive to EFT as well.

Tapping with someone when feeling negative for any reason reduces the chances of achieving a positive result. It is likely to interfere with healing. By always tapping on yourself first you are placing yourself in the best position to parent.

'Even though I am just too exhausted to deal with this right now, I deeply and completely accept myself.'

I have experienced numerous situations where this has made all the difference. How much tapping needs to be done depends entirely on what needs to be cleared. This could range from a discrete annoyance such as *'I'm annoyed that I have to deal with this again'* to a deeper, many faceted, issue that might sound like *'I knew I would be a rubbish parent. I don't know how to cope. In fact I don't want to cope.'*

Using the first example, a suitable set-up might be, *'Even though I am really annoyed in my head that I have to deal with it again'*, with a reminder phrase such as, *'annoyed in my head'* or *'have to deal with it again'*. Further articles, workshops and training can be accessed at the Positive E-Being website (www.e-being.co.uk).

The parent's personal peace procedure

An adaptation of the personal peace procedure gives parents a gentle method of addressing negative emotions and limiting beliefs that may stand in the way of their own ability to parent. Parents who are using EFT with their children really need to experience the benefits themselves first-hand in order to be truly congruent and encouraging of the techniques. At the worst, a parent's assumption that EFT is going to 'fix' their child is doomed to failure. Additionally, it is vital that a parent is able to become emotionally clear of current blocks and issues before going to help or support someone else. The more emotionally clear we are, the more present we are going to be to those we are serving.

After working through the parent's personal peace procedure at home Ben's dad, Eddie, came to the next EFT session gripping his list, saying, *'I have begun to really understand why I hold resentment for my son's special needs'* and that he was ready now *'to tackle the gritty truth head on'*.

The procedure provided a natural and gentle vehicle for Ed to resolve some of the more uncomfortable aspects that had been making him *'feel ashamed and selfish'*.

Tapping for all the family

There are many benefits to tapping within your family. My passion is sharing EFT techniques with people of all ages so that they can be at their best whatever their circumstances. Families can pick up EFT techniques and introduce them as a lifestyle choice in any set of circumstances. Here are some ideas and tips. See how they might work for you.

Never too young

Tapping for pregnancy and birth issues is just as easy as tapping for any other issue. There are hundreds of success stories concerning tapping during pregnancy. It can be used to address emotional issues such as fear and anxiety, and has also been reported to be effective on physical issues such as morning sickness, pain and discomfort, tiredness and hormonal imbalances.

Many parents use EFT in preparation for birth. It can be used to address fears, worries, physical symptoms, complications and birth choices as well as post natal issues. EFT allows mum, child and family short- and long-term calm to deal with the many changes and challenges. Likewise, EFT can be an extremely effective tool during the birthing process and throughout labour. Many people have experienced great success in achieving a sense of calm and decreasing pain during labour using EFT.

One of the best things we can do for our children is to teach them to tap continuously from an early age. This will serve to neutralise all the negative stuff they may accumulate over the years and will result in a much freer adult. A great way to do this is to start tapping with children when they are babies, particularly if there are problems such as restlessness, fear, digestion problems, colic. Birth itself can be potentially traumatic for a baby. Giving a baby the comforting effects of tapping and balance can be immensely beneficial whether or not specific problems are evident.

You can surrogate tap for your child or baby, using set up phrases such as *'I am* [baby's name], *and even though this place is new for me, I truly and deeply love and accept myself.'* You can also tap (or gently rub the spots) on your baby, using whatever facial and torso points are comfortable to reach at the time – but remember to be gentle! It has been suggested that you should tap on a baby lightly with your ring finger only, as this finger has the least muscle strength and will help ensure that you are not tapping too hard. A baby will make clear to you when they are receptive to tapping and when they are not. Sometimes, when they are crying or very upset, touching their face may only increase their frustration or aggravation. Pay attention to your baby's signals. Use of EFT is not meant to be a substitute for meeting physical needs.

Parents increasingly use EFT with young babies for a whole range of issues from encouraging sleep and relaxation to feeding and colic. The parent naturally develops gentle practices of tapping on the baby's energy system whenever needed or as part of a daily routine. Parent and baby can share positive energy in a beautifully bonding form of love, comfort, encouragement and assurance.

With a small amount of practice, and bringing energy systems close together in this focused way, parents report that they begin to develop better intuitive understanding of what the baby is communicating and how they can best fulfil their needs.

As the child grows EFT is extremely effective for helping with early signs of worry and anxiety of all types. Pain and ailments are also commonly eased with tapping, and the child quickly learns the empowering feeling of helping themselves with the support of parents.

As children reach pre-school age, temper and emotional overloads in children can be tough for all concerned. It is important that you remain calm, or regain calm, yourself, before you attempt objectively to help this overload of emotion. When you are ready, get to the child's level (crouch if necessary) and while gently holding the child's hand, tap on their friendly point (FP). Words are not necessary at the start if the child is tuned into their issue anyway. It can be enough that you are calmly there for the child and not having an adult tantrum beside them!

From nursery-age and upwards children tap daily using an inspiring song written and recorded by a keen group of young tappers. The theme of the fun *Tapping Tune* is *'Doing the best I can'* (see the Resources section). Young tappers of all ages learn the basics of tapping within a few minutes and this forms the basis of an everyday energy fitness activity.

On initial visits to a children's nursery I am accompanied by a PAT Bear in his rucksack[1]. Children are keen to help PAT (who can be a bit scared, angry, in trouble, etc.). Immediately, they see the tapping points on PAT and want to know what they are. After talking about what is up with PAT (set to the theme selected by the nursery staff), the children are eager to share their similar feelings. We talk about how negative feelings make our body and our energy system feel. We do some simple exercises around happy and sad feelings in our bodies, and talk a little about how feelings affect our health. I encourage the children to help PAT with a technique called tapping. Today, PAT is angry with his friend because his friend wants to play with someone else. PAT reluctantly agrees to come out of his rucksack if the children are willing to help him. He emerges shyly and the children sing and tap using the *Tapping Tune*. They easily pick up the tapping points while learning and feeling the benefits of *'Doing the best I can'*. Programme training, resources and case stories for a wide range of issues experienced in early years have been developed for the Positive E-Being programme.

Part of the daily routine

Encourage your children to tap daily as part of a family routine. Even though we all lead busy lives, a few of rounds of tapping each day can be really fun. A morning routine is great although many families will feel that there is no time. It is surprising, however, how much time can be filled with disruption and dispute both in the morning and at night. Getting skilled at building EFT into the routine proves to be a much more productive use of time.

Would you be willing to trade a few quality minutes tapping together in exchange for a pattern of daily family troubles?

- Be creative. It is easy to make up a game, to laugh or sing while you tap, and you can share news of the highs and lows of the day while you rebalance your energy system.
- Start the day on a positive note with the *Tapping Tune*. It is a great set up for the day, it takes about 90 seconds to complete. Everyone in the family can balance their energy systems, and you cannot help but feel happy when everyone is set up to attract positive energy from the day. Everyone you encounter will benefit from your actions.

Getting their attention

One of my key recommendations to parents is to let children experience tapping by example. Let children see you use tapping without inviting them to join in. It is human nature that they will desire something that is a little out of their reach. They will ask, *'What's that?'* Let them help you create the set-ups for a genuine need that you have. Tapping can be introduced just as easily as good dental hygiene, as a choice that children can enjoy, cherish and benefit from every day. You are more likely to have success if you make tapping happy, show by example and encourage children to feel empowered by their skills.

Tap for the positive

Children will absorb new information much more readily when you and they are free of overwhelming feelings. When they seek help, tap first to reduce emotional intensity before attempting to deal with the underlying problem. It might then be appropriate to continue tapping for what is going on underneath. If it is not a good time or situation, then the child's issues could be gently worked through at another time when there is quiet and peace.

Shortcuts to tapping

Most children happily follow full rounds of tapping using the shortcut version. After a bit of practice children usually have a couple of points that have become their favourites, and these are likely to be the ones that a child responds to best. Trust their intuition. Children are really much more intuitive than most of us adults.

Trading niggles

Tapping quietly with your child at a time when there is no conflict is an ideal opportunity to identify the root of their larger niggling issues. To set the scene, encourage children to tap along with you and invite them to help you with a real issue. For example, a 6-year-old will be able to identify what *'feeling mad'* is like, so invite them to help you tap for a minor upset that you have had at work recently. Empower your child to help you to feel differently. Done skilfully, you will have a very proud child before you, as they have genuinely helped their parent feel more positive and resourceful. Children really thrive from this kind of result. Do not forget to thank them for their help. If you still have a willing participant, then they are more likely to trade and share with you something that is bothering them. Do not push it if they are not ready or have had enough for now. Better to leave it for another time rather than forcing the issue.

Older children

For older children in the family the need for and benefits of tapping are just as relevant, especially as older children may already have established negative patterns of thinking about themselves. Difficulties that are not addressed during childhood and early adolescence can mar a child's experience of life at the time, and can also lead to difficulties in adulthood. EFT helps with current problems and empowers older children and young people to opt for more positive and healthy choices.

The good news is that some of my most persistent tappers are, perhaps surprisingly, in the young adult age group. Their emotional issues can often leave them feeling isolated and misunderstood. Once they have discovered how EFT can really work for them they are inspired to continue.

The timing for introducing the techniques needs careful thought. By practising tapping regularly at quieter, calmer times, young people are more likely willingly to tap to resolve a problem when it arises. Additionally, our energy body becomes primed to the beneficial effects of tapping. It seems that the speed of positive change in our physiology and thought field patterns when we tap is increased as a result of regular practice. Feelings around negative behaviour, temper and physical aspects can be scary for all concerned, and older children really do not wish to hang on to lousy feelings that can loom at this age. EFT 'access cards' are often used at the start of the process to help young people communicate their feelings while minimising any shame, embarrassment or guilt they may have about opening up. They consist of 31 cards each depicting an emotion or thought represented by words and photos and were created through teen project. Eating disorders, depression, friendships, anxieties, self-worth, performance and identity issues are commonly addressed using EFT for young adults. Many record their progress in their own 'Positive Energy Being' journal which is designed to be used in conjunction with their EFT session, during workshops and when tapping at home. Already many teaching assisitants, PHSE staff, teachers and school counsellors consider EFT as a natural and effective addition to the toolbox of skills. Basic EFT skills for simple applications can be provided in days.

Surrogate tapping for children

While active tapping with children is one of the best gifts I know to help clear negative emotions, there are occasions when surrogate tapping for a child will be beneficial. This is really quite simple although I recommend that you are quite familiar with the basics of EFT before you engage in surrogate tapping on negative feelings for others who cannot or are not willing to tap for themselves. It is fine, however, to tap anytime with a blessing or gratitude for other people in your life.

Guidelines for surrogate tapping.

- The first move is with you: clear your negatives first.
- Then get yourself out of the picture: be mindful of your intention.
- You can work alone or together when you surrogate tap.
- You put yourself in the other person's shoes.
- Address psychological reversal and resistance first.
- You can help to address issues with any emotional content.

With care, surrogate tapping reduces negative emotions by clearing energy disruptions, but most importantly it must always be done with the child's best interests in mind.

A full explanation and many examples of surrogate tapping are supplied in the Positive E-Being programme.

The EFT bedtime tuck

It is a nice idea that bedtime is a calm time for young people whatever their age, but clever distractions and worries tend to emerge at 'lights out' time. Negative memories of the day and fears about what is up ahead have a tendency to rise to the surface just when you would like them to settle down.

'I am really upset that I didn't get picked for the team. It's not fair.'

'What if I can't remember all my lines when I'm in front of the audience?'

'I can't face him tomorrow. I'm not going to school.'

The EFT bedtime tuck technique uses tapping to create a relaxed bedtime. The basics outlined here are for a younger child, but they can be adapted to suit the needs of all age groups.

Using a gentle version of tapping at bedtime eases the mind while also empowering young people to find their own natural resolutions. So, if at all possible, just spend a few minutes with each child doing the bedtime tuck to create a settling down ritual, tapping for the positive and negative events of the day. Alter the wording according to the child and their age needs.

The bedtime tuck

1 First the good stuff. Start with asking your child about positive or good things that have happened today: *'I got a good mark on my project'*, *'It's all sorted now; she said we were mates again'*, *'I'm really pleased that I got selected for the first team'*. This encourages the good habit of giving gratitude for the day, even with little children.

2 Taking one positive comment at a time tap together for a round. You tap on your own points while they tap on theirs. *'I'm pleased I was picked for a part in the play, I'm a budding actor'*, while beginning to tap on the friendly point (FP). Then follow with a tapping round using a reminder phrase such as 'pleased I was picked'.

3 Comfortable and relaxed with tapping in the positives, the opportunity arises to tap as well on negative feelings including worries for tomorrow. Gently invite the child to share any negatives. I suggest you call these 'wobbles and worries' (less defeating) or whatever term suits the child's age. Have a limit, say three, to avoid the huge lists that some children are keen on creating. Examples could include: *'I am worried that I'll mess up the rehearsal on Wednesday'* or *'I don't think that he will trust me again.'* Take one aspect and measure the SUD or a variation as usual (refer to Chapter 3).

4 Using EFT begin tapping on an aspect. *'Even though I'm worried that I'll mess up the rehearsal on Wednesday, I accept myself.'* The reminder phrase could be *'Worried that I'll mess up'*. Or *'Even though, I feel left out because David didn't ask me to play football and he asked Fred, I'm a good drummer'*, with a reminder phrase such as *'feeling left out'*.

5 After a couple of rounds on the negative emotion, feelings change. Your child will alter the words naturally while they are tapping. Go with it, whatever it is: *'Maybe they'll choose me tomorrow'* or *'It's nice to play with my other friends anyway'* or *'I choose to feel calm'* or *'I usually do OK so I'll just try my best'*. Go with it; children reframe with ease. Carry on tapping until they no longer feel bothered, upset, sad or angry and they are relaxed. Measure the progress using SUD rating or similar and continue as needed. Just how many bits of positive or negative you put into a night-time routine is entirely up to you and your child. Enjoy a relaxing evening.

Waking up during the night can be a really scary time for children, especially with bad dreams and terrors. If you can pop them back into bed, then tuck and tap. The speed at which the child can be re-settled with EFT is often surprising, especially if they are familiar with the relaxing effects of tapping. You can gently tap on the child and say *'Even though the dream made me scared, I am a great boy'* or *'Even though I woke up crying, I am safe and calm'*.

Supporting families

Issues within families can be intense whether they are emotional or physical, and support from an experienced EFT practitioner can be invaluable. The non-threatening and empowering elements of tapping frees participants to clear and heal often painful emotions.

Jenny wanted to share her experiences with other families who might be thinking about using EFT. In her family, uncovering and clearing what Jenny termed 'negative vibes' was crucial in helping her beautiful baby with a severe food phobia. Many layers, aspects and stages were addressed in a number of sessions before baby was comfortable to feed orally for the first time in her life. Details of how to access the full version of Jenny's letter are given in the Resources section (www.e-being. co.uk), but here are some snippets.

Case study

My beautiful daughter was born with a duct in the heart ... doctors recommended a simple procedure ... to achieve sufficient weight gain it was advised that she was tube fed. After the operation my baby had become so accustomed to feeding via the tube during the previous seven months and vomiting after most feeds that she was intensely scared of trying to eat orally. By this I mean at 13 months she would not allow ANY food or drink to her mouth.

Many specialist tests ... no medical reason had been found as to why my daughter wasn't eating ... problem was probably emotional.

Christine worked with both of us. Emotional issues that I did not realise I had ... When I cried, my baby girl would shuffle over and extend her arms to comfort me. My vibes were affecting her ... As the days passed I felt lighter, issues were clearing. Heavy weights were being lifted. We had more fun and I saw the situation from a different light.

Christine was fabulous with my baby, winning her affection and trust immediately. While we played, progress was being made. Christine has a wonderful, kind disposition. I recommend her so highly.

Three weeks later, I felt strong and determined enough to remove the tube from my daughter. Despite many, many previous attempts at feeding and removing the tube ... this time my little baby ... started eating ... my vibes had and still do affect my baby ... Christine not only helped my baby but me too to clear negative vibes.

Three weeks after taking the tube out we went on holiday. There were many other parents there who obviously did not know the background ... Every mealtime other parents commented on what a great eater my baby girl is and on a couple of occasions some parents asked if their kids could sit with us so that their little ones would copy mine!

>>

Case study continued

When you have been through something like this, and all that goes along with this, it is not so easy to explain everything on one sheet of paper, but when my friends at home see my baby girl eat, and when I tell the doctors who have been looking after us, they all say that what has happened is like a miracle.

Anxious feelings

Anxiety is among the most common mental health issue for children and young people. While excellent specialist help is available, it is not always easy to access. EFT provides accessibility to all young people and works well with a variety of anxieties and related conditions:

general anxiety	general phobias	school phobia	separation anxiety
social anxiety	selective mutism	panic	complex phobias

Specialist EFT trainings and workshops for therapists and professionals, who work with children and young people in a variety of settings, invariably return fantastic feedback.

Many young people have difficulty discussing the emotional aspects of anxiety, especially if they think that no one else feels the same way, or that they will not be understood. EFT provides an easy route in for young people to address all aspects of anxiety feelings and other negative influences such as tiredness, upset and frustration.

Usually young people are very in touch with how they feel physically, and all ages use EFT on specific feelings to calm the sources of anxiety. EFT is perfect for chasing pain (see Chapter 13) and settling the sensations of worry, upset, feeling sick, shaky, dizzy, faint, unpleasant thoughts and panic attacks. Although a school teaching curriculum educates young people to understanding feelings, EFT provides much needed practical solutions for reducing and removing anxious feelings quickly and safely.

Case study

Kayleigh (13) had learned to use tapping to reduce her general feelings of anxiety and a nail-biting habit. In class one day, her good friend Lucy was triggered into a frightening panic attack. Kayleigh reported,

'She had collapsed on to her chair and she was having trouble breathing. Our teacher was a bit flustered. Someone went to get help so I took Lucy's hand in mine and asked her what she was feeling. I tapped on the side of her hand and spoke for her. I said,

"Even though I have a frightening feeling in my chest, I am a good friend, Even though my chest and head are thumping, I am doing my best".

'I did three rounds which only took about 2 minutes. Lucy's tears stopped and her breathing went back to normal. Lucy stood up, smiled and thanked me. The teacher looked on, really baffled. Colour came back into Lucy's face and after a few minutes in matron's office, she was able to come back to her maths class.'

While I would never recommend relying on EFT for an emergency, there are many hundreds of cases where tapping has brought about immediate marked improvements in symptoms such as heart rate, breathing difficulties, rashes and allergy reactions (see www.e-being.co.uk).

Applications range from simple, quick fixes for a younger child who is suffering from a nervous stomach going into school through to more complex interventions such as complex phobias which require more structured sessions. Done well, EFT has the same outcome whatever the approach, and that is to remove negative disruptions at an energetic level so that the original trigger no longer has the same emotional and physiological tie for the person. They can feel better permanently. This outcome is wholly more effective than simply learning ways to be stronger and changing behaviour to match.

Simple yet still powerful tapping games are introduced to young people who are having anxious feelings. During the practice the child may give the feelings a character, personality and dimensions to help them work through the layers of feelings, addressing the intensities as they tap.

'Even though Spongebob jumps in my chest when I see...'

'Even though I can feel firey tingly spiders in my throat and cheeks when it's time to go...'

Fears and phobias

Many childhood problems come and go as part of normal development. If a current fear does not interfere with day-to-day functioning then it is worth considering allowing nature to take its course. If the fear becomes a phobia which impacts strongly, causing regular distress, it is not safe to believe the child will grow out of it.

EFT does not require willpower or pushing. Tapping on each aspect of the fear helps to uncover the hidden aspects and any underlying limiting beliefs or core issues. The symptoms gradually fade and the phobia disappears.

Young people respond well to tapping as they increase their skill and competence because they are actively taking part in collapsing their fears. Where it is helpful to reintroduce the source of a fear, tapping activities and games facilitate a natural recovery by

- easing feelings of embarrassment or shame about the fear or phobia
- helping to move from a feeling of being in danger to feeling safe
- dissolving the fears
- shifting thought processes
- altering beliefs around the object of fear.

Parents also join in to share. This is especially important if they also have the same fear or have a tendency to be anxious generally. Very often a child adopts a similar fear to a parent. This can happen very easily because fear can be downloaded from the parent inadvertently.

I regard EFT so gentle and gradual, yet I find it absolutely fascinating that in reducing the negative responses, young people's personal choices about exposure very often completely swing in the opposite direction after using EFT.

Table 22 **Young people's positive choices following EFT**

Before tapping: phobia and duration	After tapping
Severe fear of dogs in any situation/5 years	Purchased a rescue puppy one month later
Generalised phobia – about vomiting/8 years	Organised her own work experience with St John's ambulance
Severe fear of bridges and walkways/4 years	Went on a trip to aerial adventure forest
Dental phobia with panic attacks/3 years	Has been researching into history of dentistry

Unhelpful habits, rituals and obsessions of all descriptions are also very successfully altered with EFT for young people of all ages.

Bereavement

When a child or young person loses a parent, grandparent, sibling or a beloved pet EFT can be extremely useful in helping them through this uniquely difficult period. Whether feelings are intense and obvious or hidden and deep, EFT can help a young person to think and feel calmer through the various stages of bereavement.

Incorporating EFT into a counselling process provides a gentle pathway through the layers of feelings, addressing and settling each negative disruption. The techniques work equally well when used in a stand-alone application in sessions or for quick fixes. Careful listening to the feelings, questions and beliefs provides a rich source of material to form suitable set-up statements. Some of the ideas may be expressed extremely logically, others will be confused, and some are just plain inspirational. It is the young person's interpretation that is used in EFT. We have a lot to learn from children.

The Positive E-Being programme (www.e-being.co.uk) has developed a suitable handbook, training and leaflets for parents, children, organisations and schools. It contains EFT instructions, session stories and using EFT on common questions and statements like *'Will I die too?'*, *'How can Grandad breathe in the box?'*, *'Will Nan forget about me now?'*, *'Will I ever feel any better?'* or *'I don't want to be alive'.*

Depression

Rising rates of childhood depression increase the need for effective, cost-effective solutions. EFT provides an ideal vehicle of healing that does not require medication or years in therapy.

As an example of what can be achieved in the space of an hour, here are some snippets from a session. The full article, *'Chris in a dark place'*, can be read on www.e-being.co.uk.

Case study

Chris, aged 9, was stuck in a *'dark place with deep sadness'* (Mum's words). He was not a victim of bullying but … dropped into an increasingly depressive state. He looked … a 60-year-old man, drooped in the shoulders, looking at the ground, facial features grey and strained. His words … with negative gloom … He felt *'left out'* at school, *'different'* and *'not like the other kids'*.

We looked at some of the collected stories, pictures and tapping journals from other children of his age using EFT. He said, *'Oh, so I'm not the only odd one!'* I took that as comfort!

We used the distance between Chris's hands to measure the intensity of his feelings – *'how much'* instead of numbers – and started to tap on a huge range of aspects to his *'left out'* feelings. We tapped on:

'Even though I get upset because I feel left out at school, I'm still a good boy', *'Even though I always feel different from the other children …'*, *'Even though I don't like football …'*, *'Even though I don't like the games they play…'*, *'Even though they are too rough …'*

With each aspect, we re-measured the strength of his feelings continually. Chris made gradual progress with his hands getting closer together.

'Even though when I think they are talking about me I get a ringing in my ears …'

'Even though they might be talking about me and that makes me scared, I'm still a good boy.'

We explored Chris's willingness to let negative feelings go, and he said, *'I think I will always feel sad.'*

>>

Case study continued

A piece of rainbow-coloured cardboard sitting on a ledge nearby provided a tangible way to explore this further. I showed it to Chris. We tapped several rounds: *'Even though I am in the black sad area of the card, I am a good boy.'* We continued with successive rounds, altering the set-up as appropriate until we reached

'Even though I'm in the black area now, I may decide to feel differently about how people see me.' Suddenly after three more rounds, he jumped up, still tapping and announced,

'Even though I'm not in the black area any more...' and *'I don't care what other people think.'*

'Great', I said, but I wanted to be very careful that he had not just decided to pay lip-service to change. So I asked, *'What's happened?'*

'I need to get rid of it', he replied, pointing to the black bit.

'How can you do that?'

'I'd like to rip it off and get rid of it.'

'I need to be sure that you really want to get rid of it Chris. Do you think I should keep it here in my drawer in case you want to be sad again?' I was testing his willingness to reframe.

'No, I want to get rid of it forever.'

The metaphor of the rainbow of colours on the piece of card had given Chris an opportunity to let go. This boy's attitude was changing dramatically before my eyes. We continued tapping:

'What will you do with it then?'

'Rip it into bits so ... oooh small and put them into your bin.'

'We can do better than that if you like Chris.'

I brought him outside into the garden where Chris ripped up the black end of the card into tiny pieces, dropped them into the bin and said, *'I'm done with you sad thoughts for good'*. And then he stood in the bin and jumped up and down on the rubbish until he was exhausted.

His face was bright, his posture upright, he beamed broadly. He jumped out of the bin, back through the office, grabbing the remainder of the coloured piece of card and literally ran to his waiting mum, grabbed her hand and told her *'It's gone Mum, I'm not the same.'*

His mother smiled, bewildered by the dramatic changes. I heard reports from three teaching staff at Chris's school who spoke of his instant transformation on the next Monday morning. He was contributing in class, answering questions and volunteering to help. Apparently he had not actively contributed for about one year beforehand. In the playground he organised games, helped other children join in and he was happy. All the staff who noticed the

>>

Case study continued

changes asked his mother *'What happened to him?'* They could not believe it was the same boy. Staff in the school subsequently undertook EFT school training and now use tapping in many capacities.

Three years on and Chris is a well-adjusted teen at secondary school. He said that he knows that he is a *'bit different'* from the other boys at school but is content with it. The changes that he made that day have lasted. He still uses tapping when he needs to, and he does not mind if others see him do it. In fact a current teacher told me that he often shows other classmates how to tap for their difficulties.

Abuse

Despite much preventive effort, abuse of children occurs in every area of society. Many qualified professionals who attend to the wellbeing of young people have been attracted to specialist EFT training and use the adapted skills to help in the most difficult of cases of emotional, physical, sexual and domestic abuse.

Case study

Two girls aged 11 and 7 came to EFT sessions with Mum. They drew pictures, talked and tapped on their fear of their father, his drinking, drugs and the violence they had witnessed towards their mum. One of the girls drew a picture with terrified faces and blood. There were tears from them all as they tapped, but they were a welcome release. The session went from terror to calm.

In further sessions the older daughter tapped for her feelings of sadness at not having a normal father, and her hope for a safe future. Mum also benefited from individual sessions where she released negative disruptions around guilt, shame and fear of decisions that she was facing.

Mum called me three months after our initial sessions to say that she and her girls were on the other side of the country in a safe unit. She said that the sessions had helped them properly to realise what was for the best. She said that the tapping had helped her to be clear and less afraid and to make the best decisions for them all. EFT empowers change naturally, unlike anything I have ever experienced.

Working in schools

EFT provides an easy-to-use method of enhancing the emotional health, wellbeing and performance of young people and fits the many aims set out in policies such as those set out in government and national healthcare policies. The use of EFT is filtering into mainstream work with schools, agencies and pupil referral units. I liaise and train counsellors, teachers, behaviour support staff, PSHE staff, parents and children. Depending on the needs, I support individual pupils, conduct small-group work, whole school and whole class interventions and staff issues. I regularly run introductory EFT workshops with specific themes ranging from bullying issues and diversity to learning styles, panic busting and teen-power. Some training is bespoke and most are accredited programmes.

Healthy school projects in primary and secondary schools organise a variety of EFT workshops for pupil and staff wellbeing. In addition in the last three years a small research team have been conducting programmes of EFT research within education on topics such as blocks to learning, exam anxiety, confidence, anger and performance.

'I can't explain it properly, but I just don't feel so stressed about the things that were troubling me before I came to this!'
PSHE lead at EFT stress-busting workshop

'Do not be deceived by these simple techniques. Using EFT provides extraordinarily powerful and lasting effects. The results have astounded me (a sceptic by nature), my staff and my pupils. It doesn't create lots of paperwork and it is used in many classrooms without unduly interfering with the school day'
headteacher, Bedfordshire

One of EFT's key strengths is its flexibility. With basic skills staff can use it in the classroom, in circle time or in specific workshops. When appropriate, staff encourage pupils to engage EFT for quick fixes such as *'I can't do', 'He's annoying me', 'I'm getting angry'* or *'I'm getting a headache'*. Several schools I work with have installed tapping corners where pupils can sit and use easy tapping instructions on a variety of topics. Working with children in schools produces remarkable results. Children are naturally open to change. The empowering techniques of EFT elicit impressive results in areas such as learning differences, behaviour issues, performance enhancement, esteem, confidence issues, fears and physical illnesses.

For complex or serious cases EFT often provides much speedier relief than other conventional methods with issues becoming naturally resolved and physical symptoms fading automatically. A skilled EFT practitioner or trained staff member learns to move themselves out of the picture and act as a guide. Young people are empowered to make positive changes for themselves, and even from a young age they recognise that this is a very significant state to nurture.

Case study

Two months ago I worked with James, aged 10, who was displaying huge anger at home and school. A few days ago he delivered a picture and a note that read, *'I'm OK at helping myself to feel calm, and that feels good. I can see now that I was being a right pain. I feel better about myself.'*

Laura, aged 10, has various learning difficulties. She had slipped into a world of no confidence. I met with her through a local learning support group. She learned how to tap and she began to make changes straight away. Her teacher recently reported to me that Laura had asked to speak in front of her class. Laura had said, '*I used to feel bad, but now I feel like I am happy to give anything a go.*' The teacher added 'Her 10-year-old classmates were genuinely pleased for her ... she has blossomed into a confident and competent pupil.'

As common-sense indicates, an advanced EFT training status is a minimum recommendation for staff members who are dealing with more complex issues.

Case study

'I have been using EFT in school sessions for about three years. It often fits the needs exactly. Even though I am very aware of the possibilities with the techniques, I'm still consistently surprised in sessions. Frequently, a young person gets to gritty stuff quickly and makes permanent and significant shifts in their outlook with apparent ease',
J Reynolds, school counsellor

Challenging behaviour

The range of challenging or disruptive behaviours for which young people engage EFT includes anything from mildly negative, hostile and defiant attitudes, arguing, resentment, lying and truancy to aggressive behaviour, destruction of property, theft and inappropriate sexual behaviour. Often these challenges are related to indifference to social rules, a lack of concern for others and lack of remorse. Typically, with a bit of tapping layers of frustration, temper and blame subside. With more specialist EFT intervention the underlying and sometimes unconscious drivers are relieved gently and addressed. Poor self-esteem is often at the core.

Case study

In the previous eight months Molly aged 14, had been attracting attention at school. After two fantastic years in secondary school her grades, attitude and behaviour had crashed to the floor. The news that her parents were separating had been the source of extreme upset for her. When Molly first started using EFT she said *'I hate my friends and everyone; I don't want to be with anyone.'*

Molly managed to get herself 'back on track' as she called it, first by calming her aggressive outbursts at home and school. To the surprise of everyone concerned with Molly's welfare, within a month she was focusing positive interest on her passion for animals and what she needed to study to train to become a vet. A few months after our sessions Molly volunteered to help out at a lunchtime EFT anger-busting workshop at her school.

Many headteachers, SENCO staff and PSHE welcome programmes like Positive E-Being in schools and the word is spreading fast. Development of resources and specialist EFT training (see Resources section), excellent DVD material and the latest scientific research, brain scan evidence, performance and behaviour improvement figures and case studies are all helping enhance acceptance and delivery to our younger generation.

EFT with exceptional learning needs

EFT used skilfully addresses and calms negative aspects around many learning difficulties. Labels such as autism, ADHD (attention deficit hyperactivity disorder), Asperger's syndrome, dyslexia, dyscalculia (affecting the ability to acquire mathematical skills) and dyspraxia matter much less than the real experience for each person. Far more relevant is the need to pay attention to the individual's description of sensations, thoughts, beliefs and physical reactions. Using EFT the specifics are pinpointed by gently recreating the disrupted energy and settling it to bring about extended change. As always, persistent tapping is recommended in the following period to address connected aspects of an issue that would otherwise hinder positive changes from becoming permanent.

Case study

Paul, aged 12, a high-functioning autistic child, was having trouble making friends in his new school and had difficulty with reading. We had three EFT sessions together. While tapping we addressed his insecurities, feeling different and fear of talking with people. We also explored Paul's intense fear of death. This issue had been quite a surprise to everyone, including Paul. We tapped on a whole host of layers, including:

>>

Case study continued

'Even though I feel that the black tightness in my chest means that my time is running out...' until the set-up became:

'Even though some black smoke still needs to float out, I am breathing in clean fresh air now and...'

'Even though I still have some fading grey trails of powder swirling around, I feel lighter and bouncy...'

Soon Paul's school reported that he was more at ease with talking in general, and they were very pleased that he had volunteered for a forthcoming school production. Paul's support teacher reported that he was calmer, more confident and that his reading scores had improved.

The range of issues connected with learning difficulties is huge: problems with peers, behaviour, being different, self-esteem, concentration, frustration, anger and physical difficulties, beliefs and resistance to change. As mentioned before, the label does not matter as EFT can be used to remove the energetic disruptions around any feeling that has emotional content and allows the young person to gain personal insight and growth.

Case study

Sam, a 10-year-old boy with dyslexia, explained that when he tried to read the words *'they jump up and down the page'*. He could see letters within letters and outlines around those. His reading level was low. He *'hated'* reading and was *'scared of the words because they make me unhappy'*. *'These don't help either'*, he said, pointing to his special coloured glasses, *'I feel like a freak'*. His anger levels in class where high and his behaviour was beginning to be labelled disruptive. We tapped for every aspect he listed:

'Even though the words jump like beans on my page and I can't see them clearly...'

'Even though I get upset and try to read fast like the others...'

'Even though I like my friends, I heard them talking about me...'

At the end of the first session Sam exclaimed, *'The letters are not moving anymore!'* Within three sessions the wobbly outlines were gone and he was enjoying just holding a book and looking at the letters. His dad said that before using EFT he was more inclined to fling the book out of his hand.

>>

> ## Case study continued
>
> Since then, he taps in class before his reading as he finds it helps him to settle down and be calm. He taps at home with Dad before they read together. Dad reported, *'I wish we had started this two years ago; we would have saved a lot of fights and tears. His reading is so much better and so is his behaviour at home. He is a nicer child to be with.'*
>
> Sam's confidence and his enthusiasm to learn increased further. His teachers and parents are pleased that he no longer feels angry. He knows that he has a long challenge ahead of him but is in a much improved position to learn.

Examples of set-up statements used with learning issues

Poor understanding of language	*'Even though I am afraid that my teacher will ask me about this chapter tomorrow...'*
Poor expressive speech	*'Even though I'll never be able to say this poem like Jason does...'*
Unclear speech	*'Even though my words come out jumbled up like jigsaw pieces...'*
Attention and listening difficulties	*'Even though I find it hard to follow instructions from my teacher...'*
Dyslexia	*'Even though I get in loads of trouble because I can't find my things, I...'*
Difficulty with writing	*'Even though I got angry when Gina laughed at my project...'*
Problems with reading	*'Even though I get upset when Mum wants me to read...'*
Specific difficulty with maths	*'Even though I want to throw my maths homework out the window now...'*

Natural insights for solutions

During an EFT session young people typically review feelings and beliefs and naturally arrive at alternative and more positive reflections. For instance, a child may reflect while tapping, *'My dad said I was a bad reader just like him'* and within a few short rounds can be congruent with *'I'm up for exploring some new words today'*. Insights and shifts in thinking and feeling for our younger generation can be arrived at quickly and can be embedded quickly given the optimum conditions discussed in earlier chapters.

Even more fascinating, by using EFT young people arrive at inspiring and practical insights to difficulties that might not even be picked up by a professional educational assessment.

Listed below are some insights that young people have spontaneously offered during recent EFT sessions. The practical and internal insights include details about what can help to resolve their current difficulties.

Cases

Ben, aged 7, discovered through tapping that he was not *'doing so well'*, sitting on the right-hand side of the class. His parents arranged for him to move seats and a hearing test detected a minor issue.

Megan, aged 6, identified in an EFT session that her noisy class was badly affecting her stress levels and ability to learn. She found a way to muffle the background sounds using imaginary volume controls and was much happier.

Eleanor, aged 8, verbalised while tapping that, *'My teacher talks too much and then the words about what I have to do float out of my head.'* We explored this problem further using EFT and Eleanor came up with her own solution. She was confident that *'I can underline the important words in my head with a big orange highlighter pen.'* Eleanor, now 12 years old, tells me that she still uses this method.

Lydia was having difficulty concentrating. After a short introduction to EFT, and while she was tapping, she found the concentration part of her head and she described it as *'jumbled and hazy'*. The imagination part of her brain was *'calm and easy'*. She said as her imagination *'worked so well, it could spare some help'*. She was 7 years old! Together we continued tapping to work out how Lydia could transfer some spare help over to the concentration side of her head. Here was Lydia doing her own neuroscience analysis – fascinating stuff!

Lydia had also mentioned during one round of tapping that she would like to be able to write more like her friends. We used an adapted EFT technique called the 'downloading buddy store' which just took a couple of minutes. Lydia had a reading and writing assessment three weeks later and her levels had improved considerably.

Richard, aged 10, was able through tapping to pinpoint the process of what happens when he gets into a panic. He described *'a blanket coming down over my eyes'* whenever he was given a maths sheet to work on. We continued tapping on the aspects of the blanket and the worksheet. We then introduced *'a clear view in my head'* that Richard has from another type of school work. After we had finished, Richard decided that he could *'fold the blanket and keep it on the shelf'* most of the time.

I think that you might agree that this easy data is invaluable.

Performance

Performance is always enhanced by feelings of safety and confidence, and is negatively impacted when we feel scared, unsafe, or convinced that we cannot do well. The same applies in school for a particular subject or sport, for a particular exam, performance or presentation. Teachers, parents and coaches have a desire to help students perform at their best and to get past any mental blocks to performance. EFT provides quick and painless methods to use in class, on stage or on the sports field.

Studies and exams

EFT is ideal for addressing subject phobias, the *'I can't do's'* and other learning related issues. Exam and test anxiety has a detrimental effect on performance and is rife throughout the school system – from the earliest stages of learning maths and spelling through to external public exams.

Following several years of EFT training and practice I took EFT into a school setting for the first time by introducing basic techniques in the school I happened to be working in. A levels and GCSEs were looming and the 'exam wobblies' were gaining pace. I ran a series of informal group workshops for the pupils and staff, addressing several aspects of exam anxiety. The outcome was positive with pupils reporting feeling calmer in their approach to revision and exams. Using EFT before maths tests produces consistently higher test results than relaxation, breathing or similar practices. EFT 'easy exam busting' workshops have become a common feature within the Positive E-Being programme and staff can train to run them internally. At the time of writing we have begun a trial of evidence-based research into the effects of EFT workshops on GCSE performance grades.

Some exam issues are best dealt with individually.

Cases

One young man, Harry, aged 16, would physically vomit on exam days. He came for two short sessions of EFT before his GCSE mocks. This was sufficient to eliminate his anxiety completely and he has reported from university that the thoughts and symptoms have never returned.

In the middle of her AS levels, Charlie was finding the thought of more exams overwhelming. We tapped on a number of aspects. *'Even though when I can't understand the topic I ignore it and I know that's stupid...'*, *'Even though I get distracted so easily when I need to revise...'*, *'Even though I get a migraine above my eyes when it's exam time...'*, *'Even though I study hard I just can't remember anything when I take a test...'*. Charlie is still taking exams but without excess stress.

Children of all ages can address performance anxieties easily using EFT. Common themes that crop up are: hating a subject; finding it difficult; not understanding; not being fast enough; feeling stupid, embarrassed, worried, sad; not wanting to disappoint parents and teachers; scared of not been good enough to make the grade.

We move to rounds of tapping statements that reflect a shift towards a more positive reframe on the negative when we are feeling a bit better: *'Even though I know that I can get good grades if I relax...'* *'Even though I usually can remember most stuff if I relax...'*

Going back to revise after tapping or before approaching the exam hall is enough to calm nerves and create a much better state of mind to learn. Negative thoughts and beliefs and subsequent physical reactions can be extinguished from the energy body and mind forever.

Even for high performing individuals, the extra edge being on the top of your focus and mental game can make a tremendous difference in scores. EFT rebalances the disruptions and calms the negative feelings for many bright students who have tended to mess up in exams. *'Even though I really get really upset around exams....', 'Even though I worry about what Dad will say about the results and that gets me in a mess...'*

Students go on to apply the same tapping procedure with future exams, but need it less every time. They often report much less worry and panic and permanent shifts in confidence. The adrenaline is still running but the anxious thoughts, feelings and beliefs have been reprocessed in the mind and disruptions have been settled in the body.

Sports performance

You do not have to be a sports psychologist to understand the damaging effects of stress, anxiety or damaging self-talk in sports and other performance situations. It's commonplace to witness a football penalty, medal performance or golf tournament being ruined due to performance nerves. EFT is ideal for addressing the mental side of sports performance as it quickly resolves negative thinking and relaxes the body's subtle energy system. This results in a more natural approach to the game and often brings dramatically improved scores and general performance.

A growing number of professional and amateur athletes and coaches are using EFT for eliminating performance anxiety fears that would usually interfere with performance. Young people are also using the techniques for peak performance and general sporting improvement. In addition to getting harmful emotions out of the way, EFT is regularly used to improve many areas.

Table 23 **EFT success in peak performance**

Area for attention	EFT example application
Range of motion and agility	Focusing on parts of the body, movement, relaxation. Injury recovery and chasing pain. Limiting beliefs about capability of the body. Use of sub-modality focus
Body strength	Focus on core, conditioning and stability
Motivation	Yourself and others, in a positive, empowering way. Self-belief. Clearing limiting beliefs

Area for attention	EFT example application
Visualisation skills	To relax, develop optimum state and positive mental rehearsal. Using downloading resources exercise (described below)
Setting compelling goals	For peak performance. Circle of excellence exercise (described below)
Focus and control	To maintain concentration and positive emotion under pressure. Relaxation. In the zone. Coherence
Positive self-image	Develop the self-image and mental toughness of a champion. Using EFT borrowed resource states (described below)

Very often I use a young person's sporting interest and enthusiasm to help them gain strength in an area that they find difficult. To explain, I will share my experience with meeting Tommy.

Case study

Tommy's dad had died in a car accident when Tommy was 6. This devastating loss was a constant source of anxiety which impacted on many aspects of his day. At 10, Tommy was still having regular nightmares and was prone to panicking if his mum was out of contact for too long. With support from his mum, Frances, his school contacted me. Frances listed examples of his behaviour, feelings and physical reactions. Tommy would go into *'a blind panic'* if Frances was not waiting for him at the school gate (his teacher used the same phrase). His distress and constant worrying was also causing upset to the other pupils. Counselling sessions at school had helped a little, although Tommy still felt much the same. He had told his teachers and friends that he was convinced that, *'Mum will die as well'.*

In EFT sessions through tapping and gaining rapport Tommy's fears began to subside. I introduced the adapted EFT technique called the 'downloading resources exercise'. Using this exercise he was easily able to recreate his good feelings about his successes on the running track and readily 'download' those feelings at times when he would usually be starting to feel fear. Tommy, like most children, quickly learned how to enjoy and benefit from this exercise. He used it regularly so that within a few days the switch between scary feelings and calm control feelings became automatic. Being able to calm the thoughts and physiological responses in situations where usually Tommy would have been anxious was a big step.

Within two more sessions Tommy found other ways of letting his mum know that she was extra special and he continues to use his *'power sprint'* download and remains *'in calm control'.* Exercises like the one used here and the 'circle of excellence' are detailed in the Positive E-being programme.

External agencies

Outside mainstream schools, I also work with and train a wide range of external agencies – pupil referral units, special schools, educational and parenting groups and healthy school initiatives. Enquiries through local GPs and CAMH, DCSF and national young people's charities are increasing and have shared presentations with several national educational and parenting forums.

Child and Adolescent Mental Health Service	Children's services and children's centres
Public health and primary care	Careers support
Support groups	Parenting support groups
Social and health care teams	Behaviour improvement programmes
Extended schools	Youth service
Youth offending teams	Teenage pregnancy projects
Behaviour education support teams (BEST) and Targeted Mental Health in Schools TaMHS	Fostering and adoption agencies
Home Start	Support and practical help for parents with young children

The positive reputation and results of using EFT with young people is growing rapidly. One of my family workshops was recently featured, albeit briefly, on national TV as an effective tool for helping families with anxious feelings.

I have been working with a number of agencies to collate EFT studies concerning young people. I greatly admire the commitment of the staff of these agencies who work with disadvantaged and vulnerable young people to help them with the complex challenges they face:

vulnerable/at risk	substance misuse	community support
eating disorders	gun and knife crime	schemes for the disabled
drug programmes	self-harm	rehabilitation

The work is often stressful and unpredictable, requiring the highest standards of professionalism and the ability to think outside the box. I am grateful to be able to share EFT trainings and workshops in these specialist areas. Thankfully staff are often able to benefit too from learning and using EFT for their own needs, while helping others.

'We are a better team now. We didn't expect it, but this training has cleared some cobwebs for all of us. As for the kids, they love the group sessions. They keep asking to do more and that's unusual'

Tim, youth manager, addiction unit

Positive E-Being programme

In 2007 my passion for developing the usefulness of EFT in the wider field led me to found the EFT Children, Young People and Families network. The network is open to everyone involved in the emotional health and wellbeing of children, young people and families.

The network successfully creates links between the needs of young people of all ages – privately and via schools, healthcare practitioners and agencies – with the services and expertise of EFT practitioners and trainers.

Within the network the Positive E-Being programme has been developing training schemes and materials for each educational key stage, for young people, parents and families. Newsletters, specialised resources, articles, workshops, talks and Association for Advancement of Meridian Energy Techniques (AAMET) - accredited training courses are available.

We are building a community of specialist young people's EFT practitioners to exchange news, training and standards. Filming projects of children's EFT sessions, workshops and intensive applications are underway, which will help to inform a much wider audience.

There is no doubt that using EFT skilfully gives surprisingly effective, swift and lasting outcomes. For those that are committed to making children's lives better, EFT offers diverse approaches that work in so many settings. Energy psychology is rapidly gaining acceptance and the formal research within EFT is gaining pace. I encourage all connected with children and young people to learn more about how to apply this refreshing and effective approach.

1 PAT Bear and all resources for children and young people are available at www.e-being.co.uk

Appendices

Appendix 1 Meridian pathways and Chinese medicine functions

Meridian (and tapping point)	Pathway	Main functions
Small intestine (friendly point - FP)	Runs up the arm and shoulder from the little finger to the edge of the jawbone	Linked to the heart and useful for clearing all kinds of blockages, including confidence
Bladder (eyebrow - EB)	Runs down the back a couple of finger-widths away from the spine	Transforms fluids Can increase levels of courage and energy
Gall bladder (side of eye - SE)	Runs from the head to the tip of the little toe	Concerned with breaking down Generates clear thinking and a sense of calm
Stomach (under eye - UE	Runs down the body from the head to the second toe	Associated with balancing and nourishing the system Good for overcoming nausea
Governing meridian (under nose - UN)	Runs from just above the anus to the upper lip	Chi flow of all the Yang meridians Good for reducing panic
Conception meridian (chin - CH)	Down the centre front of the body, from the roof of the mouth	Chi flow of the Ying meridians Good for overcoming shame
Kidney (collarbone - CB)	Goes up the body from the sole of the foot to the top of the chest	The body's source energy - the chi we are born with - is stored in this meridian, which also governs growth, will power and short-term memory
Spleen (under arm - UA)	Runs upwards from the big toe to the armpits	Associated with learning and concentration, and transforms the energy from food into chi

Meridian (and tapping point)	Pathway	Main functions
Lung (thumb - TB)	Runs from the top of the chest down to the thumb	Linked with tears and sorrow
Large intestine (index finger - IF)	Runs upwards, from the index finger to the edge of the nose	Responsible for cleansing Detoxifying emotional release
Pericardium (middle finger - MF)	Runs from the chest to the middle finger	The 'heart protector', anxiety, tension or shock Good for low self-esteem
Heart (little finger - LF)	Runs from the top of the arm to the hand	Associated with the mind and long-term memory, chest pain and compassion
Triple warmer/ energiser (gamut point - GP)	Runs from the ring finger to the eyebrow	Regulating warmth and balancing the body's fluid levels between kidney and heart, so stimulating the lymph system Releases depression and pain
Liver (under breast - UB)	Runs from the big toes to the chest	Regulates the flow of chi Good to combat anger

Appendix 2 Emotions associated with energy meridians and tapping points

Tapping Point	Releases	Allows	Energy Meridian (and it's companion Organ)
Friendly Point (FP)	Psychological Reversal (feeling stuck or frozen), inability to let go, resistance to change, sorrow, sadness, feeling vulnerable, worry, obsession, compulsive behaviour	Acceptance, ability to move forward, letting go of the old, healing from grief, finding happiness in and connecting to the present moment, clarity of thought, joy.	**Small Intestine Meridian** (Heart)
Top of Head (TH)	Inner critic, 'gerbil wheel' thinking, lack of focus	Spiritual connection, insight, intuition, focus, wisdom, spiritual discernment, clarity	**'Thousand Meeting Points'** (meeting of all meridians)
Eyebrow (EB)	Trauma, hurt, sadness, restlessness, frustration, impatience, restlessness & dread, caution, restraint, fear, lack of confidence, hypersensitivity—emotional and physical	Peace and emotional healing, patience, harmony, calm, will power, determination and ambition.	**Bladder Meridian** (Kidney)
Side of Eye (SE)	Rage, anger, resentment, fear of change and muddled thinking	Clarity, compassion, adoration and forgiveness	**Gall Bladder Meridian** (Liver)
Under Eye (UE)	Fear, anxiety, emptiness, worry, nervousness and disappointment, feelings of suspicion	Contentment, calmness, and feeling safe. "All is well', confidence, trust, considered thought and action	**Stomach Meridian** (Spleen and Pancreas)
Under Nose (UN)	Embarrassment, powerlessness, shyness, introversion, shame, guilt, grief, fear of ridicule, fear of failure and psychological reversals, panic, bitterness, nausea, hunger, worry, nasal congestion	Self-acceptance, self-empowerment, healthy pride, compassion for self and others, communication	**Governing Meridian**

Tapping Point	Releases	Allows	Energy Meridian (and it's companion Organ)
Chin (CH)	Confusion, uncertainty, shame, embarrassment and second guessing decisions, trauma, psychological reversal, panic and worry	Clarity, certainty, worthy, confidence, self-acceptance & self-empowerment	**Central Meridian**
Collarbone (CB)	Psychological reversal, feeling stuck, fear, indecision, fear of intimacy, worry, and general stress	Ease in moving forward, security, confidence, and clarity	**Kidney Meridian - Adrenal Gland Function** (Bladder)
Underarm (UA)	Guilt, worry, obsessing, hopelessness, insecurity, anxiety about the future, poor self esteem, self pity, addiction and attachment	Clarity, confidence, relaxation, and compassion for self and others, security, faith, confidence, satisfaction, achievement, ideas & creativity	Spleen Meridian **(Stomach)**
Thumb (TB)	Judging others inferior to self, Intolerance, Prejudice	Humility, Tolerance, Modesty	**Lung Meridian** (Large Intestine)
Index finger (IF)	Guilt, Self-Hatred, Low Self- Esteem	Self Worth	**Large Intestine Meridian** (Lung)
Middle Finger (MF)	Sexual Tension, Stubborn	Letting go of the past, Generosity, Relaxation	**Pericardium** (Triple Warmer)
Little Finger (LF)	Anger, hysteria, erratic behaviour, mood swings, jealousy, yearning for love, sorrow	Love and Forgiveness, tranquillity, emotional balance, spirit, growth, zest for life	**Heart Meridian** (Small Intestine)
Gamut Point (GP)	Depression, Heaviness, Despair, Grief, Hopelessness, Despondency, Loneliness, Solitude	Hope, Lightness, Buoyancy, Elation	**Triple Warmer** (Pericardium)

Tapping Point	Releases	Allows	Energy Meridian (and it's companion Organ)
Under Breast (UB)	Anger, depression, impatience, hatred, jealousy, insecurity, attachment issues	Drive, planning and starting skills, clear intellect, agreeability, ambition, patience & sense of wellbeing	**Liver Meridian** (Gall Bladder)
Sore Point (SP)	Psychological Reversal, (feeling stuck or frozen), inability to let go, resistance to change, sorrow, sadness, feeling vulnerable, worry, obsession, compulsive behaviour. Rejection	Acceptance, ability to move forward, letting go of the old, healing from grief, finding happiness in and connecting to the present moment, clarity of thought, joy.	**Neurolymphatic Point**

Appendix 3 EFT Research

A UK EFT Research Programme is in the process of establishing a national EFT research platform. Its focus is to coordinate evidence-based trials using EFT for PTSD, depression, addiction, anxiety, physical pain. Initial research has been in collaboration with the US based research unit (www.stressproject.org).

Promising evidence-based EFT research is also in progress in the UK, in schools and other support-agency settings, evaluating the effectiveness of EFT on a variety of issues including performance, anxiety, behavioural challenges, esteem and anger. (www.e-being.co.uk)

Stress Relief and Energy Psychology

(2007©article reprinted from www.energypsychologypress.com)

In a study published in *Counseling and Clinical Psychology Journal*[1], psychologist Jack Rowe, Ph.D., of Texas A&M University's Psychology and Sociology department, tested people for stress before and after EFT. He administered a standardised test for measuring stress to 102 people before, during, and after an EFT workshop. Rowe also measured their stress levels one month before the workshop, and six months later. He found that the stress levels of participants decreased significantly between the beginning and end of the workshop. But even more promising was the finding that the effect endured, and that when subjects were re-tested six months later, their stress levels remained much lower than they had been before the event. Such was the strength of the result, that there was less than one chance in two thousand that such results could have occurred through chance.

Another pilot study of EFT examined its effects on patients about to undergo dental surgery. Research confirms that about one in three people experience moderate to severe anxiety when confronted with dental treatment. After EFT, 100 per cent of patients in the study reported a decrease in anxiety[2].

Another study examined the effects of tapping these stress reduction points on subjects who had received a minor injury that required paramedics to transport them to hospital. Those who had received this simple treatment showed a significantly greater reduction of anxiety, pain, and heart rate than those who had not[3]. A pilot study is now in progress at Marshall University medical school, working with Iraq war veterans with Post-Traumatic Stress Disorder (PTSD). Kaiser Permanente, a large HMO with over nine million members, recently tested Energy Psychology for weight lost against its best existing methods, and found it to be far superior at helping patients keep their weight down. Kaiser is also studying the effect of Energy Psychology on chronic inoperable pain. The scientific evidence for the field is being tracked by several institutions like the Energy Medicine Institute, and they update their sources as new papers are published.[4] Year after year, the objective evidence of the effectiveness of Energy Psychology is mounting.

Energy Psychology and Brain Function

In one experiment, the brain scans of subjects suffering from generalised anxiety disorder were examined. Conditions such as anxiety and depression 'can be distinguished by specific brain-frequency patterns. Anxiety has one such electronic signature.... depression has another,'[5] according to David Feinstein, Ph.D. in The Promise of Energy Psychology, which describes this study in fascinating detail.

Digitised EEG readings of subjects' brain scans were taken before treatment began. They then received twelve energy treatment sessions, and a second EEG was taken. The group receiving Energy Psychology treatment was compared to a group receiving the gold standard in experimentally validated 'talk' therapy, Cognitive Behaviour Therapy (CBT). It also compared them with patients receiving medication. The patients were interviewed three, six, and twelve months after treatment to determine whether the therapy had produced lasting results.

The EEG readouts demonstrate the regions of their brains that are functioning normally, and those with various degrees of dysfunction. The illustration below indicates the progress made by those subjects that received EFT. It shows that before treatment began, most areas of their brain revealed high or very high levels of dysfunctionality. Only a small portion of their frontal lobes shows normal or slightly dysfunctional patterning.

Brain scans over the course of twelve energy treatment sessions

After twelve sessions of energy treatments, as can be seen on the right bottom scan, most areas are normal or close to normal. Patients given CBT had similar results, but 'more sessions were required to accomplish the changes, and the results were not as durable on a one-year follow-up as were the energy psychology treatments.' Compared to giving patients drugs the brain-wave ratios did not change, suggesting that the medication suppressed the symptoms without addressing the underlying wave frequency imbalances. Undesirable side effects were reported. Symptoms tended to return after the medication was discontinued.'[6] When symptoms are suppressed, the patient may act and feel more normal. But the underlying brain rhythms remain unaffected. Antidepressant drugs are masking their symptoms, without removing them. This is like taking a painkiller when you have a broken arm. You might feel better, but left to fester, your underlying condition remains unchanged.

Energy Cures for Physical Traumas

Besides working well on psychological traumas, EFT has established a surprising track record of effectiveness in shifting, or even curing physical ailments. This is because there is virtually always an emotional component of a physical disease[7]. Cancer patients, for instance are often psychologically depressed, along with the depression of their immune system that accompanies chemotherapy.

Psychological depression left untreated often contributes to organic disease. Even if a patient has a disease that seems purely organic, such as an acute bacterial infection, releasing any possible emotional stressors cannot hurt. There are many reports of colds and flu being ameliorated or prevented by Energy Psychology.

Summary

Energy Psychology is demonstrating that a simple, fast and reliable set of stress-reduction gestures can have a lasting effect on many emotional traumas. It can also shift baseline biological measures of stress quickly. Stress and trauma often underlie physical disease, and resolving emotional issues can thus affect symptoms. The use of Energy Psychology in treatment programs is becoming widespread, and its base of research is growing. Energy Psychology holds out the promise of effective treatments for many physical conditions and psychological issues, and its methods will be found on the leading edge of medicine and psychology in the coming decade.

Resources:

Energy Psychology Press web site: **www.EnergyPsychologyPress.com**

The Promise of Energy Psychology (Tarcher, 2005). Feinstein, Eden & Craig

The Genie in Your Genes (Elite, 2007). Church

EFT web site: **www.emofree.com**

Association for Comprehensive Energy Psychology: **www.energypsych.org**

Endnotes:

1 Rowe, Jack (2005, September). The effects of EFT on long-term psychological symptoms. *Counseling and Clinical Psychology Journal*, 2 (3), p. 104-111.

2 Temple, Graham (2006). Reducing anxiety in dental patients with EFT. www.emofree.com/Research/graham-templedental-study.htm.

3 Kober, A., et. al, (2002). Pre-hospital analgesia with acupressure in victims of minor trauma: A prospective, randomized, double-blind trial. Anesthesia & Analgesia, 95(3), p. 723.

4 Feinstein, David (2007). Energy psychology: method, theory, evidence. www.EnergyPsychologyResearch.com, accessed Feb 5.

5 Ibid, Feinstein, p. 297

6 Ibid, Feinstein, p. 322

7 Russek, L., & Schwartz, G. E. (1997). Perceptions of parental love and caring predict status in midlife: A 35-year follow up of the Harvard mastery of stress study. Psychosomatic Medicine, 59 (2), p. 144.

A selection of abstracts from other EFT research studies and review articles

The Neurochemistry of Counterconditioning Acupressure Desensitization: Acupressure Densitization in Psychotherapy

Lane. J.R. (2009) Energy Psychology 1.1 Nov

Abstract: A growing body of literature indicates that imaginal exposure, paired with acupressure reduces midbrain hyperarousal and counterconditions anxiety and traumatic memories. Recent research indicates that manual stimulation of acupuncture points produce opioids, serotonin and gamma-aminobutyric acid (GABA), and regulates cortisol. These neurochemical changes reduce pain, slow the heart rate, decrease anxiety, shut off the fight/flight response, regulate the autonomic nervous system, and create a sense of calm. This relaxation response reciprocally inhibits anxiety and creates a rapid densensitization to traumatic stimuli. This paper explores the neurochemistry of the types of acupressure counterconditioning used in energy psychology and provides explanations for the mechanism of actions of these therapies based upon currently accepted paradigms of brain function, behavioural psychology, and biochemistry.

Psychological symptom change in veterans after six sessions of EFT (Emotional Freedom Techniques): an observational study

Church, D., & Geronilla, L. *International Journal of Healing and Caring*, January 2009, 9:1.

Protocols to treat veterans with brief courses of therapy are required, in light of the large numbers returning from Iraq and Afghanistan with depression, anxiety, PTSD and other conditions. This observational study examined the effects of six sessions of EFT on seven veterans, using a within-subjects, time-series, repeated measures design. Participants were assessed using a well validated instrument, the SA-45, which has general scales measuring the depth and severity of psychological symptoms. It also contains subscales for anxiety, depression, obsessive-compulsive behavior, phobic anxiety, hostility, interpersonal sensitivity, paranoia, psychotism, and somatization. Participants were assessed before and after treatment, and again after 90 days. Interventions were done by two different practitioners using a standardized form of EFT to address traumatic combat memories. Symptom severity decreased significantly by 40% (p<.001), while breadth of symptoms decreased by 29% (p<.032). Anxiety decreased 46% (p<.003), depression 49% (p<.001), and PTSD 50% (p<.026). Most gains were maintained at the 90-day follow-up.

Neurophysiological indicators of EFT treatment of Post-Traumatic Stress

Swingle, P., Pulos, L., & Swingle, M. K. (2005). Neurophysiological Indicators of EFT Treatment of Post-Traumatic Stress. *Journal of Subtle Energies & Energy Medicine*. 15, 75-86

Abstract: This research study, conducted by Dr. Paul Swingle and his colleagues (Swingle, Pulos & Swingle, 2005), studied the effects of EFT on auto accident victims suffering from post traumatic stress disorder -- an extremely disabling conditioning that involves unreasonable fears and often panic attacks, physiological symptoms of stress, nightmares, flashbacks, and other disabling symptoms. These researchers found that three months after they had learned EFT (in two sessions) those auto accident victims who reported continued significant symptom relief also showed significant positive changes in their brain waves. It was assumed that the clients showing the continued positive benefits were those who continued with home practice of self-administered EFT.

Self-administered EFT (Emotional Freedom Techniques) in individuals with fibromyalgia: a randomized trial

Brattberg, G. *Integrative Medicine: A Clinician's Journal*, August/September (2008).

Abstract: The aim of this study was to examine if self-administered EFT (Emotional Freedom Techniques) leads to reduced pain perception, increased acceptance, coping ability and health-related quality of life in individuals with fibromyalgia. 86 women, diagnosed with fibromyalgia and on sick leave for at least 3 months, were randomly assigned to a treatment group or a waiting list group. An eight-week EFT treatment program was administered via the Internet. Upon completion of the program, statistically significant improvements were observed in the intervention group (n=26) in comparison with the waiting list group (n=36) for variables such as pain, anxiety, depression, vitality, social function, mental health, performance problems involving work or other activities due to physical as well as emotional reasons, and stress symptoms. Pain catastrophizing measures, such as rumination, magnification and helplessness, were significantly reduced, and the activity level was significantly increased. The number needed to treat (NNT) regarding recovering from anxiety was 3. NNT for depression was 4. Self-administered EFT seems to be a good complement to other treatments and rehabilitation programs. The sample size was small and the dropout rate was high. Therefore the surprisingly good results have to be interpreted with caution. However, it would be of interest to further study this simple and easily accessible self-administered treatment method, which can even be taught over the Internet.

Energy psychology in disaster relief

Feinstein, D. (2008b) Energy psychology in disaster relief. *Traumatology, 141:1*, 124-137.

Abstract: Energy psychology utilizes cognitive operations such as imaginal exposure to traumatic memories or visualization of optimal performance scenarios—combined with physical interventions derived from acupuncture and related systems—for inducing psychological change. While a controversial approach, this combination purportedly brings about, with unusual speed and precision, therapeutic shifts in affective, cognitive, and behavioral patterns that underlie a range of psychological concerns. Energy psychology has been applied in the wake of natural and human-made disasters in the Congo, Guatemala, Indonesia, Kenya, Kosovo, Kuwait, Mexico, Moldavia, Nairobi, Rwanda, South Africa, Tanzania, Thailand, and the U.S. At least three international humanitarian relief organizations have adapted energy psychology as a treatment in their post-disaster missions. Four tiers of energy psychology interventions include 1) immediate relief/ stabilization, 2) extinguishing conditioned responses, 3) overcoming complex psychological problems, and 4) promoting optimal functioning. The first tier is most pertinent in psychological first aid immediately following a disaster, with the subsequent tiers progressively being introduced over time with complex stress reactions and chronic disorders. This paper reviews the approach, considers its viability, and offers a framework for applying energy psychology in treating disaster survivors.

Energy Psychology Treatment for Posttraumatic Stress in Genocide Survivors in a Rwandan Orphanage: A Pilot Investigation

Barbara Stone, Lori Leyden, & Bert Fellows (2009) *Energy Psychology: Theory, Research and Treatment, 1:1.*

Abstract: A team of four energy therapy practitioners visited Rwanda in September of 2009 to conduct trauma remediation programs with orphan genocide survivors with complex posttraumatic stress disorder (PTSD). The program consisted of holistic, multi-dimensional rapport-building exercises, followed by an intervention using Thought Field Therapy (TFT). Interventions were performed on three consecutive days. Data were collected using the Child Report of Post-traumatic Stress (CROPS) to measure pre- and post-intervention results, using a time-series, repeated measures design.
N = 48 orphans at the Remera Mbogo Residential High School Or-phanage with clinical PTSD scores completed a pre test. Of these, 34 (71%) completed a post-test assessment. They demonstrated an average reduction in symptoms of 18.8% (p < .001). Seven students (21%) dropped below the clini-cal cut off point for PTSD, with average score reductions of 53.7% (p < .001). Follow-ups are planned, to determine if participant gains hold over time. Directions for future research arising out of data gathered in this pilot study are discussed.

The Effect of a Brief EFT (Emotional Freedom Techniques) Self-Intervention on Anxiety, Depression, Pain and Cravings in Healthcare Workers

Dawson Church, PhD and Audrey J. Brooks, PhD. Integrative Medicine: A clinician's journal. In press.

Abstract: This study examined whether self-intervention with Emotional Freedom Techniques (EFT), a brief exposure therapy that combines a cognitive and a somatic element, had an effect on healthcare workers' psychological symptoms such as anxiety and depression, as well as self-rated pain and craving. Participants were 216 attendees at 5 professional conferences, and included physicians, psychologists, chiropractors, nurses, and alternative medicine practitioners. Psychological distress was assessed before and after 2 hours of self-applied EFT in a within-subjects design. Physical pain, the intensity of traumatic memories, and cravings were self-reported on a 10-point scale. A 90-day follow-up assessment of symptoms was completed by 53% of the sample, and 61% reported using EFT subsequent to the workshop. At post test statistically significant improvements were found on all scales, as well as pain ($p<.001$), emotional distress ($p<.001$), and cravings ($p<.001$). Gains were maintained at follow-up ($p<.001$) for the two global scales and most of the SA-45 subscales. On the two general scales on the SA-45, symptom severity dropped 45% at post test, maintaining a 25% drop at follow-up. Similarly, symptom breadth dropped 40% at post test, maintaining a 21% improvement at follow-up. Greater subsequent EFT use correlated with a greater decrease in symptom severity at follow-up ($p<.034$, $r=.199$), but not in breadth of symptoms ($p<.117$, $r=.148$). EFT provided an immediate effect on psychological distress, pain, and cravings that was replicated across multiple conferences and healthcare provider samples.

The Effect of Two Psychophysiological Techniques (Progressive Muscular Relaxation and Emotional Freedom Techniques) on Test Anxiety in High School Students: A Randomized Blind Controlled Study

Sezgin, N., Ozcan, B., Church, D., *International Journal of Healing and Caring*, Jan 2009, 9:1.

Abstract: This study investigated the effect on test anxiety of Emotional Freedom Techniques (EFT), a brief exposure therapy with somatic and cognitive components. A group of 312 high school students enrolled at a private academy was evaluated using the Test Anxiety Inventory (TAI), which contains subscales for worry and emotionality. Scores for 70 demonstrated high levels of test anxiety; these students were randomized into control and experimental groups. During the course of a single treatment session, the control group received instruction in Progressive Muscular Relaxation (PMR); the experimental group, EFT, followed by self-treatment at home. After two months, subjects were re-tested using the TAI. Repeated covariance analysis was performed to determine the effects of EFT and PMR on the mean TAI score, as well as the two subscales. Each group completed a sample examination at the beginning and end of the study, and their mean scores were computed. Thirty-two of the initial 70 subjects completed all the study's requirements, and all statistical analyses were done on this group. A statistically significant decrease occurred in the test anxiety scores of both the experimental and control groups. The EFT group had a significantly greater decrease than the PMR group ($p < .05$). The scores of the EFT group were lower on the emotionality and worry subscales ($p < .05$). Both groups scored higher on the test examinations after treatment; though the improvement was greater for the EFT group, the difference was not statistically significant.

Pilot study of Emotional Freedom Technique (EFT), Wholistic Hybrid derived from EMDR and EFT (WHEE) and Cognitive Behavioral Therapy (CBT) for Treatment of Test Anxiety in University Students

Benor, D. J., Ledger, K., Toussaint, L., Hett, G., & Zaccaro, D. *Explore*, November/December 2009, Vol. 5, No. 6.

Objective: This study explored test anxiety benefits of Wholistic Hybrid derived from EMDR (WHEE), Emotional Freedom Techniques (EFT), and Cognitive Behavioral Therapy.

Participants: Canadian university students with severe or moderate test anxiety participated.

Methods: A double-blind, controlled trial of WHEE (n = 5), EFT (n =5), and CBT (n = 5) was conducted. Standardized anxiety measures included: the Test Anxiety Inventory (TAI) and Hopkins Symptom Checklist (HSCL-21).

Results: Despite small sample size, significant reductions were found for WHEE on the TAI ($p < 0.014$-.042) and HSCL-21 ($p < 0.029$); on the TAI ($p < 0.001$-.027) for EFT; and on the HSCL-21 ($p < 0.038$) for CBT. There were no significant differences between the scores for the three treatments. In only two sessions WHEE and EFT achieved the same or better benefits as CBT did in five sessions. Participants reported high satisfaction with all treatments. EFT and WHEE students successfully transferred their self-treatment skills to other stressful areas of their lives.

Conclusions: WHEE and EFT show promise as effective treatments for test anxiety.

Resources

EFT resources

EFT talks, sessions, workshops, bespoke programmes and accredited training can be arranged by calling 01494 766778 or emailing contact@eftworking.co.uk. Additional case studies and downloads are available as follows:

- for young people's EFT www.e-being.co.uk
- for adults' EFT www.eftworking.co.uk

Information about Healthy Options Tapping© resources can be obtained via www.eftworking.co.uk

Contact Christine Moran for information on the EFT Children, Young People and Families network for children, young people, families, educators, healthcare practitioners and anyone involved in young people's emotional health and wellbeing.

A variety of positive energy programmes are accessible by families, educators, support agencies and health professionals. Journals, workbooks, cards, PAT Bear, music and videos, training materials and manuals can be seen on www.e-being.co.uk

Recommended EFT reading

Attracting Abundance with EFT Carol Look LCSW (2005) Author House

The Healing Power of EFT and Energy Psychology D Feinstein, D Eden and G Craig (2006) Piatkus

Books that explore the changing paradigm

The Genie in Your Genes: Epigenetic Medicine and the New Biology of Intention Dawson Church (2009) Energy Psychology Press

Energy Medicine for Women Donna Eden with David Feinstein (2008) Tarcher Penguin

The Field: The Quest for the Secret Force of the Universe Lynn McTaggart (2003) Harper Collins

The Biology of Belief Bruce Lipton (2005) Mountain of Love

The Power of Intention Wayne W Dyer (2004) Hay House

How your Mind Can Heal your Body: David R Hamilton (2008) Hay House

Molecules of Emotion Candace Pert (1997) Simon and Shuster

The Brain that Changes Itself Norman Doidge (2007) Viking Adult

The Quantum Mind and Healing D Chopra (2004) Hampton Roads

Recommended websites

www.aamet.org/ – Association of Advancement of Meridian Energy Therapies – Therapies, research and education in the fields of energy medicine and energy psychology.

References

Ader R, Felton DL & Cohen N (eds.) (1991) *Psychoneuroimmunology* (2nd edition), Academic Press, San Diego, CA.

Chopra D (1990) *Quantum Healing: Exploring the Frontiers of Mind/Body Medicine*, Bantam, NY.

Church D (2008) *The Genie in your Genes: Epigenetic Medicine and the New Biology of Intention*, Energy Psychology Press, Fulmer, CA.

Craig G (2009) *EFT for PTSD*, Energy Psychology Press, Fulmer, CA.

Craig G (2011) *The EFT Manual: Everyday EFT (Emotional Freedom Techniques)*, Energy Psychology Press, Fulmer, CA.

De Kooker M (2001) *Psychoneuroimmunology*, An overview, online, www.wellness.org.za/html/pni.html (accessed 27 August 2003).

Dilts R (1990) *Changing Belief Systems with NLP*, Meta Publications, Capitola, CA,

Dorfer L Moser M Bahr F Spindler K Egarter-Vigl E Giullén S Dohr G & Kenner T (1999) 'A medical report from the stone age?', *Lancet*, 354(9183), pp1023–5.

Durbach D (2000) *The Brain Explained*, Prentice-Hall, NJ.

Dyer W (2004) *The Power of Intention: Change the Way you Look at Things and the Things you Look at Will Change: Learning to Co-create your World your Way*, Hay House, London.

Feinstein D (2008a) 'Energy psychology: a review of the preliminary evidence', *Psychotherapy: Theory, Research, Practice, Training*, 45(2), pp199–213.

Feinstein D (2008b) 'Energy psychology in disaster relief', *Tramatology*, 14(127), p128.

Feinstein, D (2010) 'Rapid treatment of PTSD: why psychological exposure with accupoint tapping may be effective', *Psychotherapy: Theory, Research, Practice, Training*, 47(3), pp385–402.

Feinstein D, Eden D & Craig G (2005) *The Promise of Energy Psychology: Revolutionary Tools for Dramatic Personal Change,* Penguin, NY.

Feinstein D, Eden D & Craig G (2006) *The Healing Power of EFT and Energy Psychology,* Paitkus, London.

Gage FH (2002) 'Neurogenesis in the adult brain', *Journal of Neuroscience*, 1 February, 22(3), pp612–13.

Green B (2005) *The Fabric of the Cosmos: Space, Time and the Texture of Reality,* Penguin, London.

Groesbeck G & Bach D (2008) Integral Awakened Mind: EFT and Brainwaves, online, www.3earthfriends.com/eftandbrainwaves.html (accessed 30 December 2010).

Hamilton DR (2008) *How your Mind Can Heal your Body*, Hay House, London.

Hamilton DR (2010) *Why Kindness is Good for You, Hay House,* London.

Hebb DO (2002) *The Organization of Behaviour: A Neuropsychological Theory,* Psychology Press, New edition (June 15, 2002), London.

Hui KKS Liu J Makris N Gollub RL Chen AJW Moore CI, Kennedy DN Rosen BR & Kwong KK (2000) 'Acupuncture modulates the limbic system and subcortical gray structures of the human brain: evidence from fMRI studies in normal subjects', *Human Brain Mapping*, 9(1), pp13–25.

Lane C (2009) The neurochemistry of counterconditioning; Accupressure desentisation in psychotherapy, Energy Psycology: *Theory Research treatment*, 1(1), pp31–44).

Lipton B (2005) *The Biology of Belief: Unleashing the Power of Consciousness, Matter and Miracles,* Mountain of Love, Santa Rosa, CA.

Massey M (1979) *The People Puzzle: Understanding Yourself and Others*, Reston Publication Company, Reston, VA.

Mollon P (2007) 'Thought field therapy and it's derivatives: rapid relief of mental health problems through tapping on the body', *Primary Care and Community Psychiatry*, 12, pp123–7.

Nader K Schafe GE & LeDoux JE (2000) 'The labile nature of consolidation theory', *Nature Neuroscience Reviews*, 1(3), pp216–19.

Oschman JL (2006) 'Trauma energetics', *Journal of Bodywork and Movement Therapies*, 10(1), pp21–34.

Pert C (1997) *Molecules of Emotion*, Simon and Schuster, New York.

Richter-Levin G (2004) 'Amygdala, the hippocampus and the emotional modulation of memory', *Neuroscientist*, 10(1), pp31–9.

Scaer RC (2001) *The Body Bears the Burden: Trauma, Dissociation and Disease*, Haworth Press, Binghampton, US.

Silvert M (2000) 'Acupuncture wins BMA approval', *British Medical Journal*, 321(7252):11.

Tortora G & Grabowski S (1996) *Principles of Anatomy and* Physiology, 8th edn, HarperCollins College Publishers, NY.